RAPE INTERVENTION
RESOURCE MANUAL

RAPE INTERVENTION
RESOURCE MANUAL

Compiled and Edited by

PATRICK   MILLS,   Ed.D.

Counselor-Counseling Center
Marietta College
Marietta, Ohio

With Contributions by

Lee Sachs, Ed.D.

Private Practice
West Babylon, New York

CHARLES C THOMAS   •   PUBLISHER

Springfield • Illinois • U.S.A.

Published and Distributed Throughout the World by

CHARLES C THOMAS ● PUBLISHER

Bannerstone House

301-327 East Lawrence Avenue, Springfield, Illinois, U.S.A.

© *1977, by* CHARLES C THOMAS ● PUBLISHER

ISBN 0-398-03594-6

Library of Congress Catalog Card Number: 76-22635

With THOMAS BOOKS *careful attention is given to all details of
manufacturing and design. It is the Publisher's desire to present books that
are satisfactory as to their physical qualities and artistic possibilities and
appropriate for their particular use.* THOMAS BOOKS *will be true to those
laws of quality that assure a good name and good will.*

Printed in the United States of America
R-2

Library of Congress Cataloging in Publication Data

Mills, Patrick.
  Rape intervention resource manual.

  Bibliography: p.
  Includes index.
  1. Rape victim services--Handbooks, manuals, etc.
2. Crisis intervention (Psychiatry)--Handbooks,
manuals, etc. I. Sachs, Lee, joint author. II. Title.
HV6558.M54   362.8'8   76-22635
ISBN 0-398-03594-6

PREFACE

THIS manual was written with the purpose of providing practical, tested, and relevant material to those women and men who will be confronting rape crises on a daily basis, the Rape Crisis Interveners. It is also intended to be a resource manual for those people responsible for the training of RCIs. These trainers can then use the manual as a source of ideas which they might apply in their individual training programs.

The majority of the information contained herein has been obtained from fifty-four Rape Crisis Centers throughout the nation. The Rape Crisis Centers have cooperated in the writing of this manual by sending me their training manuals, outlines, and suggestions they thought to be of importance in the training of their volunteers. I have then edited that material by taking what I thought to be the best from each and including it in the *Rape Intervention Resource Manual.* A rough draft of the manual was then distributed to selected Rape Crisis Centers for their input and review prior to writing the final draft.

Throughout this manual, you will probably recognize parts of your own training manual, or parts very similar. This is because a lot of sharing and cooperation exists among the various Rape Crisis Centers; this sharing is truly fantastic and I hope it continues.

Complimentary copies of this manual have been sent to those Rape Crisis Centers and persons who have cooperated with me by sending along their training manuals, by completing the RCC Questionnaire, or by offering moral support in my endeavors. This was my way of saying "thank you very much for all you have done."

In addition to sending complimentary copies of the book to those Rape Crisis Centers assisting the author, I will be sharing any royalties due from the sales of this book with several Rape

Crisis Centers which have contributed most towards the growth of this book. It is my intention of supporting, in a very direct way, the high purposes and humanitarian goals towards which Rape Crisis Centers across the nation seek to work.

In closing, let me say I hope your trust in me to produce a resource manual of use in the training of your volunteers has been rewarded. To those Rape Crisis Centers which have freely given of their energies and cooperated in the development of this book, I feel very warm when I think of you and cannot thank you enough. Without your genuine sense of caring and sharing, this manual could literally never have been written. Please let me hear from you regarding your reactions to the manual and any suggestions you have for improving its content; I would enjoy such encounters.

So, until next we meet, I am ...

Experiencing Life,

Patrick Mills

CONTENTS

	Page
Preface	v

Chapter

1. SHOULD YOU FORM A RAPE CRISIS CENTER? 3
   Legal Revision Alternative........................... 3
   Women Helping Women Alternative 4
   Humanizing Procedures Alternative 5
   Community Education Alternative 5
   Other Alternatives 6
   Now What? 7
2. ASSESSING THE NEED FOR A RAPE CRISIS CENTER 9
   Laws 9
   Statistics 10
   People to Interview 10
   Who Should get the Results? 12
3. ESTABLISHING A RAPE CRISIS CENTER (RCC) 14
   Legalities of Establishing a RCC 14
   What are your Motivations for or Philosophy
      Behind Establishing a RCC?...................... 20
   What Services will you Provide? 21
   Affiliation and Physical Setting 25
   Hours of Operation.................................. 26
4. PRELIMINARIES TO THE TRAINING PROGRAM 28
   What Training is Necessary to be an Effective
      Rape Crisis Intervener (RCI)? 28
   Who can Assist you with your Training
      Program?.. 29

Chapter   *Page*

What are some Characteristics of Effective
Rape Crisis Interveners (RCI)? 31
When will you Screen your Volunteers? 33
Who are the Volunteers? 38

5. THE TRAINING PROGRAM (HELPING HELPERS HELP)....... 40
Means of Training................................. 41
Pretesting Volunteers............................. 44
Psychological Reactions of the Adult Victim.......... 68
Psychological Reactions of the Child Victim.......... 73
What is the Helping Process?...................... 77
Empathy Training 79
Helping Skills.................................... 95
Secondary Helping Responses...................... 105
Special Helping Skills 109
Problem Solving................................. 112
Processing the Contact 128
Counseling a Rape Victim 129

6. MEDICAL PROCEDURES 145
Suggested Physician and Nurse Procedure for
Treatment of Alleged Sexual Abuse 146
Medical Information for the RCI 157

7. LEGAL PROCEDURES 169
Police Guidelines: Investigating a
Sex Offense 169
Functions of Rape Crisis Centers During
the Legal Process 179
Third Party Reporting 180
Special Problems in the Courts 182
Suggestions for the Victim to Consider 182
Lay Advocacy Terms to Know 186

8. REFERRAL PROCESS................................... 193
9. EVALUATION MATERIALS 198
10. FACILITATING GROUP COHESIVENESS.................... 210
11. HINTS ON SELF-PROTECTION 214

Chapter *Page*

12. GROUP RAPE 222
13. PROBLEMS CONFRONTING RAPE CRISIS CENTERS 226
    Funding 226
    Reporting the Assault 229
    Volunteer Drop-out 230
    Liaison 231
    Handling Reactions................................. 233
    Remaining Problems................................. 233

Appendices
    A. Rape Crisis Centers 235
    B. Results of the Rape Crisis Center Survey.......... 241
    C. Revision of the Rape Laws 261
Bibliography... 278
Author Index 283
Subject Index 285

RAPE INTERVENTION
RESOURCE MANUAL

CHAPTER 1

SHOULD YOU FORM A RAPE CRISIS CENTER?

FOR any number of reasons, from being a rape victim yourself, to a realization that the incidence of rape is increasing in your community and you want to do something about preventing it, to at least wanting to lessen its impact on the victims and their family and friends, you are now in the "thinking about" stages of forming your own Rape Crisis Center (RCC) as one alternative to meeting the need.

There exist other choices you can make in fulfilling your need to do something about rape crises; perhaps these other choices may even have a more profound, long-lasting, and more far-reaching effect than would forming a RCC. Let's at least consider what other alternatives may exist.

LEGAL REVISION ALTERNATIVE

As you will find from reading about the legal mess surrounding rape, there is a great need for new legislation in the area. Perhaps you might wish to form a "women's legal action group" which would have as its purpose the revision of your state's present statutes on rape. If your group could accomplish this goal, your work might well result in a law which treats the victim not as the defendant, but as a woman having the right to see her assailant brought to justice and punished accordingly, without her having to go through a very harrowing and often humiliating, degrading, and debilitating experience in the court room. By working on the legalities of rape through a legal action group, you might also increase the reporting of rapes by women who have in the past been frightened of the court experience. By increasing the reporting of the crime of rape, you will also increase the likelihood of the rapist being

3

caught and brought to trial, as well as increasing the public's awareness, thereby promoting changes in your state's criminal statutes. Your work through a legal action group may also result in a revision of the penalties for the crime of rape, changing from death or life imprisonment to five to ten years without parole. By doing this, you might find that juries and judges would be more willing to hand down a guilty verdict, thereby increasing the likelihood that the rapist will in fact be punished.

Through the work of your legal action group, you may also be able to obtain revisions in the rules of evidence for proving the crime of rape, thereby increasing the likelihood that the prosecuting attorney will want to take the case in the first place.

So, the legal revision route might, in the long run, be more beneficial and do more about reducing the incidence of rape directly than could forming a RCC. (See Appendix C for an example of proposed revisions for rape laws.)

WOMEN HELPING WOMEN ALTERNATIVE

One of the reasons so many RCCs and Women's Crisis Centers are being formed is that, traditionally, the woman who has been raped comes into contact only with men throughout the entire process of reporting the assault, obtaining medical attention, the legal and trial experience, and seeking out a person with whom to talk, such as a psychologist, counselor, or other helper.

Perhaps through a social action group or community health board, you could exhort those responsible to place more qualified women in these significant positions to assist the rape victim. For example, you could recommend that women be responsible for interviewing the victim when the crime is reported at the police department, that women physicians be placed on the hospital staff and be responsible for the medical examination of the victim, and that mental health centers have women on their staffs to provide psychological and emotional support to the victims. If women who have been raped know they will not have to confront doubting, insensitive men along the way, but will instead have concerned, knowledgeable, and sensitive women to assist them, the now valid fear of many women to even report the crime may disappear. This may then increase the likelihood of the rapist being apprehended, brought to trial, and punished. This may serve as a deterrent to potential rapists rather than reinforcing the rapists' contempt for the law as seen in the number of repeat offenders.

HUMANIZING PROCEDURES ALTERNATIVE

Many women have the rape experience compounded by the procedure used by the police in interviewing the victim and the hospital staff in conducting the medical examination. These procedures are typically so humiliating, degrading, callous, and mechanical that any person, female or male, would do anything to avoid having to go through such an experience. This is just what happens: Women will not report their rape because they have heard about or already experienced the complete annihilation of a woman's psychological being resulting from the inhumane treatment rape victims often receive in moving through the system.

You and your social action group could see that such procedures are revised so that a woman need not experience the second rape of her personhood. This would again help increase the probability that a woman will report a rape. If this were done, the law enforcement and mental health professions may lose one of their favorite cop-outs in responding to questions as to why they are not doing more to understand and solve the crime of rape. Their cop-out has been that as the result of women not reporting rapes more frequently, they can't do much about solving the crime because they don't fully understand it, as they only have a small sample to work with. Estimates as to the actual incidence of rape range from four to ten to twenty times the reported number.

COMMUNITY EDUCATION ALTERNATIVE

Another choice open to you in attempting to do something

about rape, would be to form a community education group. This group would be responsible for making your community aware of the many myths surrounding rape, destroying them, and supplanting them with knowledge about rape. You could form consciousness-raising seminars at the elementary, junior, and senior high levels. You could make presentations to police and sheriff's departments, as well as provide in-service workshops for hospitals and mental health centers.

You would generally be helping people become comfortable about discussing rape by informing them, thereby reducing some of the fear, mystique, and taboo of rape as a topic for discussion. This taboo surrounds the victim of rape with walls of silence. You may also find as the result of your community education groups, that some of the other alternatives discussed may be a natural outgrowth of this increased community awareness.

OTHER ALTERNATIVES

Self-defense programs can be organized where women not only learn tactics to defend themselves against a rapist, but more importantly instill in women a sense of confidence and self-assurance which may then help women not appear an **easy mark** for potential rapists.

Organize support for your police and sheriff departments in hiring more personnel, both women and men, and assist them in gaining the respect and confidence from the community necessary for them to conduct and undertake new aggressive campaigns against rape.

You can organize support for tax bond issues which would:

- provide for better lighting on streets and in parks;
- place emergency direct telephones to the police departments in locations such as parks, campuses, and along streets. They should be made to stand out, perhaps by use of flashing lights;
- provide schools with more money for special workshops or

presentations on rape, sexism, employment opportunities for women, and related topics.

Community mental health centers can be asked to offer assertive training programs and sexuality seminars.

Help start youth centers and programs for youth so these young people can be assisted in developing a constructive purpose in living and are not constantly faced with boredom or the need to join gangs to have any "fun." (Juveniles accounted for 22% of the persons processed on forcible rape charges in 1973. Total arrests for rape offenses increased 13% over the 1972 figures for persons under 18 years of age in 1973. [Kelley, 1974])

You can see that our penal system can do something to provide rehabilitation and therapy for rapists by having competent and effective personnel.

Finally, increase your own knowledge and understanding of the crime of rape, so you are never in a position of thinking "All women who get raped were probably asking for it and probably could have done something to avoid it."

None of these alternatives need to be exclusive of each other or of forming a Rape Crisis Center. Each can be a part of the total program of the Rape Crisis Center; however, establish your own priorities and decide where you will begin. Do not spread yourselves too thin by trying to accomplish everything at the outset.

NOW WHAT?

Where do you stand now after considering the other alternatives to forming a RCC? You say you are still interested in beginning a Rape Crisis Center? You want to do something directly for the women who have already experienced sexual assault and who need someone right now to provide them emotional support throughout their crisis?

You might begin by gathering some much needed information regarding the need for a RCC in your community. You can then realistically assess whether there exist resources, both financial and human, which you can draw upon in organizing, staffing, and supporting your RCC.

You should attempt to get at least three or four other women interested in working together with you in researching the need for a RCC. You will provide each other the moral support necessary to carry you through the frustrating experiences that many times occur when you are trying to obtain information from the police, prosecutor's office, hospital, and mental health center, as well as any interviews you can arrange with rape victims themselves.

CHAPTER 2

ASSESSING THE NEED FOR A RAPE CRISIS CENTER

YOU and others making up the study group should each decide to be responsible for a particular area of your needs assessment. For example, one person can be responsible for interviewing a person in the police department, another can interview a representative of the hospitals, etc. The remainder of this chapter is devoted to discussing sources of information and people to interview while conducting your needs assessment.

LAWS

A couple of the easiest places to begin your needs assessment is by obtaining copies of your state's present statutes and pending legislation on rape. You can usually obtain copies of your present statutes by writing to the justice division, criminal division, or department of legal affairs in care of your attorney general at your state capitol. The author has found the attorney general's offices to be very cooperative. If they don't have the information at hand or are not responsible for such requests, they will usually refer your request to someone who can respond to it.

You will usually be able to obtain copies of any legislative revisions of the criminal code regarding rape pending in either of your state houses by writing to your state legislative council, legislative service office, or legislative research service in care of your state capitol. You may also be able to obtain a great deal of cooperation in obtaining this material by writing your district representative and/or senator, especially if an election is approaching.

9

STATISTICS

You will also want to obtain statistics on the crime of rape, first in your community, then county, next your state, and finally nationally. Statistics often do not convey the human suffering which goes along with the assaults, but people who may fund your center might like to have some cold, hard data (with which it is often very hard to argue). One of the very best resources to obtain is the annual report *Crime In The United States*, printed by the U.S. Department of Justice under the direction of the Director of the Federal Bureau of Investigation in Washington, D.C. Request the Uniform Crime Reports for at least two years past and then the present year. In this way, you can see trends and develop graphs to convey your message. The results of your community, county, and state statistics are very likely to be contained therein, as almost 11,000 city, county, and state law enforcement agencies contributed to the Uniform Crime Reports in 1973. This may be the only resource you may need in order to discuss the statistics of rape — if your community is listed. Many colleges and public libraries receive this publication on a regular basis and you might be able to refer to copies through these sources.

PEOPLE TO INTERVIEW

The National Organization for Women (NOW) has developed a set of three interview forms to assist you in speaking with the police, a representative of the court, a representative of the hospital, and guidelines for talking with rape victims themselves. You can obtain these forms and other helpful information from their "Rape Task Force Kit."[1] NOW's material in the "Kit" is excellent. It will assist you in how to go about the interviewing, what questions are asked, why the questions are asked, and what to do with the results once they are compiled. Questions similar to those provided by the Chicago Women Against Rape are necessary in any needs assessment. These are:

[1]Order from: National Organization for Women, Inc., 5 South Wabash, Suite 1615, Chicago, Illinois 60603.

Hospital Questionnaire
1. Does your hospital accept rape victims? If not, to which hospital do you refer them?
2. Does your hospital have uniform procedures for dealing with rape victims? What are they?
3. Does a gynecologist see the rape victim in the emergency room?
4. If unaccompanied by police, is a victim treated immediately, after the police are notified, or after the police arrive?
5. What is the cost of emergency room treatment for rape victims?
6. Does your hospital provide any follow-up treatment?
7. What is your hospital's policy on juvenile rape?
8. What laboratory tests are done? What is done with the tests? Do you make duplicate sets of results?
9. Does your hospital cooperate in gathering medical evidence?
10. Does your hospital provide immediate psychological help?
11. What sort of information regarding pregnancy and venereal disease does your hospital provide?
12. Does your hospital provide a private waiting area for rape victims?

Police Questionnaire
1. Does your precinct handle the investigations of rape cases?
2. What questions does the investigating officer have to ask at the scene of the crime?
3. Does your precinct have Spanish interpreters?
4. Is a line-up standard procedure when suspect(s) are apprehended?
5. Does your precinct have a photographer? If not, who takes photos? Are photographs of the scene standard procedure?
6. Who investigates sexual assaults in your precinct?
7. Does your precinct have a States Attorney on call at all times? Is she or he ever at the station?

Questionnaires should also be developed for interviewing your State or district attorney and chief prosecutor as well as the treatment rape victims themselves have received from the above personnel.

WHO SHOULD GET THE RESULTS?

Now that you have gathered all pertinent information from the police, the court representative, the hospital, the mental health center, and the rape victims themselves, you need to publicize your findings. This is necessary so you can hopefully gain public support from as broad a base as possible.

A suggestion is that you first put the information together in a form similar to a news release to newspapers, radio and television stations. If you are in a small community with no such media, send the results to members of the city council, police or sheriff's departments, school board members, hospital board members, etc. Make sure you have put your names and addresses on the releases so people can contact you for interviews. The author recommends that you send copies of the release to those people you interviewed, so they are given the opportunity to respond to questions arising from your needs assessment and to change degrading, ineffective, and inappropriate practices that your findings may have pointed out. Some changes will occur as a result of your report and that is what you want to have happen. If you can present your report as a means of feedback to the police, prosecutor, hospital, etc., rather than a condemnation of these services, you will be more likely to receive their support in the future. Anybody or any organization deserves the right to change; if given a choice by the tone of your report, it will be much more likely to occur. This will also serve to foster better relations between you and the people or organizations you will have to come into contact with as a RCC.

Publishing the results of your needs assessment *may* be all that is needed in order to effect a change in the system and people dealing with victims of rape. A recommendation however, is that you follow up on your findings several months later to be sure that changes *have* occurred. If there are any important areas that have not been dealt with, notify the media once again and push for an awareness in the community that little progress has been made.

What do you do for the rape victims who have already suffered from the inadequacies of the system and those women who will be future victims of rape? This is where your original idea of establishing a Rape Crisis Center can have its immediate and direct impact on the women who have and who are going to suffer sexual assaults.

CHAPTER 3

ESTABLISHING A
RAPE CRISIS CENTER (RCC)

A GENERAL discussion of some of the less talked about considerations when planning a RCC will be presented here. There are two excellent resources you can utilize which offer a detailed set of guidelines on how to organize your RCC. One of these resources is *How To Organize A Women's Crisis-Service Center* developed by the women at the Women's Crisis Center.[1] The second resource offering detailed guidelines for establishing a RCC is *How To Start A Rape Crisis Center* developed by the women at The Rape Crisis Center.[2] The latter manual will probably meet your needs more directly as it is only about RCCs, whereas the former is more concerned with establishing a multipurpose women's center.

LEGALITIES OF ESTABLISHING A RCC

What was true of Hotlines and Suicide Prevention Centers starting in the 60's, is probably true now of Rape Crisis Centers and multipurpose women's centers: The people beginning such services very rarely think about the legal implications of and restrictions on a RCC and its staff while the center is being organized. After all, who would want to make problems for a center established to be of help to women and which is people-centered, one which will at all times be working for the interests of its patrons? Well, the parents of a minor child who has contacted your center may cause problems, or the rapist and his lawyer may bring civil action against your center for something you may have said about him, or it is possible that a victim

---

[1]Women's Crisis-Service Center, 306 North Division Street, Ann Arbor, Michigan 48108.
[2]The Rape Crisis Center, P. O. Box 21005 Kalorama Street Station, Washington, D. C., 20009.

who thinks she was not given the kind of care you said you provide may question your service. Also, what happens if the court subpoenaes your records or one of your staff members to provide evidence during a trial?

These are only possibilities and they may never occur, but you should know where you stand legally in these kinds of situations. This section of the manual will attempt to provide samples of areas which you will want to investigate and then hopefully develop guidelines for dealing with such occurrences. Some of the areas discussed may or may not deal with your center, depending on what services you provide and the status of your staff, professional or paraprofessional. In any case, you should contact a lawyer while you are organizing; s/he can then advise you in these and other matters along the way.

To Be or Not To Be Nonprofit, Tax-Exempt

Depending on whether you see your center as a stimulus for legal/social change and on how actively you wish to push for change in your state's rape statutes, you may or may not be granted nonprofit, tax-exempt status.

If you wish to lobby publicly for change in your state's rape laws, you probably will not be granted nonprofit, tax-exempt status. If you are organizationally attached to an already non-profit, tax-exempt organization, that organization will probably not allow you to lobby for changes in the laws. This however, does not prohibit the members of your center from lobbying as private citizens. Just do not use your center's name in doing so.

Obtaining nonprofit, tax-exempt status can be a mixed bag. On the one hand, you may be able to obtain monies for your center much easier from granting agencies and private contributors, if they know they can use the contribution as a tax exemption. On the other hand, this restricts your center from advocating change politically.

The whole issue of whether to become incorporated as a nonprofit, tax-exempt service can best be dealt with by writing your state's director of the Internal Revenue Service, attorney general, or even better, discussing it with an attorney whom you may wish to be a resource for your center.

To find an attorney sympathetic to your center's purposes, consult your local bar association's directory. Another suggestion is to speak with other human care services in your community to see whom they might suggest as sensitive, person-oriented attorneys whom they have also used. After obtaining the names of some possible attorneys to assist your center, then it is up to you to get an appointment and sound them out. Again you may wish to obtain guidelines on selecting an attorney from your local bar association.

Dealing With Minors

Women in all age groups are subject to an assault by a rapist. This obviously includes minors, so through your attorney you should investigate what the legal implications are for your center in being of help to minors. Some possible implications include need for parental consent prior to treatment, confidentiality of your records from parents, and so forth.

Confidentiality of Records

Your center will need to be fully aware of your legal limitations and restrictions regarding the issue of your center's records of calls and face-to-face interviews.

Briefly, confidentiality is a legal abstraction which provides a person some freedom from legal pressures to divulge information gained as a result of the specific relationship of the parties involved. Generally, all staff members, professional and paraprofessional, have an obligation to their clients never to disclose personal and private information without the *written* consent of the client.

Typically, the privilege has been granted legally to cover the doctor-patient relationship (including in most states dentists, registered professional nurses, and licensed practical nurses), the lawyer-client relationship, the clergy-penitent relationship, and depending on what state you reside in, registered or licensed psychologists, social workers, and school counselors.

Once this privilege is invoked, it allows a person called as a witness to refuse to answer without being cited for contempt of court. Nonprofessional staff of a RCC have no legal protection and if necessary, they or their records can be subpoenaed to appear as a witness or provide evidence in a court action.

To assist you in your training program by driving home the importance of confidentiality among your volunteers, you may want to utilize the following group exercise which originally came from the Hotline in Xenia, Ohio.

Confidentiality Exercise

Immediately move into the exercise without telling the group it has to do with confidentiality by saying, "Now we are going to do another exercise and the more you put into this exercise, the more you will personally benefit from it. It may cause you to feel nervous or uptight, but that's all right."

INSTRUCTIONS: "On these sheets of paper we are providing you, write a secret you would least like the other people here to know about you. You can go to a private part of the room if you do not want someone looking over your shoulder." Have the group come back to the center of the room and distribute envelopes in which they are to place their secrets, seal and sign the envelope.

Pick up the envelopes and then proceed in one of the following ways: (1) pick one envelope out at random and ask that person, "How would you feel if I were to read this to the group?" or (2) give the envelopes to different people in the group and have them break down into dyads to process the exercise, or (3) have the trainer put the envelopes in her/his pocket and tell the group you will finish the exercise tomorrow.

FEELINGS TO FOCUS UPON: The following feelings are usually aroused when using this exercise — honesty, betrayal, hesitancy to self-disclose, trust, catastrophic expectations should the secret become known, trainer's power over them, etc.

APPLICATIONS TO RCC: (1) Are not you, as a helper, really asking the rape victim to tell you a secret? (2) The rape victim does not know what you are going to do with her secret. (3) How much courage, guts, honesty does it take for a rape victim to let her "terrible" secret come out? (4) How will anonymity help a rape victim who calls to share her secret? (5) Will the rape victim, as perhaps the group members did, envision catastrophic results from someone knowing her secret? (6) Who has the right to the information about the secret? (7) What about sharing the secret with a third party, even when you as the helper think this third party can help the rape victim?

NOTE: This exercise can arouse many very strong feelings in the participants; it is therefore very important that the trainer allow plenty of time for processing the exercise.

The bottom line on confidentiality is to discuss the entire issue with your attorney and develop guidelines to cover the disclosure of confidential information and to be sure each volunteer clearly understands these guidelines.

Transportation of Clients

Depending on whether your center will provide transportation for the victim to and from the police department, hospital, and court, your individual staff members or center may be liable for suit if an accident should occur while transporting a victim and either party is injured. Determine areas of liability in this regard. By incorporating, the liability may be spread over the entire center rather than the individual involved, but this is not necessarily so.

Accidents on the Center's Premises

Assuming you have a walk-in center or a physical facility acting as an office, your center or individual staff members may be liable for damages occurring on its premises from clients as well as staff members themselves. Again, incorporating may help spread the liability for damages. Find out!

Giving Advice

The crux of this issue is that when information (medical, legal, psychological) is offered as advice and harm occurs, the RCC may be held responsible. As a general rule, the RCC staff should: GIVE NO ADVICE UNLESS YOU ARE PROFESSIONALLY QUALI-

FIED TO DO SO AND ARE WILLING TO ACCEPT RESPONSIBILITY FOR OFFERING SUCH ADVICE. This is especially true in cases where the victim is a minor.

This does not mean you cannot quote existing law or first aid procedures out of legal texts or Red Cross manuals. The important point is, when you begin interpreting information and implying it is relevant to a particular victim, you are giving advice. Discuss it with your lawyer.

Errors of Omission or Inaction

Your center may also be liable for criminal as well as civil action should your center not act in particular cases. For example, if you do not notify the authorities that one of your clients is threatening suicide or making a premeditated threat to kill another person, your center may be liable. In the former case, in some states it is still illegal to attempt or commit suicide. The latter case is self-evident as to why authorities should be notified.

Illegal Activities

Often times, victims seeking your assistance will divulge the fact that they are using illegal drugs, wish to obtain an abortion not legal under the law in terms of weeks of pregnancy, or that they have stolen something of value, etc. On the one hand, sanctioning illegal activity may seriously jeopardize the future of your center. On the other hand, since your center is functioning in the capacity of a nontraditional helping service, you may choose to violate a particular law for the welfare of a particular segment of your clientele. In either case, the decision should be made with full knowledge of the consequences. Such issues will necessitate the RCC drawing up guidelines for dealing with such occurrences.

Your Protection

Hopefully, you are not so uptight about the legal implica-

tions and restrictions on your center and its activities that you
are ready to give up. If you are uptight, hopefully you will seek
out legal assistance and be cautious in your activities. As is
stated in many law buildings, "Ignorance of the law is no excuse."

Your center can, however, obtain protection to cover both the
center and its clients in the form of insurance against the possibilities of personal injury, theft, and fire. It may also be possible to obtain liability or malpractice insurance which would
cover your staff in cases of legal actions. Look at the options.

WHAT ARE YOUR MOTIVATIONS FOR OR PHILOSOPHY BEHIND ESTABLISHING A RCC?

As a result of your needs assessment, you may already know
why you want to begin a RCC, but perhaps some responses
others have given to the question "Why?" may help you for-
malize your philosophy of service or care.

In the author's survey, the most frequent answers given to the
question "Why did you think it was important to begin a RCC
rather than rely on already existing helping services?" included:
(1) No agency existed which specifically dealt with the problem
of rape or was trained or staffed to handle reactions of rape
victims; (2) existing agencies were not meeting the special needs
of rape victims; (3) because we are women and feminist
oriented, we can understand and feel compassion for the
women more easily; and (4) no one in the community would
support or be sensitive to the immediate needs of rape victims.
It would seem that the common theme running throughout
these responses is "Women helping women can do it better and
will do it now!"

To help you draw together your various ideas for a rationale
or philosophy statement, a sample statement follows[1] —

> The Rape Crisis Team, an organization of volunteer women,
> states that its purpose is "to be supportive to women who
> have been raped or sexually abused." The F.B.I. estimates

---

[1]Reproduced by permission of the Rape Crisis Team, Grand Rapids, Michigan.

that one rape occurs every 10 minutes in this country, and that at least 80% of all rapes go unreported to legal authorities. Members of the RCT are concerned about the welfare of victims and are committed to providing them with access to community resources which they might need. Because the crime of rape is surrounded by much misunderstanding and mythology, and because until recently, it has not been discussed or recognized publicly as the serious problem it has become, victims are vulnerable to further abuse by legal and medical agencies, whose personnel lack skills and understanding necessary for working effectively with them.

The RCT seeks to work with these women in a nonjudgmental, supportive fashion, providing them with carefully researched sources of medical, legal, and counseling assistance, if this is what they choose. A client makes all of her own decisions about how she wants to proceed, and the goal is to enable her to regain her own sense of strength and self-respect as a person. Through the Team's substantial research, it is clear that no where else in the community is such a service available.

Team members believe that due to the present circumstances, concerned women, acting collectively, can work to assist victims and to promote a more realistic and compassionate understanding of the problems of rape in the community. All volunteers are currently women because the Team recognizes and supports the significance and necessity of women helping each other. Further, because all women are potential victims, there appears to be a greater commonness in concern and larger possibility for understanding the effects of, and problems related to, rape.

The structure of the Team reflects its philosophy, its belief in the importance of women working together to deal with this destructive crime, and in the viability of operating a democratic organization of shared responsibility and committment.

WHAT SERVICES WILL YOU PROVIDE?

Based upon your needs assessment, you know what services

are already provided for in your community and what needs are going unmet. The needs assessment survey should probably be your guide for what services you will offer rape victims. On the one hand, to duplicate already existing services would put your center in a position of competing for monies, personnel, and good will in the community. On the other hand, if you believe already existing services are inadequate, abusive, or sexist, you may decide to duplicate their services until the quality of care your clients will receive from them is acceptable.

Immediate Crisis Counseling

This is definitely the primary service which RCCs provide to rape victims. This includes helping the woman express her immediate feelings, giving information about medical and legal procedures, helping her decide whether she is going to report the assault to the police, providing transportation to the hospital, and discussing ways in which she can relate the incident to lover, family, or friends.

This service probably requires that the majority of training program time be devoted to learning helping behaviors and appropriate medical and legal information.

Lay Advocate Or Companion Program

This service revolves around your center providing volunteers to be with the victim on an outreach basis. That is, the RCC volunteer will accompany the victim to the hospital, police department, and through the court proceedings, if the victim so wishes. The purpose is to provide at least one person who will be supportive, sensitive, and understanding of the victim's feelings and behaviors over many days or months in the case of a court trial.

Responding to a question in the author's survey of RCCs, 76.60 percent of lay advocates were allowed to accompany the rape victim through the medical examination, 74.47 percent of the RCC volunteers were allowed to accompany the woman during police questioning, and 82.98 percent of the RCCs said they are allowed to accompany the victim through the preliminary hearing and/or court trial.

The lay advocate/companion is not always in the same room during the medical examination and/or police questionning, but may be just outside the door or room. This is often done at the request of the RCC volunteer, so s/he cannot be subpoenaed to appear as a witness as to what evidence was gathered during these procedures. In other cases, this is done at the request/order of the attending physician or police officer.

Walk-In And/Or Phone Service

To have a choice, you must obviously have an office where the women may come. Of those responding to a question in the author's survey of RCCs dealing with how contacts are made to the center, an average of 4.02 percent of the contacts were the result of having walk-in capabilities; twenty-five of the forty-seven responses had no contacts made to them in this manner. However, an average of 80.57 percent of the contacts were made by telephone, with sixteen of the forty-seven responses saying that at least 90 percent of their contacts came in this manner.

One of your first necessities would be obtaining phone service since that is how the majority of RCCs receive their contacts with rape victims. This does not, however, rule out the possibility of having walk-in facilities.

If you are going to conduct face-to-face interviews with your clients on a follow-up or long-term basis, it would seem advantageous to be able to tell the women where your office is located and meet with them there.

The decision as to providing walk-in service and face-to-face counseling also depends on the referrals available in your community for competent and sensitive counseling. If none exist, or if you are not satisfied with the service provided, then your decision may be to offer face-to-face counseling as well as telephone counseling.

A Speaker's Bureau

This is often the second most important service a RCC provides its community. The speaker's bureau makes presentations to any interested group on rape, rape prevention, what to do if raped, etc. The speaker's bureau may also conduct workshops for police and medical personnel to assist them in becoming more sensitive in their dealings with sexual assault victims.

Follow-Up Care

This service is seen as being necessary for any RCC to offer to the rape victims. This service involves helping interviews being available to the woman following the initial call or contact and is provided on a regular basis.

The rape crisis and its aftereffects for the victim usually unfolds over a series of weeks or months. This is due to various predictable stages victims typically pass through, and as a result of the trial occurring months later. The trial can often reignite or bring to the forefront issues, concerns, or feelings the victim has tried to suppress by not thinking of them. It is often necessary for the woman to seek out a helping person at this time to really adjust to or resolve some of her feelings.

Some of the concerns a Rape Crisis Intervener will probably deal with on follow-up contacts are: the legal issues of the case; relearning how to relate to others, especially men; again becoming comfortable with expressing affection; and redefining her sexuality.

Based on the results of the author's survey, the average number of follow-up interviews with each woman in a typical case is approximately four with a range from as few as one interview to as many as ten interviews. The majority of respondents said they had no specific time schedule for follow-up appointments, but followed up as necessary or when the rape victim requested such contacts. Two of the RCCs had follow-ups six months following the crisis and one center said they followed up one or more years later.

If you do not believe you have the staff-time to provide adequate and necessary follow-up, be sure your center has competent referral resources who can provide such long-term care.

Other Services

There exist any number of other services you may wish to provide rape victims, as well as women in general. Some of the following ideas will be more typical of a multipurpose women's center rather than just a Rape Crisis Center, but may include sexual discrimination information, divorce counseling, gay counseling, problem pregnancy counseling, abortion counseling/referrals, self-defense groups, and venereal disease education/referrals.

What services you will provide will need to be decided on grounds of feasibility, financial resources available, staff required, referral resources available, size of your community, and legalities involved. If you wish to be primarily a RCC, be careful not to overextend yourselves and lose sight of your original goals.

AFFILIATION AND PHYSICAL SETTING

Will you be part of a larger organization? This question concerns aligning your center with an already recognized agency, such as a hospital, mental health center, crisis intervention service, or YWCA. In the survey of RCCs, 57.45 percent of the respondents said their RCC was part of a larger organization.

Some reasons for associating with an already existing service are —

- it will be unnecessary for you to find separate housing for your office;
- you avoid difficulties in obtaining office furniture, rent and utilities monies;
- you can share referral resources and library materials;
- better communication between community based groups;
- facilitating formation of a physical coalition of feminist and/or community groups having a genuine impact on the community;
- obtaining more rapid credibility with the public;

• the existing service can often act as an intermediary in negotiations with police, hospital, medical, and legal officials.

The above advantages may all be offset by the fact that your philosophy and that of a potential parent organization may be antagonistic to each other. You may not even want to convey any connection with the potential parent organization, e.g. a church.

Will you have an office? Some possible physical settings for your center include churches, university/college campuses, a private home, or no specific office at all. Regarding this last alternative, 11.75 percent of the respondents in the RCC survey had no office but utilized a "divert-a-call" system whereby crisis calls were diverted to and handled from the volunteers' homes. This alternative creates its own particular problems, however, such as —

• Where will training take place?
• Where will you meet for general meetings?
• How will not having a place as an office affect the sense of the group?
• Will you conduct face-to-face interviews in your homes?
• Where will records be stored?
• If you provide transportation for the victim, is the dispatcher capable of diverting calls to another volunteer?

HOURS OF OPERATION

In considering what services you are going to provide, you will also need to realistically decide what hours these services will be available to your clients. The hours of operation will also affect the number of staff you will need to cover these services.

Of those responding to the RCC survey, 65.96 percent said they operated twenty-four hours a day, and another 12.77 percent said they operated at least twelve hours a day. For 85.11 percent of the respondents, these hours of operation are available seven days a week.

The question of how many staff members are going to be necessary to cover these services is very important to consider. Suppose you decide to operate twenty-four hours a day, seven days a week. With two women on duty at all times and three eight hour shifts, you will need to have a volunteer pool of at least forty-two women, who will work only one eight hour shift per week. Depending upon the size of the community in which the center is located, that may be an easy or difficult number of volunteers to obtain. You must also consider volunteer drop-out, burn-out, and times when someone is unexpectedly absent: These contingencies increase the size of the volunteer pool necessary to staff the center during its hours of operation.

CHAPTER 4

PRELIMINARIES TO
THE TRAINING PROGRAM

THIS chapter discusses some of the important considerations your training staff will need to examine prior to the training program becoming a reality. You will be much further ahead if you devote time now to this phase of your center's growth rather than becoming carried away by the excitement of your first training program and plunging ahead.

WHAT TRAINING IS NECESSARY TO BE
AN EFFECTIVE RAPE CRISIS INTERVENER (RCI)?

Answers to this question will provide the basis for your training program, criteria for selection of volunteers, and evaluation of your staff. To a great extent, it is also dependent on what services your center will provide.

As the result of your needs assessment survey, your own reading, and discussions with other RCC personnel, you should have a pretty good idea of what is necessary to cover in your training program, but perhaps an outline of some of the topics and areas discussed and practiced by other RCCs may help. These include:

1. History, philosophy, policies, and functions of your RCC
2. What is rape?
3. Myths surrounding rape
4. Statistics on incidence of rape — nationally, statewide, and your city
5. Sociocultural factors supposedly contributing to the rising incidence of rape
6. Psychology and types of rapists
7. Psychological aspects of rape for the victim
   a. immediate reactions

28

    b. short-term reactions
    c. long-term reactions
    d. in the adult
    e. in the child
8. Medical aspects of rape
9. Police procedures
10. Procedures of the prosecuting attorney and court trial
11. Rape crisis intervention via
    a. telephone counseling
    b. face-to-face counseling
12. Helping skills
13. Handling reactions of family and friends
14. Difficult calls
    a. silent caller
    b. obscene caller
    c. prank caller
    d. chronic caller
    e. suicidal caller
15. What to do if you are raped
16. Rape prevention
17. Follow-up care for the victim
18. Referrals and transfer of cases

This brief list is not meant to be an example of what each and every RCC covers in their training program, but it does give you an idea of the areas you may wish to cover in your program.

WHO CAN ASSIST YOU WITH YOUR TRAINING PROGRAM?

At first, you will probably have to call in outside people to assist you in specific areas of your training program. After you have had some personal experience with your own program, and better understand what skills are necessary to be an effective Rape Crisis Intervener (RCI), then you will become more and more capable of relying on yourselves for the necessary expertise.

In response to the question, "Who conducts your training program?" in the RCC survey, 38.46 percent of the RCCs relied on medical personnel (physicians, emergency room nurses) for an average of 13.43 percent of the training program time. These people can assist you in clarifying: what medical procedures are involved in the medical examination following an assault; what prophylactic treatment for VD, bruises and wounds, and pregnancy is suggested and provided; the medicolegal implications of the examination; and what evidence is necessary to prove penetration. Much of this information will probably already be available to you as a result of your interview with a hospital representative during the needs assessment phase.

Almost 54 percent of the respondents relied on psychological personnel (psychiatrists, psychologists, counselors, social workers) for an average of 23.70 percent of the training program time. These people can help you with such skills as interpersonal communications, crisis intervention, psychological implications of rape for the victim and the rapist, and how to deal with reactions of family and friends.

Attorneys were relied upon for some help during the training program for an average of 7.77 percent of the training program time by almost thirty-six percent of the RCCs. They can be of assistance in providing information regarding rules of evidence, tactics used by defense and prosecuting attorneys during the trial, and your state's rape laws.

Police and sheriff's departments were helping 28.21 percent of the RCCs an average of 11.40 percent of the time devoted to training. Again, they can be of assistance in clarifying and giving examples of how the questioning of a rape victim is conducted, why some of the questions are asked, and what procedures they follow from the time of the assault being reported to the disposition of the case.

Paraprofessionals (women from other RCCs, Planned Parenthood Representatives, etc.) not on the staff of the RCCs responding, were relied upon an average of 21.07 percent of the training time by 41.03 percent of those RCCs responding. These are people with particular expertise, usually as the result of personal experience rather than "professional qualifications" who can provide input for any topic in your training program.

The majority of RCCs (92.31%) relied on their own staff an average of 68.36 percent of the training time in their programs. Remember, these staffs probably already had experience by participating in a number of their own training programs.

Some important considerations, or perhaps requirements, of these outside people providing part of your training program, are that they are very supportive of your efforts, have a strong feminist orientation or consciousness, are free from sexist bias, and are generally willing to work with and for women. However, as noted by one RCC worker, in the beginning you may find your staff doing more training in both the factual and attitudinal areas of professionals rather than they training you.

WHAT ARE SOME CHARACTERISTICS
OF EFFECTIVE RAPE CRISIS INTERVENERS (RCI)?

The answer to this question will help you decide what qualities you will be searching for in your volunteers and may also help you develop criteria for accepting or screening out prospective volunteers.

Of those responding to a question asking, "Do you screen your personnel?", 68.89 percent of the respondents said "Yes." The means utilized for screening range from a sophisticated test to simply allowing volunteers to screen themselves out as training progresses.

Some of the qualities the staffs of RCCs are looking for in prospective volunteers include:

willingness to work; sensitivity to people; concern for women; expertise in counseling/nursing/caring; ability to actively listen to a caller in a way that focuses on the caller's feelings and concern; knowledge of the subject; stable life situation; aware of own feelings and able to share them or set them aside in an appropriate manner; motivation; commitment; flexibility; willingness to learn; must be a woman; conveys a nonjudgmental attitude; conveys empathy; have interpersonal skills; be a feminist; warmth; desire to work with and for women; common sense; ego strength; and responsibility.

As you can see, there isn't a great deal of difficulty in selecting a number of desirable traits you would want to see in your volunteers. The difficulty arises in defining each of these qualities in a manner which can be easily observed by more than one person; in other words, attempt to make the criterion more objective by removing some of the subjective judgments required.

Why objectify the criteria? Primarily so that when a prospective volunteer is accepted or screened out, you can offer the woman some specific feedback rather than making a global statement such as, "You seem to be too emotional" or "We have accepted you because you seem to really have it together." Neither of those remarks provide a woman with any feedback she can use, but instead may make her angry or happy. They don't offer the woman a choice in deciding whether to change or improve upon the quality you said was "good" or "bad."

How do you go about making some of your criteria more objective? The first place to begin is to decide which qualities you think are necessary for a person to be an effective RCI. You can select some of these qualities from the list provided or discover your own.

After you have decided what qualities are necessary for effective RCIs, then simply define each skill, quality, trait, or characteristic. Do not go on to the next criterion until you and the other people making up your training staff clearly understand what is meant by that word or phrase describing a skill or trait.

Some questions you will want to ask yourselves which may assist you in objectifying a word or phrase are these:

1. What would your prospective volunteer be *doing* if s/he were displaying this trait or skill?

2. What specific things would the prospective volunteer be *saying* which would reflect this trait or skill?

3. *How* might someone else know the prospective volunteer is displaying this trait or skill?

4. *When* will the prospective volunteer be displaying this trait or skill?

5. *Where* or under what circumstances will the prospective volunteer be displaying this trait or skill?

All of the above questions are focused upon obtaining a more specific, clearer and behavioral definition of the quality your training staff will want to observe in an effective RCI. You can place each of those criterion on a scale, say from 1 to 5, and then rate each prospective volunteer in terms of that trait, skill, characteristic, or quality.

WHEN WILL YOU SCREEN YOUR VOLUNTEERS?

Will you attempt to screen your volunteers prior to, during or after the training program? Of those responding to the question, "What means do you utilize for screening?", 68.75 percent of the responses were answers implying RCCs were observing the volunteers during the training program and then providing feedback to the volunteers following the training program, at which time the volunteer was either accepted or denied duty as a RCI.

That approach is especially appealing, because although you may have already given the prospective volunteers some feedback regarding areas needing improvement prior to the training program, allowing them to participate in the training program affords them the chance to change their behavior and hopefully, to make themselves more fully functioning individuals, even if they aren't accepted for RCI duty. At the end of the training program, you can again assess their functioning and provide feedback on what you observed during the program.

On the following pages, there appear three examples of interview forms used by three different RCCs in conducting the interview of the prospective applicant prior to the training program. You may wish to use these as models for any similar forms which you develop as part of your screening process.

What Happens to Women Screened Out?

This is a very necessary question to answer as it may affect the number and quality of the volunteers you receive in the future, as well as having an impact on your center's reputation

Volunteer_____

Interviewer_____

INTERVIEW FORM FOR SCREENING OF COMMUNITY CRISIS
CENTER VOLUNTEERS[1]

I. Explanation of screening and training
    A. Importance of screening and training of volunteers
        1. The volunteers at the Community Crisis and Information Center
            are from time-to-time confronted with people who are having a
            crisis at the time of their calling. The volunteer in that
            crisis situation must respond as a counselor would respond.
            It is this important aspect of the volunteer's job that re-
            quires screening and training.

II. Global Assessment
     A. Please tell us why you are interested in being a volunteer.
     B. What sorts of things about yourself will help you as a volunteer?
     C. What do you think your weaknesses might be as a volunteer?
     D. Have you had any past personal experiences which you think might help
         you as a volunteer help others?
     E. For many people, an experience in which they themselves were helped
         by a good listener, a counselor, or a group of friends can be valuable
         in helping them be good helpers themselves.
         1. Have you ever been in any sort of encounter group or sensitivity
             group?
         2. Have you ever seen a counselor yourself?

III. Committment
      A. The Director of the Community Crisis and Information Center thinks
          that in order for the Center to offer a good service to the community,
          the people who volunteer should receive training to develop their
          particular strengths and skills. This training may take up to 40
          hours, plus additional training as needed.
      B. Would you be willing to come to these training sessions?
      C. Since it is important to know your own strengths and limitations when
          you try to help others, part of the training will include opportuni-
          ties to receive feedback from the trainers, and some tests on where
          your own strengths are. Would you be interested in this?

IV. Particular Interest
     A. There are two major roles at the Community Crisis and Information
         Center. They are both equally important and necessary to the Center.
         1. One is the administrative role which involves typing, fund rais-
             ing projects, publicity, etc.
         2. The other is the telephone role which involves mainly information
             giving and some crisis counseling.
         3. The training would prepare a volunteer for either role she or he
             wanted.
     B. Assuming that you were trained, of these two roles, which do you think
         you are more interested in?
     C. Why?
     D. If the volunteer selected the second, the counseling role:
         1. What do you think helps people who are in a crisis situation, and
             who ask for help?
         2. What do you think people who ask for help don't need?
         3. Suppose someone called up and said something like this (provide
             an example). What sort of thing do you think someone should say?

---

[1]From the Community Crisis and Information Center of Fort Collins, Colorado.
Reproduced by permission.

4. Suppose another person called up and said something like this: (provide second example) What sort of thing do you think some-one should say?

V. Description of the rest of the screening process
   A. There are two more steps of this screening process:
      1. The first step is to give you an opportunity to respond to a few practical situations which you might encounter at the Community Crisis & Information Center.
      2. The second step in the screening process is the training program itself. Your trainers will keep you informed as to your progress during the training and a decision will be made as to your sta-bility at the end of the training program.

* * * * * * * * * *

APPLICATION TO VOLUNTEER IN THE RAPE CRISIS PROGRAM[2]

Name_____ Phone_____

Address_____
      (street)   (city)   (state)   (zip)

Check the areas in which you are interested in working:

telephone crisis intervention_____   legislation_____

publicity_____   court watching_____

community education_____   other (what)_____

Education and/or work experience relevant to this kind of service_____

_____

Have you ever had any empathy training? yes___no___; if yes, where_____

_____and for what purpose_____.

Have you ever done any volunteer telephone work? yes___no___: if yes, what kind

_____and where_____.

Would you be available for training daytime___or evening___.

Would you be available as a volunteer weekdays___, (day)___ (night)___; weekends

___, (day)___ (night)___.

How did you hear about the Women's Centre Rape Crisis Program?_____

_____

Have you ever been assaulted or raped? Did you report it? Why or why not? If you reported the incident, please describe your experience with the police and courts_____

_____

[2]From the Rape Crisis Program, Kalamazoo Women's Centre, Kalamazoo, Michigan. Reproduced by permission.

(use reverse side if necessary)

What can you gain from being a telephone volunteer? and
What do you think you can give to the program?_____

_____

_____

If you were trying to impress us, what would you tell us?_____

_____

_____

Tell us about a good and a bad experience you've had helping someone._____

_____

_____

_____

_____

Are there any kinds of people you feel uncomfortable around?_____

_____

_____

_____

_____

Are you willing to make a six month committment to the program?

* * * * * * * * * *

RAPE CRISIS COUNCIL
EXPLORATION OF OUR ATTITUDES[3]

As you are introducing yourself to another person, please focus on the following
questions and answer as honestly as possible:

1. How willing are you to compromise your clothing, language, etc.?

2. Do you believe rape is possible? Explain your position.

3. Why did you volunteer for the on-call or counseling committee? What's in it
for you?

___

[3]From the Chester County Rape Crisis Council of West Chester, Pennsylvania. Reproduced by permission.

4. What qualities do you have that would make you effective in a helping relationship with a rape victim?

5. What qualities might work against your ability to be effective in a helping relationship with a rape victim?

6. If you were raped, how do you think you might respond?

7. What's your attitude toward the police?

8. How do you react to the pressures and responsibilities of being on-call to meet victims or counseling victims? (i.e. having victim dependent on you for information, answers, emotional support, etc.)

* * * * * * * * * *

in the community.

Throughout the entire screening process, it must be remembered that you are looking for *potential*: potential to relate to other people in a meaningful and open manner, potential to learn what facts are necessary to do the job effectively, and potential to understand the concerns people can and do experience. If you wish to obtain those women who have already developed the necessary skills to be an effective RCI, you would probably not even have a training program. As one of the necessary ingredients of a well functioning group is a sense of trust, cooperativeness, and cohesiveness among the staff, not having a program in which some of these characteristics can be learned and conveyed would do great harm to the center's spirit. These feelings of trust, cooperativeness, and cohesiveness are especially important when some of your staff begin to suffer from burn-out symptoms or become discouraged as the result of an especially frustrating or demanding experience with a victim. It is the author's belief that group togetherness and warmth cannot come from people thinking themselves already highly skilled or Messianic to the helping services. You may also find that these people who are supposedly already expert helpers are not going to want to work the difficult hours, do the paper work, run errands, etc., which are needed to have an effective service. So be careful how and whom you screen out.

What do you do with those women you think would not be effective RCIs? You are probably now aware that there is more to operating an effective RCC than just duty as a RCI. A suggestion is that you offer those people screened out the opportunity to be of help to your center by working with the resource or referral file and keeping it up-dated, helping with your public relations program, serving on your speaker's bureau, or working with record keeping and statistics. In this manner, you are providing them the opportunity to serve your center and rape victims, with the understanding they can always apply again and go through training in an attempt to become a RCI. This will also allow your more effective RCIs to have more time to take part in in-service workshops to maintain and increase their proficiency as helpers.

WHO ARE THE VOLUNTEERS?

You now have a tentative outline of your training program, you know who in the community can assist in your training program, you have established criteria for volunteers, and you know what services and coverage you are going to provide. You should also now know how many volunteers you will need to staff your center. Now, the next important area must be considered, i.e. Whom are you going to have as volunteers?

At first, as you probably have little money to spend on a campaign to attract volunteers, the group members will have to rely on each other to ask acquaintances and friends to volunteer. As you are a new organization, and haven't really tested your service, policies, and procedures, this may be the best way to begin. You are more likely to obtain greater understanding from these volunteers as the result of foulups and confusion that can be expected from an untested service.

After your center has been in operation for a few months, you can then begin to reach out into the community and seek people less well known to yourselves. These people can be solicited from college and universities, the nursing profession, teachers, housewives, policewomen, and senior citizens' organizations. You can make these people aware of your need for volunteers by advertising in the newspapers, spot announcements on radio and television, placing posters and pamphlets in schools, churches, etc.

The majority of your volunteers will probably be between the ages of eighteen and thirty-two years old, but RCCs have volunteers younger than eighteen and as old as seventy. More than 90 percent of them will be women, according to the survey results, and approximately 16 percent are likely to be rape or sexual assault victims.

If you have monies to provide salaries, results of the RCC survey indicate almost 75 percent of these salaried persons will be professionals, whereas 91 percent of your staff are likely to be unpaid paraprofessionals.

At first, you will probably also need more people to undergo training than you really need. This will be necessary so you can begin your center fully staffed for all services, as a few of your volunteers will probably drop out of training. As you begin to lose people from burn-out, you will be able to anticipate your needs for new volunteers in the future. Based on the survey results, the average number of people going through typical training programs will be approximately fourteen.

You are now prepared for the training program itself.

CHAPTER 5

THE TRAINING PROGRAM
(HELPING HELPERS HELP)

THIS chapter is the core of the manual as well as being the probable core of a RCC's training program. Contained in this chapter are many training tools and forms which you may want to adapt for your own program. These can be used as handouts or as devices to assess the growth taking place in your volunteers.

Prior to typing the final draft of this chapter, the author received some criticism of the material contained herein that the material "... was too long and 'involved' ... (the volunteers) are *not* PROFESSIONALS ... (there was) not enough emphasis on women's natural empathy ..." Perhaps the drift of the criticism is contained in a statement which one RCC says to its volunteers, "Since you're a woman, you already have most of the background you'll need (to be an effective helper)."

The author considered deleting some material, but finally decided against it. In fact, even more has been included. This was done not to confuse or befuddle anyone but instead to serve the purpose for which the manual was intended, i.e. to be a "resource" manual for RCCs. You still have the *choice* of what and the quantity of material you will include in your own training program. Not every RCC's training program should include everything in this manual, but when you want more, the manual will be waiting for you to draw from it.

As to an inference made by some that the author is suggesting you should become "mini-professionals": Women, or anyone else, "never" underestimate your potential for growth! If, after reading this chapter, you also believe too much is asked of you, the author's response is "I need goals and something higher than myself to aim for and perhaps the material in this chapter can serve that purpose for you."

MEANS OF TRAINING

The aim of the training program is to impart information, provide practice sessions to increase the volunteers' skill repertoire, and develop the ability to use herself/himself as an instrument for change. Emphasis should be placed on the volunteer's natural abilities and her/his normal desires to help people, then integrating these characteristics into a style which is comfortable for her/him.

One of the more difficult tasks of the training program is to teach an ability to listen which will avoid having the volunteer form a premature conclusion about the nature of the woman's concern. Often, volunteers are almost panicky about knowing what to do with each and every probable concern a rape victim might come to the RCI with, i.e. they take on a problem-centered rather than a person-centered orientation. The trouble with providing specific answers to each and every concern a person might have is that once the volunteer runs out of advice given her/him about how to handle a specific complaint, s/he then freezes and is unable to use her/his own creativity and ingenuity. Attempt to convey to your volunteers the importance of growing as a helper, not as a person programmed with X amount of information which is spewed out when problem A, B, or C is presented by the rape victim.

The typical training program is composed of three means of teaching; the didactic, the growth group, and the role-playing sessions. The didactic mode is primarily used to impart information such as crisis theory, psychological reactions of the rape victim, medical procedures, and legal procedures. This information might best be conveyed through a training manual which the volunteers can do at home, so that they do not waste valuable training time listening to lectures. To insure that your volunteers have read the material, you may want to develop *short* quizzes on assigned reading.

The growth group is usually used to develop a sense of trust, openness, sharing, cohesiveness, personal awareness, and as an introduction to communication skills. The personal awareness aspect of the growth group is very important, since it is necessary for the volunteers to understand their needs as well as their own hang-ups. By working through their own concerns and having an awareness of the feelings accompanying their self-disclosures, the volunteers develop an appreciation for how the crisis victim may be feeling and can more fully understand how some of their own concerns may interfere with or facilitate the helping process. The growth group experience should occur very early in the training program.

The other primary means of teaching is role-playing. No amount of discussion about problems, techniques, or resources can really prepare a volunteer to answer crisis calls or go out on outreach teams. Only practice can provide the "gut-level" confidence which enables the volunteers to be effective without becoming completely unglued.

Role-playing should not be a time for putting people on the spot or an opportunity to show off. Instead, the practice sessions should be a time for trying things out, finding out what works and what doesn't, making and correcting mistakes, and generally becoming comfortable with the responses the volunteers will be using with rape victims.

A recommendation is that the training staff not begin by role-playing typical calls or situations arising with rape victims at the outset. RCIs need to learn these helping skills one at a time by working with real confusion, hesitancy, anger, frustration. These feelings can best be dealt with by having the volunteers talk about a concern or problem real or important to them, not through made-up feelings and thoughts. The person practicing the skill then knows what it is really like to work with a person having a real problem.

Later on, the situations in which to practice the helping responses can be more like actual calls or contacts with rape victims. Below are some samples of suggested role-play situations.[1]

Suggested Role-Play Situations

1. A woman has been raped and has no way to come to you.

---

[1]Reproduced by permission of the Madison Rape Crisis Center of Madison, Wisconsin.

She wants your presence. What do you need to do to prepare yourself?

2. A man called wanting to know if a rape was reported on Jane Doe last night. He knew the boyfriend of the girl who was allegedly raped. He referred the boyfriend to the Rape Crisis Center because he was so upset, as was his girlfriend. You have the log book right in front of you. What do you do?

3. A woman was raped by an old acquaintance while walking her dogs. She calls, feeling guilty and upset because she was afraid to fight and is afraid to be independent anymore. This incident really shakes her confidence in herself and her trust in people. What do you say?

4. A woman was hitchhiking at 12:00 at night wearing a halter top and cut-offs. A man picked her up, drove to a dark side street and raped her at gun point. She was so exhausted she sarcastically asked if she could have her ride home now — he gave her the ride. You find out through the conversation she is on drugs and has been in and out of therapy. How do you handle this?

5. A boyfriend calls secretly because he's concerned about his girlfriend. She was raped eight months ago but won't talk about the incident. She only states "feeling dirty." The boyfriend is afraid for her because the rapist keeps sending the girlfriend threatening letters. What do you advise?

6. A man's voice states he is so horny he is afraid he is going to rape someone tonight. He has done it before, so he says, and has been receiving therapy for this problem. What would you do?

7. A young woman calls and sounds very nervous and upset. She was fixing dinner when someone rang the doorbell. The man at the door said he was collecting her bill for the newspaper which he delivers. Although he wasn't the usual guy who comes around, she let him in. He proceeded to throw her on the floor, rape her, then left. How do you feel about this? What do you say?

8. You answer the phone at 3 AM to hear heavy breathing, then, ... "What do you do if you've been raped?" Screams and hangs up. Calls again yelling obscenities. What might you

say to discourage the caller from calling back?

PRETESTING VOLUNTEERS

You may wish to conduct an evaluation of your training program and its impact on your volunteers. One way to accomplish this is to administer various questionnaires assessing the volunteers' present level of knowledge and expertise in interpersonal skills functioning. You can then score these questionnaires and develop group norms, and will have a record of each person's performance prior to training. Following the training program you can readminister the questionnaires to see whether changes in the direction of increased knowledge and interpersonal skill functioning have occurred. Pre- and posttesting your volunteers will also afford you the opportunity to provide some specific and definitive feedback to the prospective volunteer. By pretesting your volunteers, you are also given an opportunity to make each training program unique in some respects, as you will have volunteers with varying degrees of knowledge regarding rape and interpersonal functioning.

The typical pretesting device used by RCCs is a survey form attempting to assess the volunteer's present level of knowledge about rape and some of her/his attitudes towards rape and its victims.

One of the most comprehensive such surveys is shown following this paragraph. Many of the questions asked on the survey are from material contained in the book *Patterns In Forcible Rape* by Menachem Amir. This book exploded many of the fallacies and myths surrounding rape. It was out of print at this writing but you may wish to check with your local library. Some of the questions contained on the "Information and Attitude Survey" are true and/or false, depending on your state's laws. You should check into these possibilities before using such a survey. Some other questions you may wish to ask can be based on the needs assessment survey you conducted and can pertain to procedures used by the police, hospital, and prosecuting attorney in your area.

Information and Attitude Survey[2]

Please answer True or False or fill in the blank as the question requests. This is *not* a test to determine whether you will be accepted as a volunteer. *It is* to assess areas to be covered in volunteer orientation, so we can emphasize concepts necessary.

(True or False)

F Rape is a rare occurrence in our society.

T Under some circumstances, intercourse without the woman's consent is within the law (legal).

T A woman can press charges against her husband for assault without giving up the marriage.

F Rape of a healthy adult woman is impossible.

T Rape of a healthy adult man is possible but may not be legally defined as rape.

F Most women who are raped have somehow enticed or invited the attack.

F When walking alone at night, stay close to the fronts of buildings, as far as possible from the street.

F Rape victims are usually young and attractive.

F Most rapists of white women are black.

T Most rapists of black women are black.

F Rapists rarely repeat their crime.

F Nurses, waitresses, and go-go dancers are more likely to have loose morals than the population at large.

T Pregnancy can be one result of rape.

F,T The community is generally supportive of rape victims.

T It is illegal to display one's genitals in public.

F,T It is legal for a husband and wife to have oral sexual relations if they wish.

F If hitchhiking, always sit in the back seat.

F Most victims "ask for" attack by the way they dress.

F If one realizes rape is inevitable, one should just lie back and enjoy it.

F Rapists cannot get "normal sex".

F Victims of sexual assault are unlikely to contact VD.

F Psychological tests reveal that most rapists are crazy.

F Most attacks take place in lower class neighborhoods.

---

[2]From the Center Against Sexual Assault, Phoenix, Arizona. Reproduced by permission.

 F If a person stays inside after dark, she is generally safe from rape.

 F Many women enjoy rape, even have orgasms.

 F Mishaps rarely happen to hitchhikers who travel in pairs.

 F Women invite attack by being where they shouldn't be, i.e. walking down streets at 3 AM, going to bars unescorted, etc.

 F Rapists suffer from overwhelming sexual impulses.

 F Rape victims rarely feel guilty about the incident.

F,T A person having sex with a minor because he believes her to be of age is not guilty of a crime.

T,F A person who gets another person drunk or drugged in order to have intercourse is guilty of rape.

F,T Rape victims generally receive support and understanding from their families.

 F If a woman fights a rapist, he is likely to kill her.

 F If the attacker tells the victim he has a weapon and will use it, she must still physically resist, or she will be said to have consented.

F,T Verbally urging the attacker to stop is not "resistance".

 F Castration of a rapist will insure that he will no longer act in violent ways.

FILL IN THE BLANKS

What do you think are the immediate needs of the assault victim:

_____

_____

_____

_____

How can society begin to prevent rape?_____

_____

_____

_____

_____

What does the current method of prosecuting rape cases indicate about the status of women?_____

_____

_____

_____

You may also wish to cover some policies or procedures used by your center in working with rape victims. One form is contained on the following pages, dealing with the RCI's responses to a rape victim in which the referral has come from the police.

RAPE CRISIS COUNCIL LISTENING SKILLS PROGRAM[3]

A neighboring city's police chief calls your city's police department requesting the Rape Crisis Center's phone number. Your city's police give your crisis phone number to the police chief. The neighboring city's police chief then gives the number to the rape victim and the victim calls the Rape Crisis Center. The RCC tells the victim to expect a call from the on-call Rape Crisis Team member. The RCC answering then calls the on-call counselor and leaves the victim's name and phone number. The on-call counselor then calls the victim.

As the on-call counselor:

1. How do you introduce yourself to the victim? What do you say? How do you approach the victim?
2. What do you need to know from the victim?
3. What do you need to tell the victim?
4. How do you judge the urgency of the victim's need to meet with you?

You set up an appointment to meet personally with the victim:

1. Where?
2. When?
3. How do you approach the victim in person? What do you say?
4. What do you do if the victim clams up with you?
5. What do you need to know?
6. What do you need to tell the victim?
7. How long does this initial interview last?
8. How do you end the interview?

---

[3]Reproduced by permission of the Chester County Rape Crisis Council of West Chester, Pennsylvania.

9. When do you meet again?

The victim calls the RCC to reach you on Saturday night about 1 AM the next weekend. The RCC calls you to get in touch with the victim. You call. The victim tells you that she is very upset, panicky, nervous, not eating, having nightmares. She doesn't think she'll be able to make it through the night staying alone in her house in the country. Her husband is a salesman, and has left for two weeks to take care of business in another state.

As the on-call counselor:

1. What do you say?
2. What do you do?
3. Do you continue with her on the phone?
4. Do you arrange to meet with her?
5. Where would you meet with her?
6. How long will your interview continue?

On the following Tuesday, the victim calls the police department or the DA's office to find out whether or not they have arrested the alleged rapist. The police or DA tell her, "Yes, they picked him up Sunday night." She calls the RCC to reach you. You call her back. She wants to know the next step she needs to take since the alleged rapist has been caught.

1. What do you say and do?
2. What information do you need to find out and from whom?

The preliminary hearing has been set up for the following Monday at 9 AM. You call the victim to let her know about the hearing. She tells you that she's been thinking it all over and really doesn't want to press charges now.

1. What do you say and do?

The victim is to appear at the justice of the peace's office at 8:15 AM on Monday before the hearing to meet with the Assistant DA who will represent her. He has a copy of the police report and he's investigated the case. She calls you through the RCC to find out why they won't talk to her before Monday.

She's panicky, doesn't know what to expect, still hedging on whether or not to prosecute — she's concerned that the alleged rapist is sick and should not be sent to jail.

1. What do you say over the phone?
2. Is there anything you need to do?
3. Do you again meet with her personally before Monday? If so, what do you tell her?

In the meantime, you've called the first person on the "Will attend hearings and trials list" to get others on the RCC staff to attend the hearing at 9 AM on Monday.

On Monday morning, you meet with the victim and the Assistant DA at 8:15 AM before the hearing. The hearing is held and ends at 1:30 PM with the case to be sent on to the grand jury. The defendant is out on bail until the grand jury convenes (sometime within the next six months). The victim wants to keep in touch with you between now and the trial.

1. What do you say and do?
2. Any alternatives you can offer her since you are now involved in another on-call crisis with another victim?
3. If you have chosen to offer alternatives to the victim, how do you refer her and to whom?
4. What do you do if she will not see anyone but you?

Three months have passed since the hearing and the victim has continued to call you, especially on weekends when she is lonely. By now, the initial shock and trauma have worn off slightly and she just wants to talk to you.

1. Do you continue to meet her requests?
2. How long do you continue the relationship?
3. She is now sharing much more of her family life and more of her personal life with you. What do you do with all of this?

The trial date has been listed for next week.

1. Do you call the victim to set up a meeting prior to the trial?
2. What might the victim be feeling?

3. Is there anything you should tell the victim in reference to the trial?

You meet the victim in the Assistant DA's office prior to jury selection. She seems quite nervous and wonders what testifying will be like.

1. What do you tell the victim?
2. What can you say to reduce some of the anxiety?
3. While you wait for the trial to begin, what do you say to the victim?

The trial has begun. The victim has given her testimony. She seems relieved. The trial has proceeded and now you are waiting with the victim for the jury to return.

1. What do you say to the victim?
2. In the many hours of waiting, what do you talk about?
3. Do you offer to go with the victim for lunch or dinner if the jury breaks for lunch or dinner?
4. How do you prepare the victim for the outcome of the trial, whether the verdict is guilty or not guilty? The jury is returning. The verdict is given.

NOT GUILTY	GUILTY
1. What do you say?	1. What do you say?
2. What might the victim be feeling?	2. What might the victim be feeling?
3. The victim is upset about the implication she was lying. What do you say?	3. How do you deal with the relief the victim might be showing?

The victim is about to leave the court house. The trial is over and she is ready to return home.

1. What do you say to the victim?
2. Do you arrange any other meetings?
3. Now that the trial is over, do you keep any type of contact with the victim?

* * *

Another area you will want to assess besides the volunteer's knowledge of the subject and procedures, is the volunteer's present level of interpersonal functioning. This primarily involves a person's ability to be empathic and convey an understanding of the victim's emotional world by emitting helpful responses.

One stimulus/response test you may wish to adapt, using more relevant examples and responses for rape crises, was developed by Dr. Robert Carkhuff, called the "Index of Discrimination," contained in his book, *Helping and Human Relations*. He designed the test primarily for screening purposes to select volunteers to undergo an intensive but short-term training program in helping. The test is composed of sixteen "Helpee stimulus expressions" to which there are four possible "Helper responses." Each of the four alternatives has varying degrees of facilitation (i.e. offering the client empathy, genuineness, respect) and action orientation (i.e. a response which helps develop directions for exploration and forward movement). The volunteers then receive a score for each response they have chosen and then a total score for all sixteen responses. The higher the total score, the more potential the volunteer has to become an effective helper. This test is already being used by some of the RCCs with whom this author has had contact.

An adaptation of this test for use by crisis intervention services is contained in the book *Crisis Center/Hotline: A Guidebook to Beginning and Operating*, by Ursula Delworth, Edward Rudow, and Janet Taub, which is an excellent resource to have in your library.

Two other tests you may wish to utilize as pretests for interpersonal functioning are entitled "The Simulated Therapy Program" and the "Counselor Excerpt Completion Test" developed by Dr. Lewis Leitner. These two tests are contained on the following pages. Before these are used for RCC purposes, you may wish to revise some of the stimulus material to conform to more typical contacts in a RCC.

* * *

The Simulated Therapy Program[4]

General Instructions

Please read the following very carefully and note the changes in the instructions as you go along. It is important that you respond as naturally as possible and, therefore, please do not change any of your responses once they are written down. Thank you.

Please Read These Instructions Carefully

Imagine that you are talking to someone (perhaps a friend), in private, who says something to you like you will find in the comments below. What would you say back to them? Please write your responses, as if you were actually speaking to the person, beneath each statement. Remember to write your response as if you were actually talking.

Comment 1. I feel miserable today — like I have no friends. Nobody likes me and they always leave me out when they do something. What do I do?
You would say —

Comment 2. Boy, am I mad!! Everybody tells me what to do and what not to do. Everybody pushes me around and they better leave me alone!!
You would say —

Comment 3. This is really exciting!! I had a great day and I really feel good inside. It's unbelievable!!

---

[4]Reprinted by permission of Lewis A. Leitner, Stockton State College, Pomona, New Jersey.

You would say —

Please do not change any of your responses.

Please Read All of these Instructions Before You Go On.

Imagine that you are involved in the following conversations. Read each of them carefully and then respond, as if you were talking to person 1 in the available space. You should try to be as helpful as possible in responding to person 1. Please write as if you were speaking directly to the person.

Remember: 1. Be as helpful as possible.
2. Write as if you were actually speaking.
3. Please do not change your written responses.

Conversation U

Person 1 — I'm at the end of my rope — no where to turn.
Person 2 — So you think you've got a problem.
Person 1 — Can't you see? I don't think I can make it any more!
Person 2 — Make what?
Person 1 — Living!! The problems and the pressures are too much. It can't be worth it.
Put your own response here:

Conversation M

Person 1 — Man! It's a better day than usual.
Person 2 — What do you want to talk about?
Person 1 — Like I said, it's just a good feeling.
Person 2 — Something has happened to you!

Person 1 — Oh, lots of things, but this is too good to tear down into little pieces.

Put your own response here:

Conversation E

Person 1 — Sometimes I just get so depressed, I just don't know what to do!

Person 2 — You mean sometimes you feel like you're never going to get up again.

Person 1 — Right! I just don't know what to do with myself. What am I going to do?

Person 2 — You're wondering if you'll ever be capable of coming to a decision.

Person 1 — I feel trapped by my problems. So many of them to worry about.

Put your own response here:

Conversation B

Person 1 — I'm angry right now and I'm not sure why.

Person 2 — That's impossible.

Person 1 — Well, it's tough for me to say it and I'm not exactly positive of what's bothering me.

Person 2 — People know themselves better than that.

Person 1 — Listen, I've tried, but this has happened before. What's going on?

Put your own response here:

Conversation H

Person 1 — I can't stand some people I know! They just kill any good idea I come up with.

Person 2 — Sounds like you know some really stifling people.

Person 1 — I sometimes feel like hitting some of them.

Person 2 — You want to just let loose and teach them a lesson.

Person 1 — I think of it sometimes, but some of them have a lot of power over me. You know, they are in charge of something.

Put your own response here:

Conversation L

Person 1 — I feel good today, like I'm going to make it!

Person 2 — You sound like you're really going somewhere.

Person 1 — The future looks really good; I'm really happy about it.

Person 2 — That's a wonderful feeling to have.

Person 1 — I can feel it all over and I've got to talk about it!

Put your own response here:

Please Read All Of These Instructions Before You Go On

Imagine that you are involved in the following conversations, read each of them carefully and then respond to person 1 as if you were person 2, in the space available. In other words, write down what you feel person 2 would say to person 1. Please write as if person 2 were talking directly to person 1.

Remember: 1. Write as if you were person 2.
2. Write as if person 2 were actually talking.

3. Please do not change your written responses.

Conversation C

Person 1 — I don't think I can go on any more!

Person 2 — You are in trouble now and feel like quitting — like giving up.

Person 1 — Yeah! I've had it. The pressure is too much.

Person 2 — You're at the bottom and need some good alternatives.

Person 1 — I've got to get help. I need something — somebody.

Put your idea of what Person 2 would say here:

Conversation O

Person 1 — I'm really excited about doing good things!

Person 2 — What's the matter?

Person 1 — The future is exciting; I want to get there.

Person 2 — Aren't there things you have to do now?

Person 1 — Oh, just school, but that's no real problem.

Put your idea of what Person 2 would say here:

Conversation S

Person 1 — I hate doing certain things and I keep getting pushed into them.

Person 2 — You're in a position that sounds very disagreeable to you.

Person 1 — Well, you know how it is — being forced to do something against your will.

Person 2 — Like being against a wall and not being able to defend yourself.

Person 1 — I want to fight it, but my anger just gets in the way and I don't know what to do!

Put your idea of what Person 2 would say here:

Conversation J

Person 1 — Some of my teachers — they just keep me down. I really hate them!

Person 2 — There is bound to be a conflict once in a while.

Person 1 — I guess so, but this is really getting to me.

Person 2 — You've got to try to understand them.

Person 1 — I can understand some things, but this may be just too much for me to take.

Put your idea of what Person 2 would say here:

Conversation G

Person 1 — I am so depressed! I just don't know where I am going.

Person 2 — Everyone feels that way once in a while.

Person 1 — But this time I'm really at the bottom.

Person 2 — You know it won't stay this way all the time.

Person 1 — That's true, I do feel slightly better at other times, but this time ...

Put your idea of what Person 2 would say here:

Conversation A

Person 1 — I feel really strong today — really feel it.

Person 2 — You've got lots of energy and it is coming to the top.

Person 1 — I could run a mile and better than that I can really face up to my problems today.

Person 2 — You want to use that energy to help yourself.

Person 1 — Sure! When I help myself it's the best kind of success.

Put your idea of what Person 2 would say here:

Once again, Please read these directions carefully.

Question 1.

Disregarding your own written addition to each of the previous twelve conversations between Person 1 and Person 2, please go back and rate Person 2 only as to how well (in the sense of being helpful) Person 2 is responding to Person 1.

Use the following rating scale:

    Level 1. Person 2 not being helpful

    Level 2. Person 2 slightly helpful

    Level 3. Person 2 is being helpful

    Level 4. Person 2 is very helpful

    Level 5. Person 2 exceedingly helpful

Please place your ratings here:

Person 2 in Conversation U__   Person 2 in Conversation C__

Person 2 in Conversation M__   Person 2 in Conversation O__

Person 2 in Conversation E __   Person 2 in Conversation S__

Person 2 in Conversation B__   Person 2 in Conversation J__

Person 2 in Conversation H__   Person 2 in Conversation G__

Person 2 in Conversation L__   Person 2 in Conversation A__

Question 2.

Using the same scale you used to rate Person 2 in each of the twelve conversations, go back and rate your own helpfulness in responding to Person 1 in each of the twelve conversations.

Remember, keep this scale in mind when you rate:

Level 1. not helpful
Level 2. slightly helpful
Level 3. helpful
Level 4. very helpful
Level 5. exceedingly helpful
Place your own helpfulness ratings here:

Conversation U ___   Conversation C ___
Conversation M___   Conversation O ___
Conversation E ___   Conversation S ___
Conversation B ___   Conversation J ___
Conversation H ___   Conversation G ___
Conversation L ___   Conversation A ___

Question 3.
Looking at only the six conversations where you were asked to respond as if your were Person 2, choose the three Person 2's you could imitate best.
The three Person 2's I could imitate best were from:

Conversation ___
Conversation ___
Conversation ___

Expert Ratings for Therapists-in-Excerpts in the Simulated Therapy Program

STE — U — low functioning therapist — overall rating-1.25
STE — M — low functioning therapist — overall rating-1.50
STE — E — high functioning therapist — overall rating-3.25
STE — B — low functioning therapist — overall rating-1.50
STE — H — high functioning therapist — overall rating-3.00
STE — L — high functioning therapist — overall rating-3.0
STE — C — high functioning therapist — overall rating-3.50
STE — O — low functioning therapist — overall rating-1.50
STE — S — high functioning therapist — overall rating-3.25
STE — J — low functioning therapist — overall rating-1.75
STE — G — low functioning therapist — overall rating-1.50
STE — A — high functioning therapist — overall rating-3.00

The Overall Scale for Rating the Facilitative Core Conditions[5]

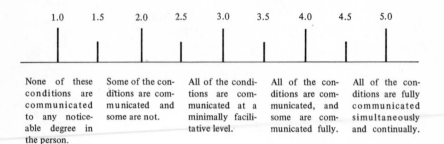

1.0	1.5	2.0	2.5	3.0	3.5	4.0	4.5	5.0

None of these conditions are communicated to any noticeable degree in the person.

Some of the conditions are communicated and some are not.

All of the conditions are communicated at a minimally facilitative level.

All of the conditions are communicated, and some are communicated fully.

All of the conditions are fully communicated simultaneously and continually.

Instructions: Gross ratings of facilitative interpersonal functioning.

The facilitator is a person who is living effectively herself and who discloses herself in a genuine and constructive fashion in response to others. She communicates an accurate empathic understanding and respect for all of the feelings of other persons and guides discussions with those persons into specific feelings and experiences. She communicates confidence in what she is doing and is spontaneous and intense. In addition, while she is open and flexible in her relations with others, in her commitment to the welfare of the other person she is quite capable of active, assertive, and even confronting behavior when it is appropriate.

*   *   *

Counseling Excerpt Completion Test[6]

PART ONE

Instructions:

Read the following statements as if the person (clients) were actu-

[5]Carkhuff, R.: *Helping and Human Relations: A Primer for Lay and Professional Helpers,* Volume I: Selection and Training (New York, Holt, Rinehart, and Winston, 1969) p. 115.

[6]Reprinted by permission of Lewis A. Leitner, Stockton State College, Pomona, New Jersey.

ally talking directly to you. Below each statement write down your response to the person, being as helpful as you can (realizing that this is only part of a longer interview). Remember, write your statement as if you were actually speaking to the person.

Client 1: I can't believe the stupidity of some of the people around here. I just can't get a straight answer from anyone about anything. I just get madder and madder ...

_____

_____

_____

_____

Client 2: I just don't know what I'm going to do about my new roommate. You know; it's like she took an instant dislike to me and we hardly ever say anything to each other now ...

_____

_____

_____

_____

Client 3: I feel so low now, like I just can't do anything. I have no energy so I just sit around and mope. I really don't know what to do ...

_____

_____

_____

_____

PART TWO

Instructions:

Imagine that you are involved in the following interviews. Read each of them carefully and then respond to the client as if you were the same therapist who is already responding. In other words, write down what you feel this therapist would say next to this client. Please write as if the therapist were speaking directly to the client.

Counseling Excerpt One

Client: You sit there acting like you know it all. Give me nothing. Not what I want. Just sit and nod.

Therapist: What do you want?

Client: I want a human being there, a real live one. A good guy who likes me. Not another stone wall father passing judgment all the time.

Therapist: Do I remind you of your father?

Client: You certainly do!

Therapist: How do you feel about being treated that way?

Client: Like hell! Like a baby or something. Who are they to be treating me like this? Who the hell do they think they are? I could kill them. They've got power over me. They can do anything.

Therapist: What could they do to you?

Client: Anything. They can do anything they want. I'm helpless.

Therapist: What associations do they have? Anything that occurs to you.

Client: I don't know. Just that it gives me a terrible feeling.

This same therapist's next response would be:＿＿＿＿＿

＿＿＿＿＿＿＿＿＿＿＿＿＿＿＿＿＿＿＿＿＿＿＿＿

＿＿＿＿＿＿＿＿＿＿＿＿＿＿＿＿＿＿＿＿＿＿＿＿

＿＿＿＿＿＿＿＿＿＿＿＿＿＿＿＿＿＿＿＿＿＿＿＿

Now, list below the cues upon which you based your above "imitation" of the therapist. In other words, how did you choose what you wrote down as being representative of the above therapist? Please list these cues (the things you imitated) in order of their importance.

1. ＿＿＿＿＿＿＿＿＿＿＿＿＿＿＿＿＿＿＿＿＿＿＿

2. ＿＿＿＿＿＿＿＿＿＿＿＿＿＿＿＿＿＿＿＿＿＿＿

3. ＿＿＿＿＿＿＿＿＿＿＿＿＿＿＿＿＿＿＿＿＿＿＿

4. ＿＿＿＿＿＿＿＿＿＿＿＿＿＿＿＿＿＿＿＿＿＿＿

5. ＿＿＿＿＿＿＿＿＿＿＿＿＿＿＿＿＿＿＿＿＿＿＿

Counseling Excerpt Two

Client: Well, my dad was a hard man. At least he seemed tough when I was a kid. Mean sometimes. Wanting me to keep pushing, get good grades, work for him in the house all the time. He doesn't seem hard to me anymore. He seems soft now, in fact, Mother was always criticizing him for not being more aggressive on his job. They argued a lot. She was always crying to me about him, I hated it. He was assistant city attorney for thirty years. Never did get the number one job. He said he never wanted it. But I don't know. I think he did.

Therapist: How do you feel about your father?

Client: I hated him when he made me do things. I hated him to be mean to my mother. But I felt sorry for him too.

Therapist: And your mother?

Client: She was complaining all the time about him and crying. I felt sorry for her. Sometimes I couldn't see what was so bad about him. Sometimes I thought she was right. But why should she always cry to me about him?

Therapist: How do you feel about her crying to you?

Client: It tore me up. Why me? Why couldn't she keep it between them? Why get me into it? I was just a boy.

Therapist: What did you feel toward your mother for doing this?

Client: I hated it! I hated every minute of it.

Therapist: And her? How did you feel about her?

Client: I hated it. I don't know. It wasn't her fault, I guess. She couldn't help it. She needed someone to talk to.

This same therapist's next response would be:_____

_____

_____

Now, list below the cues upon which you based your above "imitation" of the therapist. In other words, how did you choose what you wrote down as being representative of the above therapist? Please list these cues (the things you imitated) in order of their importance.

1. _____

2. _____

3. _____

4. _____

5. _____

Counseling Excerpt Three

Client: I never did have a very high opinion of myself. I thought I was pretty lucky to marry my husband. My family thought so too, I think. They never said so, but I sensed it. I was like the ugly duckling in the family. I'm not as pretty or sharp as my sister.

Therapist: Now this affair has opened up all the old wounds?

Client: Yes, that's exactly it. It's like I'm back where I started. All those years wasted. Just when I thought I had finally succeeded at something. It was all just a dream.

Therapist: You feel now that nothing you built in your marriage matters, that you've lost everything.

Client: Well, not really. We're still there living together with our children. But all my self-confidence is gone. I feel completely battered.

Therapist: In other words, even though your specific achievements are still there — your home, your children, your place in the community — your sense of personal worth is lost. Something you felt about what you had accomplished is gone — but not actually what you had accomplished.

Client: Yes, of course, we've still really got what we had at the beginning of the summer. It just seems hollow and meaningless to me.

This same therapist's next response would be:_____

_____

_____

_____

Now, list below the cues upon which you based your above "imitation" of the therapist. In other words, how did you choose what you wrote down as being representative of the above therapist? Please list these cues (the things you imitated) in order of their importance.

1. _____
2. _____
3. _____
4. _____
5. _____

Counseling Excerpt Four

Client: Are you interested in my dreams?

Therapist: Why do you ask?

Client: I don't know. I know that therapists are supposed to be interested in dreams. I just wondered.

Therapist: Yes, they can be useful. Did you have a dream you wanted to tell me about?

Client: I had a great one this morning just before I got up. I was being chased. I was running as fast as I could but the crowd chasing me kept getting closer and closer. It seemed like I was trying to reach a safe place. But I couldn't seem to get there.

Therapist: It seems you were afraid. What occurs to you about being fearful?

Client: Sure, I'm afraid about a lot of things. Like losing my job. Having my wife leave me. Going crazy completely.

Therapist: But now, what are you especially afraid of now?

Client: Now? Well, now, I suppose its mostly being here. You. Whether you can help me. Whether I can ever get any better. I guess that's it.

This same therapist's next responses would be: _____

_____
_____
_____
_____

Now, list below the cues upon which you based your above "imitation" of the therapist. In other words, how did you choose what you wrote down as being representative of the above therapist? Please list these cues (the things you imitated) in order of their importance.

1. _____
2. _____
3. _____
4. _____
5. _____

Counseling Excerpt Five

Client: I can't stand to look at that girl. They can't fire her, so she still works in the office, only she's someone else's secretary now.

Therapist: She still bothers you?

Client: Yes, I think of her sometimes out of the clear blue. Other times it's after I happen to see her near his office.

Therapist: She still gets to you? How do you mean?

Client: Well, I think of her seducing him, probably thinking I'm no good, that I'm an old bag, or something. He's sort of innocent. She probably wound him around her finger.

Therapist: So now, even though you've got the situation with your husband somewhat in hand, you still are troubled about the other woman.

Client: I guess she hits home more. She's a woman like me. It's harder to be objective.

Therapist: Do you mean she's more like direct competition, or that you feel inferior relative to her?

Client: She's younger and prettier and she's got no responsibilities. I hate her! Still that's not fair either. She probably didn't mean any harm either.

This same therapist's next response would be:_____

_____
_____
_____

Now, list below the cues upon which you based your above "imitation" of the therapist. In other words, how did you choose what you wrote down as being representative of the above therapist? Please list these cues (the things you imitated) in order of their importance.

1. _____
2. _____
3. _____
4. _____
5. _____

Counseling Excerpt Six

Client: My husband, he's a wonderful man really. He's kind and generous. He's good to the kids and me. Then this thing came up. (cries) It'll never be the same again.

Therapist: Oh?

Client: I don't think I'll ever get over it. Nothing will ever be the same again.

Therapist: Please tell me about it.

Client: Yes, of course, I've got to settle down. It happened this summer when our kids and I were at our lake cottage. He was staying alone in the city during the week and coming out to stay with us for long weekends. He had an affair with his secretary the month we were gone. That's it. But I can't get over it.

Therapist: It really gnaws at you?

Client: Yes, that's it. I keep thinking about him and her, and keeping saying to myself, "How could you do it to me? How could he do it to me?"

Therapist: You put it on a personal basis — as if he were actually doing it to you — thoughtlessly or deliberately directing it against you?

Client: Well, it's sort of like that, yes. He must of known how I'd feel, and he did it anyway. How could he

come to me on weekends and go to bed with me —
all the time thinking of that other woman? (cries)
Therapist: It really hits you on a sore spot.
   Client: That's right. It makes me feel like nothing. He
   didn't even think of me. I was just there, but it was
   as if I didn't really matter.
This therapist's next response would be: _____
_____
_____
_____

Now, list below the cues upon which you based your above
"imitation" of the therapist. In other words, how did you
choose what you wrote down as being representative of the
above therapist? Please list these cues (the things you imitated)
in the order of their importance:
1. _____
2. _____
3. _____
4. _____
5. _____

*   *   *

PSYCHOLOGICAL REACTIONS OF THE ADULT VICTIM

Acute Crisis Period

VICTIM'S RESPONSES: There are two typical types of responses
which might be seen in the adult rape victim. The first is called
the "expressive" type in which the woman responds with relief
to the opportunity to discuss the assault and will be quite
verbal and talkative (Burgess and Holmstrom, 1974). The most
prominent feelings are fright, anxiety, anger, and disbelief
(Donadio and White, 1974). These may be apparent from her
uncontrolled crying, shaking, tenseness, and restlessness. The
anger is a likely result of her feelings of powerlessness. She may

second-guess herself — "Did I fight hard enough? Did I do everything possible to resist?" (Flynn, 1974). In speaking about the emotional distress this second-guessing may cause the victim, Dr. Brussel (1971) states that "the victim who is beaten into almost senselessness may suffer far less emotional trauma than the woman who submits to rape, even when her life is threatened." Dr. Brussel's reasoning is that those women who suffer these severe beatings don't know what was happening, as they were beaten into semi- or unconsciousness, therefore do not consciously experience the degradation, humiliation, and terror. They are thus plagued less by the thoughts which others who do submit experience to a greater degree. A second reason those who are beaten into senselessness may experience less emotional trauma is that the wounds and injuries coming from these severe beatings serve as testimony not only to others but to the victim herself. She thus *knows* that she did everything possible to avoid being raped. This gut-level knowledge thereby decreases the likelihood of other- or self-inflicted re-crimination. This second-guessing phenomenon of self-recrimination has been thought of as a potential source of the guilt frequently experienced by victims of rape and can lead to severe depressions.

The second response type is called the "controlled" style. (Burgess and Holmstrom, 1974). The woman may appear in control, composed, or subdued, speak clearly and fluently, but generally respond in a quiet and guarded manner. It is reported that women often say they appeared calm because they were afraid what their reaction might have been if they had let go — they don't want to become hysterical; other victims said their calm appearance was the result of wanting to be strong so others would not become upset, but would believe things were fine; still others appeared subdued out of sheer physical and mental exhaustion. Women Organized Against Rape (WOAR) in Philadelphia report that the controlled style is typical of the majority of cases with which they deal. WOAR adds that the RCI should therefore not assume the victim has not been as-saulted, as the calm, composed style may be the woman's typical way of coping with crises or an expression of her relief to be alive following the assault.

The rape victims' immediate concerns are usually:

1. Should she tell her parents, family, or friends?
2. Should she press charges?
3. Will she be able to identify the rapist and how will she react to seeing him?
4. What will be the nature of publicity regarding her rape?
5. Concerns about pregnancy and VD.
6. How to care for herself in the days following the assault, e.g. repair of broken windows or doors, not wanting to be left alone; if she was robbed she might need money for immediate needs. (Donadio and White, 1974; Fox and Scherl, 1972)
7. Will the rapist return to retaliate prior to or following the trial?

RCI's RESPONSES: At this time, the RCI's attitude of warmth, calmness, empathy, and firm consistency will be of primary importance. The woman should be assured that her feelings are similar to those experienced by other rape victims. This will help her realize she is not alone in her feelings, that others also share these reactions and they made it through the crisis. The RCI will also want to assess the victim's strengths and weaknesses, so the RCI neither does too much nor too little for the victim.

The RCI can also assist the woman by naming some of the feelings she is experiencing, which helps to remove some of the confusion a variety of feelings may bring. This is also the first step in reducing the victim's anxiety. It is essential that the RCI assist the victim in discussing the assault. If people refuse to discuss the assault at this point, the victim may assume they are too embarrassed or ashamed. This will then heighten either of these feelings that the victim may already be experiencing or cause her to now feel shame and embarrassment where there was none before. However, don't push her to say anything she isn't ready to discuss.

Interim Period-Apparent Adjustment

VICTIM'S RESPONSES: At this stage of the crisis, the victim's defense mechanisms play a vital role in helping her cope with the assault (Fox and Scherl, 1972). Defense mechanisms of intellectualization and rationalization assist the victim by placing the incident on a more cognitive or objective level. Denial of affect, especially feelings of anger and hostility towards the rapist, assists the victim in not compounding any guilt as the result of her thinking, "How could I even think of killing the bastard or cutting off his balls? Nice people don't think that way, so if I think that way, I must not be nice." Thus the victim might begin to feel guilty for such fantasies and feelings if it were not for denial of affect. A third defense mechanism used by the victim is suppression, where the victim consciously tries to forget or forces out of her consciousness any desires or impulses not in keeping with her own self-concept.

It is also at this time when the victim will be less interested in discussing the assault, since she tries to take up the day-to-day activities of her life (Fox and Scherl, 1972). Her real desire to discuss the assault will resurface at a later time.

RCI'S RESPONSES: As the result of the defense mechanisms operating to protect the victim, the RCI should not confront or challenge the victim for their use as she needs these defenses to cope on a day-to-day basis.

As typically there will be little contact with the victim during this period, the RCI can best spend her time in talking with the victim's family or friends, assisting them in helping the victim. The family may have feelings that the woman has been ruined, made unclean, was responsible in some way, or feeling embarrassment and shame: All must be dealt with so as not to compound the victim's concerns.

As should be the case throughout all phases of the crisis, the RCI can be most effective by helping the victim anticipate certain feelings or reactions. By preparing the woman, the impact of certain feelings such as depression can be greatly reduced; this will also help to reduce a feeling of "strangeness" or "unrealness" often accompanying these strong feelings. A word of caution however in anticipating victim responses is to be on guard against "programming" the victim to have certain reactions. This is also known as a self-fulfilling prophecy, whereby the RCI, expecting certain responses from a sexual assault victim, actually provides cues to the victim on what she "should" be experiencing; the victim does have these reactions thereby confirming the prophecy.

Period of Resolution

VICTIM'S RESPONSES: This stage is often the result of the victim being reminded of the assault. This can occur by receiving a summons to appear in court, seeing a man resembling the rapist, having to go for a pregnancy or VD test, or becoming depressed as the result of not being able to get the incident out of her mind. The defense mechanisms, which were once useful, are no longer helping her cope. This will be the beginning of a process through which she will learn to integrate the experience and have it become part of her past (Fox and Scherl, 1972).

Two primary concerns need to be dealt with here. The first is her feelings toward herself. She may feel guilty, dirty, or damaged. The second major concern to be dealt with is her feelings toward the rapist. The typical feelings will be anger, rage, or hostility (Fox and Scherl, 1972).

Other concerns likely to arise during this stage are the woman's wishing to discuss her sexuality — her present sexual activity, loss of virginity, etc. Losses, especially relationships with men in the past, are another common theme. Former engagements and other breakups in male-female relationships often lead into a conversation of how to handle future relationships with men (Burgess and Holmstrom, 1973). There will be a general distrust of people at home, on the street, and among strangers (Flynn, 1974).

RCI RESPONSES: The RCI must let the victim discuss the many feelings arising at this time, so the victim can realize on her own that she is not responsible or to blame for the assault.

The primary RCI responses are encouragement and exploratory, i.e. they assist the woman to open up about what she has
been suppressing so she may now fully explore her feelings and
thoughts.

Regarding the feelings of anger experienced by the victim
towards the rapist, again these must not be reacted to with
shock or embarrassment by the RCI. If the anger cannot be
fully ventilated, it may be turned inward against herself, thus
compounding guilt which might then lead to severe depression. By providing a free and supportive environment for the
victim to share these strong feelings, the victim is less likely to
experience the constant obsessive "thinking about" the assault.
If these feelings are not allowed to be expressed, the RCI may
unknowingly increase the likelihood of flashbacks. Flashbacks
were common to those who were given drugs to stop a bad trip
on acid. This caused the trip to be cut short, which is thought
to be one reason for flashbacks among acid users. It seems the
mind needed to complete the trip and when this wasn't allowed
to happen, flashbacks occurred. The same may be true for rape
victims, who need to complete the expressions of anger towards
the rapist.

During this period, the RCI must be alert to eating and
sleeping habits of the victim, any obsessive-compulsive behavior being engaged in, or generalized phobias. Any of these
disturbances can be considered within normal limits if they are
short-lived and are nonpsychotic, i.e. a person's mental functioning is not impaired to the extent as to interfere grossly with
the individual's capacity to meet ordinary demands of life (Fox
and Scherl, 1972).

If the RCI does not think she can effectively deal with some
of the stronger reactions of the victim or cannot devote the time
necessary for this process to unfold, it is wise to suggest to the
victim the availability of mental health professionals.

PSYCHOLOGICAL REACTIONS OF THE CHILD VICTIM

Short-Term Effects

VICTIM'S RESPONSES: Depending on which source you read,

the immediate reaction of the child to a sexual assault is either emotional withdrawal as contrasted to the adult victim's tearful crying (Peters, 1973) or is similar to the expressive and controlled styles characteristic of adult reactions (Burgess and Holmstrom, 1974). The bodily complaints are again typical of those reported by the adult victim and the prominent feeling reported by both children and adult victims is fear. However, the fear in the case of children is not only the result of the attack but is also a fear of what her/his parent's reactions might be, that is, did s/he do something "dirty" or "sinful" (Burgess and Holmstrom, 1974).

Accompanying this fear is a great deal of confusion or mixed feelings as to how s/he should now feel towards the assailant, expecially if the assailant was a relative or friend of her/his parents whom the parents have told the child s/he could trust (Peters, 1973).

If the child is under six years of age, s/he will be inclined to blame herself/himself and also take on any guilt reactions the parents may be experiencing. If the child is over six years of age, it is reported that s/he will tend to focus any guilt on her/his sexual feelings, especially if s/he is beyond puberty (Peters, 1973). It is, therefore, very important that the helping person now clarify the resulting confusion regarding her/his own sexuality, so the child is not left with any long-term sexual misconceptions and will be more likely to adjust to a normal adult sexual life.

The parents are the most important people affecting how the child copes with the sexual assault. If they deny anything serious has occurred and ask the child to remain quiet out of their own embarrassment or shame, the child's ambivalence can be intensified and the child will be deprived of the necessary support needed to fully discuss and then adjust to the rape.

Long-Term Effects

VICTIM'S RESPONSES: Again, depending upon which sources

you read, there may or may not be long-lasting effects on the child as the result of the sexual assault. Schultz states, "Most sexual assaults do not affect the child's personality develop-ment, particularly where neither violence nor court appearance has occurred." And in discussing the results of a court trial on the child, he goes on to state, "Most of the child sex victims who would be damaged by the court experience have indicated personality disturbances before the offense" (Schultz, 1973). However, Peters states that he has "... treated a number of adult women whose sexual disorientation or psychoses were directly traceable to a childhood rape incident — usually in-volving a relative or family friend" (Peters, 1973). Burgess and Holmstrom also seem to say there are long-lasting effects of the assault on the child when they state, "The long-term process includes (1) changes in motor activity (truant from school, arguments with classmates, etc.); (2) nightmares, and (3) phobic reactions" (Burgess and Holmstrom, 1974). Finally, Dr. Peters is also quoted as saying that a child rape can cause serious problems in adult life, "ranging from frigidity with fear of intercourse to a type of aimless promiscuity ... (without) sexual gratification" (Peters, 1973). It would appear that the future does not hold much promise for the child rape victim unless prolonged and intensive psychotherapy is provided to both the child and her/his parents.

RCI RESPONSES: In working directly with the child rape victim, the RCI will want to be cognizant óf the following tasks developed by the women at the Women Organized Against Rape of Philadelphia, Pennsylvania:

1. It will be necessary to assess the child's cognitive, life experience age. Once determined, the RCI will be able to respond to the child in a manner s/he can understand, using language appropriate for her/his mental age. Do not be mislead by street-wise young women.
2. It will be necessary to ascertain what the rape means to the child and deal with the assault on that level. To the young victim, rape may mean social ostracism (or acceptance) from peers, intense fear of living in her/his gang-infested

neighborhood, questions about her/his sexuality and so on. For all children, there will be distress about her/his parent's reactions. Remember, the younger the child the greater the likelihood that the rape was family-related either by relatives or friends. The child involved in a family-related rape will be particularly concerned about her/his family believing her/him and/or possible repercussions in the family.

3. It is necessary to tell the child why s/he is in the hospital and what is going to happen to her/him, e.g. in the case of a very young child, "You've come to the hospital because you may be hurt and the doctor wants to make you better, but first he has to look at you." By making the unknown known, the RCI will alleviate some of the fear and lessen the fright of the hospital. Focus on why the child is in the emergency room, but don't go into long, involved, elaborate explanations as these will only be more confusing. Be honest. Explain the pelvic exam and the entire medical procedure in language appropriate for the child's age, e.g. "The doctor is going to look at your bottom to see if you are hurt." As you speak with her/him, observe her/his expressions to determine her/his understanding. Again, be honest. If you are calm, treating the exam as a normal process, you will be doing much to lessen the child's anxiety.

Although there is much the RCI can do to help the child directly, most of the RCI responses will be directed toward the parents, who can then assist the child in coping with the crisis. The following is a brief list of tasks developed by the Women Against Rape in Chicago, Illinois and the Women Organized Against Rape of Philadelphia, Pennsylvania which the RCI will want to keep in mind when s/he works with the parents of the victim:

1. Be aware of the legal implications for the RCC and RCI in working with minors.
2. The parents should act as a buffer between the child and the authorities. This includes the police, medical and legal authorities. The parents should screen from the child

any particularly insensitive procedures or questions.

3. It is necessary to help the parents focus on their child's pain. Parents' own confused and negative feelings and hang-ups will cloud the issue. For example, the issue is not whether their daughter/son should have been playing alone or was on the streets at night, but that their child has just experienced a painful situation and s/he needs their help.

4. In order to help the parents focus on their child's pain, it will be necessary to constructively channel parental feelings. Usually, the parents will be in a crisis state also. Provide feedback to counteract parental feelings of guilt. Help them to channel their anger appropriately, (prosecution of the assailant) not at their child.

5. It is important to give parents some pointers on how to respond to their child. Stress the connection between parental feelings and attitudes about the assault to their child's own feelings about self and the assault experience. Encourage the parents to be available to their child, not to press the child to talk but neither to cut off discussion. Point out that it is beneficial for the child to continue her/his usual routine and activities but that this may require some parental encouragement.

6. As with any victim, it is also necessary to alleviate the anxiety of the unknown situation by informing the parents of legal and medical matters. Be sure the parents understand the medical examination is for the child's well-being and that it provides legal evidence.

7. As has already been mentioned, in talking with adolescents it is important to distinguish between rape and their own sexuality. When a young person is raped, it is often difficult for the child to draw this distinction, in which case s/he may be affected in her/his current and future dealings with the opposite sex. A referral may be necessary here.

WHAT IS THE HELPING PROCESS?

The helping process can be envisioned as a "V." The "V"

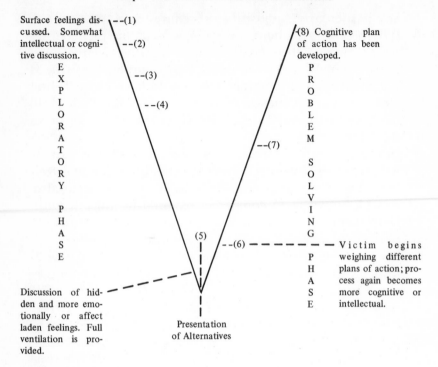

Surface feelings discussed. Somewhat intellectual or cognitive discussion.

E
X
P
L
O
R
A
T
O
R
Y

P
H
A
S
E

--(1)

--(2)

--(3)

--(4)

(5)

--(6)

--(7)

-(8) Cognitive plan of action has been developed.

P
R
O
B
L
E
M

S
O
L
V
I
N
G

P
H
A
S
E

Discussion of hidden and more emotionally or affect laden feelings. Full ventilation is provided.

Presentation of Alternatives

Victim begins weighing different plans of action; process again becomes more cognitive or intellectual.

analogy looks something like this:

At point (1), the victim makes contact with the RCC experiencing potential feelings of anger, fear, disbelief, shock, guilt, uncleanliness, feelings of being different, helplessness, worthlessness, unrealness, etc. Here, point (2), the RCI responds to the victim with empathy, warmth, genuineness, respect, acceptance, etc. The RCI uses open-ended responses, paraphrasing responses, and reflection of feeling responses to assist the victim in ventilating or unloading her feelings, clarifying confusion, and offering emotional support, point (3). The RCI's responses help develop a sense of trust between the RCI and the victim so the helping process can continue down towards a full exploration of the victim's emotional world to deeper levels of understanding (4). The RCI is now focusing on less evident feelings of the victim, perhaps feelings the victim was suppressing or not owning (5). At the bottom of the "V" the victim's concerns have been fully explored and it is now necessary to begin discussing with the victim various plans of action or alternatives as to how she may more effectively cope. At this point (6), the process of problem solving has begun; thus it becomes more cognitive in that the victim must now begin dealing with the pros and cons of various alternatives presented.

As the problem-solving phase continues, various alternatives are ruled out as having little likelihood of success (7). At this point a structure or set of guidelines is being developed, so by the time the helping process reaches point (8), the victim has a definite idea of what she is going to do, at least for the immediate future. By leaving the victim with a specific plan of action, the RCI has given her a sense of hope, lessened feelings of helplessness, shown the victim she is worthwhile, and finally, that she can cope. The helping process has allowed her the opportunity to select her own alternatives and to judge each on the probability of success or failure. This is also important in giving the woman a sense of control over her present circumstances.

The model of helping is appropriate both in cases where the woman has just experienced the assault (and needs to ventilate, receive support, and discuss her immediate needs) or where the woman has experienced the assault weeks, months, or even years before (and is now wanting to discuss residual effects the assault has upon her life and is seeking new means of coping with her relationships with men or redefining her sexuality, etc.).

EMPATHY TRAINING

One of the first steps in the helping process is conveying to the victim that the RCI is able to perceive the mood and feelings of the victim. This is called empathy. A model of empathy training has been developed by N. Kagan, D. R. Drathwohl, and R. R. Carkhuff used by the Drug Education Center in East Lansing, Michigan and adopted for use by the Women's Crisis

Center in Ann Arbor, Michigan. This model is presented on the following pages.

Empathy Training Manual[7]

INTRODUCTION: A person with a problem usually has feelings that she is unaware of at a particular moment. Before she can decide on a course of action to solve the problem, she must become aware of her feelings and be able to understand them. The RCIs' job, as peer counselors, is to facilitate that understanding.

The process we use to do this is called *empathic understanding*. Empathy is very different from sympathy. Sympathy is agreement of feelings; empathy is understanding of feelings. Sympathy is subjective — you feel what the other person feels. Empathy is objective — you perceive and appreciate what the other person is feeling. When a person asks for help, she is not asking for someone else to feel as confused or unhappy as she does. She is asking for someone else to help her understand what she is feeling and why.

Through this manual you will learn the means by which you can provide that help. Empathic understanding is a skill — it is to listen, to understand, and then to communicate. It is not enough just to listen, you must also communicate your understanding to the woman.

The attempt to understand another person seems to require something very basic; that is a desire to understand — in a word, caring. Because you are here (at the training session), we (the trainers) assume you do care, and the purpose of this training session is to enable you to translate your concern and caring into action.

I. Beginning to Use Feeling Words

The focus of this training session will be on learning a skill. This is not a sensitivity group, nor a group in which we will

[7]Reprinted by permission of the Women's Crisis Center, Ann Arbor, Michigan.

bare our innermost selves. We are here to learn empathy. However, as we will be dealing with feelings, particularly our own, we will probably feel more comfortable if we get to know what life experiences have brought each of us here. For this reason, and also to begin to become more conscious of feelings, the following exercises are provided.

A. Feeling Word List

This exercise will help you in building your feeling word vocabulary. You may each make your own lists individually, or you may do it as a group, collectively, on a blackboard. The idea is to try and think of as many feeling words as possible, using the adjective form of each word as opposed to the noun form, e.g. angry, spiteful, sorrowful as opposed to anger, spite, sorrow. It may be easier to arrange your feeling words by those you like experiencing and by those you don't like experiencing; you may also want to list feelings according to intensity, e.g. furious, angry, annoyed, etc.

B. Time Line

In this exercise, each of us will gradually depict the day we just had (today), up to and including the present (now). Your picture or time line should show how you felt during different events that occurred in your day. For example, confusion might be drawn as 🌀 and happiness as ☺ . Draw it the way you felt it!

After everyone has finished drawing, we will go around the circle, each person explaining her time line, beginning with the trainers. The purpose of this exercise is to help you become more aware of feeling words and how using them helps to clarify feelings. As you listen to others' time lines, listen for the feeling words. You will have an opportunity after each time line is presented to comment on the speaker's use or nonuse of such words.

II. Owning Feelings

Now that we are becoming more aware of feelings, and of

different kinds and shades of feelings, our next task is to become conscious of when people are owning or not owning their feelings. As a helper, your major function is to bring the victim to the point where she is freely and genuinely owning her feelings. In order to do this, you must have a clear idea of what it sounds like when someone is owning or not owning her feelings.

For illustrative purposes, three different levels of owning of feelings have been established:

LEVEL 1. The speaker avoids accepting any of her feelings, or she expresses feelings vaguely. When feelings are expressed, they are always seen as belonging to others, determined by the emotion, or as being outside of herself. She avoids identifying or admitting to any feelings. She discusses or intellectualizes about feelings in a detached, abstract manner. Example:

> The speaker, with flushed face, hotly declares, "Angry? Not me! You're the one who's getting angry. I'm just arguing my point of view."

LEVEL 2. The speaker can usually identify her feelings and their source, but tends to express them in an intellectualized manner. She seems to have an intellectual grasp of her feelings and their origin, but she has little emotional proximity to them. Example:

> The speaker blandly admits, "Yeah, I think I get a little hurt when boys don't want to go out with me, but I usually get over it."

LEVEL 3. The speaker almost always acknowledges her specific feelings and can express them with emotional proximity, i.e. as belonging to her or inside her. At the same time, she shows awareness that her feelings are tied to specific behavior of her own and of others. She shows immediate and free access to her feelings, expresses them in a genuine way, and is able to identify their origin or source. Example:

> The speaker says, "It really hurts me when you don't listen and you always ask me to do things you know I don't want to do. I feel so insignificant and small when you do that."

We have said that your task as a RCI peer counselor will be to help the woman own her feelings; however, you must also learn to recognize and own *your own* feelings during the counseling exchange, and to keep the two sets of feelings separate. Even though, outwardly, it appears that the woman is the only one who is experiencing feelings, and as tempting as it is to pretend that we are strong and all-knowing, peer counseling can only be effective when both RCI and client are operating at the same level — the feeling level.

We have therefore designed the following exercise to help you in learning to listen for feelings — both the client's and your own. Each member of the group will state a problem briefly, presenting it in terms of how it makes her feel. When she has finished giving the problem, each member of the group, or listeners, will provide the following feedback:

1. Using the "Owning of Feelings Rating Scale" above, say whether you think the speaker was at LEVEL 1, 2, or 3 in relating her problem to us. The point is to give listeners practice in hearing owning of feelings; the issue is *not* for us, as speakers, to learn how to give a LEVEL 3 response.

2. If you experienced feelings of your own while the speaker was stating her problem, try to recognize what they were and share them with the group. The presence or absence of any specific emotion depends heavily on your past experiences; the purpose of this part of the exercise is to show that different people may react to the same situation with totally different feelings.

Example:

Speaker: I have a problem with visiting my mother. I went there today to give her her birthday gift and all she did was gripe at me for not being there on her birthday which was last Sunday. I know I'm inconsiderate sometimes, but she doesn't make any effort to understand me and the kind of schedule I'm on. Whether it's her birthday or not, she's always criticizing me for neglecting her.

Listener 1: I think you presented this problem at a Level 1, as you didn't mention any feeling words (Part 1). I felt angry at your mother for being so selfish (Part 2).

Listener 2.   It sounded like a Level 2 to me because your voice sounded like you were feeling hurt (Part 1). I felt hurt that your mother doesn't understand you (Part 2).

Listener 3:   I think it was Level 1 and 2 because you were expressing feelings in your voice (Part 1). I started feeling guilty and kind of nervous about your having to face your mother with a late birthday gift, knowing what you were in for (Part 2).

Note the different reactions to the speaker's problem. One listener felt angry, one felt hurt, and another felt guilty and nervous. It is tempting and natural to project our feelings as listener on to the speaker. Many times the listener's feelings *do* match those of the speaker, but this can never be presumed! This is the reason that we must learn to recognize our own feelings as listener and keep them separate from the speaker's.

All three listeners in the example given above recognized that the speaker was not really owning any of the feelings she had about her problem with her mother. Even though her voice indicated she had definite feelings about it, she did not show, by her words, that she was aware of these feelings. Thus, a different speaker could present that same problem at a more emotional level, such as:

"Everytime I visit my mother it brings me down. Just because I was late with her birthday gift she starts griping at me for neglecting her. I get so angry at her for laying these guilt trips on me all the time, and it hurts me that she doesn't try to understand what a busy schedule I have."

Obviously, this is much closer to Level 3 owning of feelings than was our first example. Try to recognize your feelings now that you have read this second example. They will probably seem more obvious to you since the speaker was more obvious with hers. But there is still more work for you as a RCI peer counselor to do in helping a woman to explore all of her feelings about her mother in relation to the problem. Your next task is learning how to respond empathically to the speaker.

III. Empathic Understanding and Listener Responses

We have learned what it means to own one's feelings and how a person sounds when she does so. Now we will concentrate on the skills that a RCI peer counselor must use to help a speaker focus on her feelings.

By her responses, a RCI peer counselor can show the speaker that she is interested in the woman's problems, that she can be trusted, and that she is truly hearing the woman's messages. Pure empathic responses fall into a fairly limited pattern of word choice and sentence structure to allow the speaker the greatest amount of freedom to explore her feelings for herself.

For purposes of learning good empathic responses, we differentiate among three kinds of responses, defined as follows:

THE REFLECTING RESPONSE: Here, the listener rephrases what she perceives as key words or phrases from the speaker's own expressions while presenting her problem. Essentially, the listener's expressions can be thought of as interchangeable with those of the speaker in affective content and meaning in a reflecting response. The listener is responding so as neither to subtract from nor to add to the expressions of the speaker, but to mirror or reflect them back to her.

THE ADDING RESPONSE: The listener communicates her understanding of the speaker's words by expressing feelings at a level deeper than the speaker was able to express herself; she hears at a level beyond the speaker's admission or awareness. The adding response uncovers feelings that were hinted at but were not clearly expressed by the speaker. (The listener must exercise caution when using the adding response, as it involves risk on her part. She must be prepared to accept the speaker's denial of feelings expressed in her adding response — the listener may be too far ahead of the speaker or the response may become an interpretation.)

THE DETRACTING RESPONSE: The listener minimally acknowledges the speaker's feelings, or communicates less about the feelings than the speaker herself expressed; the listener subtracts from, or responds to other than what the speaker is expressing — the listener is falling behind the speaker.

Obviously, we are going to try to avoid ever giving a detracting response. As far as the other two types — reflecting and adding — there is no hard and fast rule about which is better. Whatever response helps the speaker to have a greater ownership and understanding of her feelings is the best response, and this you will learn as you gain more and more practice as an empathic RCI peer counselor. You are becoming more empathic as you are increasingly able to respond to a speaker as though you were she, in her world.

In order to illustrate the above three types of responses, the following examples are presented. In the interest of continuity and clarity, we shall work with the problem presented as an example in Part II, "Owning Feelings."

Example 1:

> Speaker: My mother is right, I am inconsiderate sometimes. But she never makes any effort to understand the kind of schedule I'm on. She's always criticizing me for neglecting her.
>
> Reflecting: She criticized you a lot for things you have no control over.
>
> Adding: It sounds like you're really angry. Or — It must hurt when your mother treats you so unfairly.
>
> Detracting: Oh well. You know mothers. They never understand anyway.

In this case, where the speaker names no feelings but merely outlines the problem, a true reflecting response would contain no feeling words. Note that the reflecting response merely paraphrases the speaker's words. This tells the speaker that the listener is really hearing what is being said. It also gives the speaker a slightly different view of the problem, from which she might gain a new perspective by her response at that point to her listener. The speaker might even be able to now express some of her feelings about the matter.

On the adding response, we used two different responses to show that we very often have to choose between two or more strong feelings that we are hearing. Either of these responses would be appropriate, but we try not to use two different feeling words in one response to avoid confusing the speaker.

Thus, if we use the word "angry" the speaker is very apt to pursue her feelings of anger, and if we use "hurt," she is apt to start exploring in that direction.

Example 2:

    Speaker: I get so angry at my mother for laying all these guilt trips on me. Can't she understand what a busy schedule I have?

    Reflecting: It really makes you feel angry that she never understands you.

    Adding: I sense your anger, but then, it sounds like you're feeling hurt too.

    Detracting: I guess you'll just have to learn to put up with her, but I don't blame you for feeling angry.

When the speaker *is* expressing her feelings, your responses will be correspondingly different, i.e. the reflecting response repeats the feeling word or words she may have used, while the adding response introduced a different, though related feeling. Here the speaker *already knows* she is angry but hasn't owned the hurt as yet.

The detracting response is two-fold in its error: the first part of the response is obviously wrong for it offers ready-made quick advice; the second part is more subtly incorrect. The feeling of anger is acknowledged, but saying, "I don't blame you ..." implies that perhaps the feeling of anger is not appropriate for the speaker to feel. For example, "It is not right to feel angry at your mother, but you have my permission to feel angry." Or — "I forgive you for feeling angry." It sounds too much like a value judgment on the part of the listener.

For exercises in this part, you may either have a discussion and question-answer period, or you may practice making your own empathic responses to the above speaker or still, some among you may wish to contribute new speaker situations.

IV. Interpersonal Process Recall (IPR) (Kagan, 1975)[8]

Everything we have done up until now has been by way of introducing you to the various aspects of being an empathic

---

[8]Kagan, N.: *Interpersonal Process Recall: A Method of Influencing Human Interaction.* East Lansing, Michigan State University, 1975. Reprinted by permission.

listener and RCI peer counselor. Now, we will combine all these aspects — identifying feeling words, owning of feelings by speaker and listener, and listener responses — and put them into practice by working with each other. This will be accomplished through the use of the IPR practice model.

IPR is a model of assisting the listener in learning helping responses by processing (recalling) but not evaluating the speaker-listener exchange. The model was originally developed by Dr. Norman Kagan of Michigan State University. The IPR model consists of the interaction between the speaker and listener and the recall or processing of the interaction. Each step is more clearly defined below:

INTERACTION: the process whereby the speaker presents a personal problem to a listener who is acting as the helper. This interaction is audiotaped or videotaped and is usually not more than five or ten minutes in length. During this period, the listener attempts to respond in an empathic manner, using the knowledge which she has gained thus far from the training sessions.

MUTUAL RECALL: the process whereby a third person helps process the speaker-listener dialogue by asking the speaker-listener to relive feelings and ideas each had had during their exchange. The recall person does not actively become part of the helping process between the speaker-listener, but is more interested in helping the participants tell each other what they wanted and really thought and felt during the recorded session. Questions which a recaller may wish to ask during the tape playback include:

1. What were you (the speaker) thinking?
2. What were you (the speaker) feeling?
3. What pictures, memories, or words were going through your (the speaker's) mind?
4. What did you (the speaker) think the other person (the listener) was feeling?
5. What did you want the other person (the listener) to think or feel?
6. Was there anything you (the speaker) wanted to say but couldn't find the right words to use?

7. Do you (the speaker) recall how your body felt — can you recall any specific part of your body reacting more than other parts?
8. What did the sex or physical appearance of the other person (the listener) do to you?
9. How did you feel about your role as listener?
10. What would you (the listener) say were the speaker's dominant feelings in relation to her problems?
11. If you had it to do over again, what responses would you (the listener) now use?

The recall person's approach should be characterized by exploratory, brief, open-ended questions, some about thoughts, some about feelings; listening rather than telling, interpreting, counseling, or teaching; and avoidance of communication blocks by remaining nonjudgmental and nondiverting.

Both speaker and listener are encouraged to participate in the recall and either can stop the tape whenever anything is recalled by them. In the first few IPRs, the trainers will do the recalling, but later the trainees will be expected to take over. This may be engaged in without observers, but in learning the recall or inquirer role, it may be useful to have two to three observers whose principle role is to give feedback to the inquirers.

GROUP DISCUSSION: After the recaller is finished playing back the tape and asking her questions, any member of the group who has further ideas to express or questions to ask may do so. In general, the group should follow these basic rules of providing feedback:

1. Focus feedback on behavior rather than the person.
2. Focus feedback on observations rather than inferences.
3. Focus feedback on description rather than judgment.
4. Focus feedback on exploration of alternatives rather than answers or solutions.
5. Avoid telling what you saw "right" or "wrong" but instead there could have been "more" of this or "less" of this.

Each trainee in the group must do two speaker roles and two listening roles. The two roles may be thought of as the two sides of the same coin; one is just as important as the other in learning the empathy model.

During the recall, we do not concentrate only on the listener's role. You will find that as speakers you will also gain valuable insight into the way empathy works by experiencing it in relation to your own feelings and problems. To experience empathic understanding in this way is to become convinced of its value. If you know that it works, your learning of the skills will be greatly facilitated. Finally, IPR is a complex model requiring forty to sixty hours of training and includes a variety of exercises and films. The above format is only one facet of IPR training.[9]

Special Notes About the Listener's Role

In learning the empathy model, you might be tempted to ask direct questions of the speaker because you're not that certain of your ability to hear the feelings which s/he is expressing. Please try to resist this temptation. Asking the speaker if s/he is feeling angry often confuses her/him or puts her/him on the defensive. Making a statement such as, "It sounds like you're angry" gives the speaker the option of accepting or rejecting that feeling word, and often encourages her/him to find the right feeling word in its place. We are facilitators, not inquisitors.

Another point here is that as a listener, you may at times find that your personal feelings are interfering with your ability to listen empathically to the speaker. For example, you may suspect that s/he is being much less than honest with you and you may find yourself growing impatient or even angry with her/him. This is the time for you as listener, to openly discuss your feelings, being careful that s/he understands: (1) that your main desire is to help and you are sharing your feelings with her/him only because they are interfering with your ability to be helpful, and (2) that you first let the speaker know that you

---

[9]You can obtain more information on IPR by writing Dr. Norman Kagan at 434 Erickson Hall, Michigan State University, East Lansing, Michigan 48823.

understand her/him and are not trying to take her/his feelings away from her/him.

The final point has to do with a listener's tendency to offer solutions for the victim's problems, whether or not s/he asks for them. During our empathy training we will not be dealing with solutions — only feelings. The Women's Crisis Center's problem-solving training will be offered to you at a later time: You will then learn some techniques for solutions.

V. Group Feedback and the Role of Trainers

The role of the trainers is to help the volunteers develop the empathic skills they will need to do counseling. The trainers are open to any feedback and criticism you may have. If you feel uncomfortable with what the trainers are doing, or if you are having difficulty understanding what is going on, feel free to interrupt at any time and talk about it. For instance, you may wish to discuss how the trainers are causing you to feel, or whether they are helping or hindering your learning process. Points like these can be raised by an individual or by the whole group, and are vital to a successful training experience.

Throughout the program, the trainers will be giving you feedback on how well you are developing the skill and aspects that you need to work on. The tendency is to feel that your competence or value as a person is being judged. This is not the case. Learning is a matter of trial and error, and you will learn more if you are willing to accept feedback given appropriately from both trainers and your peers.

At the end of your training program, we will have evaluations — of trainees and of trainers. The evaluation process is done within the group, with each person being required to contribute. It works like this:

Beginning with the trainees, each trainee in turn begins her/his own evaluation by stating how well s/he believes s/he learned the empathy model during the program and whether s/he feels ready to go on the telephones. Then, each of the other trainees offers comments regarding that trainee's understanding of empathy, and whether s/he would feel comfortable going to her/him with a problem. Finally, the trainers give their comments and final evaluation of how ready the trainee is for phone counseling.

After each trainee has finished with the above process, there will be individual and/or group feedback on their perceptions and feelings regarding their trainer's effectiveness. At all times, we must keep our comments and criticisms constructive.

One final note, most trainees complete their program of training successfully; however, it is not uncommon for trainers to request some trainees to meet with them one more time for additional practice. More rarely, there are times when trainers must conclude of a trainee that s/he cannot do phone counseling at the present time. The reasons for these decisions will be spelled out as clearly as trainers are able, and trainees should also try, as far as possible, to understand such reasons. As uncomfortable or undesirable as the evaluation process may seem, it is the only way of insuring our community that women who come to the RCC for help will in fact receive competent help.

* * *

As a means of practicing what was learned through the "Empathy Training Manual," the training staff may wish to then have the volunteers respond to the stimulus expressions on the following form.

Instructions[10]

Name_____

As a volunteer for the Community Crisis and Information Center, you will be answering the telephone and talking with people, especially women, who are in need of your assistance. Many of these persons call the Crisis Center when they are in desperate need of contact, acceptance, and understanding from you. Some of the calls will also need a practical referral for

---

[10]Reprinted by permission of the Community Crisis and Information Center at Fort Collins, Colorado.

services in the community. Whether the call is an urgent crisis for the client, or whether the call is a request for information from you, you will be placed in the role of a helping person. A helping person offers acceptance of the crisis victim and her/his problem and attempts to understand the problem. The kind of understanding that is the most helpful to clients is empathic understanding, or trying to feel and communicate to the other person what it is like to be feeling the way s/he feels at that moment. If the caller communicates a sense of desperation to you, it will be helpful to show in a warm accepting manner your understanding of those feelings of desperation and hopelessness. If a caller is feeling frustrated and at wit's end, your role as a helper would be to communicate a sense of the person's frustration.

The following nine statements are similar to calls you would be receiving as a volunteer. You are to read each statement and try to experience, inside yourself, what it must be like to be in the caller's shoes. The questions you will be asking yourself are: "What is it like to be feeling and thinking like the caller? What would it be like to feel so desperate, or confused, or lost? How can I convey the sense of my understanding to this person, so that s/he feels in touch with me? How can I communicate my concern and caring? How can the caller best hear my understanding?"

After each stimulus expression or vignette there are two blanks provided. In the first blank, please let us know how you personally felt about the caller's expression. What feelings did *you* experience as you read the call? Tense, anxious, angry?

In the second blank, please write your response to the caller — what you would say to this person. Focus on your understanding of the caller, and try to convey to the caller your emotional understanding and empathy.

Stimulus Expressions:

1. I don't know if you can help me, but I've tried everywhere else that I could possibly go. I just don't have anybody else to listen to me and try to understand what's happening to

me. I've been so edgy and nervous lately. I can't even seem to get a good night's sleep.

I feel ...

I would respond ...

2. I am really tempted to drop the whole thing. I don't know if I want this thing over my head for so long. I've heard the grand jury may not sit for a long time yet and then it can take quite a while for the trial. I don't know if that's what I want. I just want to be left alone and let it be in the past. I don't want the defense attorney jumping all over me. I get so upset just thinking about it, so I'd rather not do it.

I feel ...

I would respond ...

3. I am afraid to talk to you about this but I'm afraid of what I'll do. He's screaming again. Yesterday — I know how bad this is — but, yesterday, he just wouldn't stop screaming. I was just going to slap him once to make him stop. I really don't remember all of it. I couldn't help it.

I feel ...

I would respond ...

4: I think I must be going crazy. A few weeks ago I couldn't help crying, at nothing. Now I talk all the time and can't stop walking back and forth. There is nothing you can do for me. After this age, there's not much to live for anyway. I know my husband wants to get rid of me. But I can't blame him. I'm no good to anyone. I've been acting just like an animal.

I feel ...

I would respond ...

5. I'm depressed. There's nothing else to say ... (Pause) ... Um, ... I don't know ... (sigh).

I feel ...

I would respond ...

6. Our marriage is really going badly after it. Soon after I came home from the hospital, he approached me sexually when I was still very hurt and I said, "Not yet honey. I'm still not ready." Well, he didn't understand, then he got angry and now we hardly even see or talk to each other.

I feel ...

I would respond ...

7. I just layed there; it was so unreal, just like I was watching what was going on. This couldn't be happening to me. After he left, I must have still layed there for a long time before I came back to the real world and called the police.

I feel ...

I would respond ...

8. What kind of place is this? I've called you people twice now and you've done absolutely nothing except wait on the line. If you can't help people then you shouldn't call yourself the Community Crisis and Information Center and I'm going to make sure you lose that title.

I feel ...

I would respond ...

9. I feel so sleepy ... uh ... I took them ... I had to ...

I feel ...

I would respond ...

* * *

HELPING SKILLS

In order to respond with empathy, the RCI needs something to respond to, i.e. material provided by the victim. Two responses which will make it easier for the crisis victim to speak with you are called "open-ended responses" and "encouraging responses."

Open-ended Responses

Open-ended responses are questions asked by the RCI of the victim to which the victim cannot respond with a simple "yes" or "no," but must expand upon what is said. A response which begins with a stated or implied, "How, What, Why, or Please tell me more about ..." usually are the type of questions which help a person respond with a lengthy answer.

Examples of open-ended questions:

How do you feel right now?

How does your husband act toward you now?

What are some of your reasons for not wanting to tell your parents about the assault?

What were you doing when the assault occurred?

Please tell me more about what you mean when you say you feel worthless.

Please tell me more about your treatment by the doctors?

Why do you feel guilty about the assault?

Why is it you want to move?

An important aspect of your open-ended responses as a RCI is the tonal quality of your voice. A slightly lower pitch than your conversational voice conveys your interest and a type of intimacy which helps establish an "I-Thou" relationship. Also, *decreasing* your rate of speaking and *increasing* the tentativeness in your questioning differentiates therapeutic open-ended responses from a legal interrogation or cross-examination.

An open-ended response may best be understood when compared to a closed approach of questioning:

Open: Please tell me more about your family?

Closed: Are your parents understanding?

Open: How do you feel when a man looks at you?

Closed: Do you feel naked when a man looks at you?

Questions which begin with "Do you, Are you, Have you, Will you, Is she, Did you, Has he ... " will always be closed and should be avoided.

Open-ended questions are extremely useful in a number of situations during the helping process:

1. Beginning the first interview, e.g. "Rape Crisis Center. Mary speaking. *How* can I help you?
2. Beginning a second interview, e.g. *"How* have things been going since we last talked?"
3. Helping the woman elaborate on a point, e.g. *"Please tell me more about* your feeling of helplessness."
4. Helping the woman give examples of specific behaviors, e.g. *"What* do you do when you get depressed?"
5. Helping the woman focus her attention on her feelings,

e.g. *"How* did that cause you to feel?"

Encouraging Responses

Once the woman has been helped to begin talking by the use of open-ended responses, the next task is to facilitate her continuing to talk. You really need to say very little in order to encourage the woman to continue talking, elaborating, and explaining. Simple "um-humms," repeating one or two words from what she has just said, one-word questions such as "Then?" are often all that is needed.

More examples of the type of responses which aid in helping a woman to continue to talk about her concerns are:

1. "Oh?" "So?" "Then?" "And?"
2. "Go on." "Tell me more." "Continue."
3. "Right," "Yes." "Um-Humm."

Be careful not to overwork the "um-humms." Some people report that beginning helpers often "um-hum" them into the ground.

Attending Behavior

For those RCCs also having walk-in facilities or having an advocate or companion outreach program, your volunteers will also need to be aware of their nonverbal behavior, which can either facilitate or inhibit a helping encounter. This nonverbal behavior, when used appropriately, is often called "attending behavior."

Appropriate attending behavior shows a woman that you respect her as a person and that you are interested in what she has to say. Attending behavior helps to establish a secure atmosphere in which the woman will feel free as well as encouraged to discuss whatever is on her mind.

Four primary activities which characterize good attending are:

1. The RCI should be physically relaxed and seated in a natural posture. If the RCI is comfortable, s/he will be

better able to listen to the woman and attend to her.

2. Leaning slightly forward in your chair and maintaining an open posture (one in which the RCI's arms and legs aren't crossed tightly) as the woman begins to talk about her concerns emphasizes your interest. You're implicitly saying "I'm with you, it's all right, please continue."

3. The RCI should initiate and maintain eye-contact with the woman. However, eye-contact, like "um-humms," can be overdone. A varied use of eye-contact is most effective. Staring fixedly will probably make the woman uneasy and feel on the spot. The basic rule is: If you're going to listen to someone, look at the person.

4. The last major characteristic of appropriate attending behavior is that the RCI's comments follow what the woman has just said. By directing one's comments and questions to the topics provided by the woman, the RCI will not only help her develop an area of discussion, but the RCI's responses will help reward the woman's free expression.

Specific behaviors you will want to use are:

1. Relax physically, feel the presence of the chair as you are sitting on it.

2. Let your posture be comfortable and your movements natural. For example, if you usually gesture with your hands, feel free to do so as you are talking with the woman, but be careful these gestures do not become distractions.

3. Use eye-contact by looking at the woman with whom you're speaking.

4. *Don't jump topics and don't interrupt.* If you are afraid you're going to forget what was said or you can't think of anything to say, go back to an earlier part of the conversation and ask a question about that or just remain silent rather than asking an awkward question.

5. There is no need to talk about yourself or your opinions when you are concentrating on attending skills. It is sometimes very hard to keep yourself quiet when you are truly interested in the other person, but your task as a RCI is to learn how to help your clients talk while you do the listening and responding.

6. Avoid distracting behaviors, such as checking your watch every few minutes, wringing your hands, picking at your fingernails, filling out forms, etc.

In summary then, your goal as a RCI is to listen attentively and to communicate a warm and friendly "waiting-for-you, my time is yours" atmosphere through a relaxed open posture, use of varied eye-contact, and verbal responses which indicate to the client you are attempting to understand what she is communicating.

Now that the assault victim has been made to feel comfortable and she knows you are attentive to her, she needs to believe you can understand the sequence of events, or the informational/cognitive portion of her message. This is where the RCI will want to use "Paraphrasing" or "Reflection of Feeling" responses.

Paraphrasing Responses

Paraphrasing focuses on the content or information present in the woman's message. Using paraphrasing responses, the RCI feeds back the essential content or data portion of what the woman has just said, using new and unique or different words by the RCI.

It is:

1. A tentative statement, but not verbatim restatement.
2. A response focusing on thoughts, content, subject matter, description, or factual data.
3. A response by which the RCI feeds back the crux or central part of the woman's message in the form of a summary response.

It is used to:

1. Encourage, support, and reward client talking because it says the RCI does understand.
2. Increase the woman's comfort level, as talking about content or facts is less threatening than discussing the victim's feelings.

3. Clarify confusing material by being a synopsis or summary of what the client said.
4. Tie comments together.
5. Highlight issues by stating them concisely.
6. Check the RCI's understanding and perceptions of what the woman is saying.

It is not:

1. A verbatim restatement of what the woman has just said.
2. A parroting response.
3. Focusing on the feelings of the woman.
4. A response in which all the details and facts are recounted for the woman.
5. A response stating, "You are ...!" but one which says, "It seems to *me* that ..."

Below are some examples of paraphrasing responses during an exchange between a client and a RCI:

Client: "This is one of the things he said indicated that I was still upset about the assault (blows nose, wipes eyes, sniffles, cries)."

RCI: "The doctor thought that the tears were caused by some remaining strong feelings about the assault."

Client: "(Bawling) ... For no reason at all, I begin to cry. I just feel like crying and never stop crying. I don't know why."

RCI: "You don't know why you get these feelings that you can't stop crying."

Client: "I really can't decide if I'm right or wrong. If it is wrong, I think I'd try to break it. I do it so completely automatically that I really don't have time to think before it happens."

RCI: "It seems you really can't decide whether it's right or it's wrong, but it just seems to happen."

You will notice the RCI summarized the essential content of the client's message, focusing *only* on content, and used words familiar to the RCI. Perhaps an analogy which will help is to imagine the paraphrasing responses as a newspaper's account of an incident. Typically, a news story only deals with the facts and a description of what happened in summary form, using words similar to but not exactly the same as the people involved in the incident.

Now that the RCI has made the rape victim comfortable, helped her begin exploring her concern, and conveyed her understanding of what happened by her encouraging, open-ended, attending, and paraphrasing responses, it now becomes necessary for the RCI to assist the woman in sorting out and clarifying some of her feelings so the victim can better understand her own emotional state. This can be accomplished by the RCI combining what was learned in the "Empathy Training Manual" with a response called "Reflection of Feelings."

Reflection of Feelings

The skill of reflection of feelings requires that the RCI be able to convey to the victim a sense that the RCI can deeply sense some of the emotional or perceptual world which the victim is encountering. This will help to establish more rapport, a greater sense of trust, and can facilitate the client's movement toward more complete self-awareness.

Using this skill, the RCI is asked to focus upon and respond to the feelings or affect expressed and unexpressed by the victim, rather than focusing upon the content of the message. This means focusing upon how the woman is speaking, not on what she is saying. For example, a woman may speak more quickly when communicating enthusiasm or excitement, but speak more slowly when communicating discouragement or sadness.

It is:

1. A tentative statement, but not verbatim restatement of the feelings being experienced by the assault victim, e.g. *not* "I'm mad"; "You're mad."
2. A response focusing on affect, feelings, emotion, or attitudes of the woman.

3. A response in which the RCI feeds back the essential affect or theme feeling expressed by the woman.
4. A response by the RCI which neither exaggerates nor lessens the feeling level expressed by the client.

It is used for:

1. Encouraging, supporting, and rewarding the woman's feeling talk.
2. Increasing the woman's emotional expressions, as feelings are more personally meaningful or more stress provoking than subject matter. The "work" of the relationship becomes much more difficult.
3. Conveying empathic understanding, as the RCI's response should be an accurate reflection of the woman's emotional state, neither too deep nor too shallow.
4. Helping the woman recognize and "own" her feelings. This builds better self-understanding and enables her to deal more effectively with recognized feelings.
5. Ventilating or unloading feelings.
6. Checking the RCI's understanding and perceptions of the woman's emotional world, thus remaining with her.

Being alert for and responding to both expressed and unexpressed feelings of the rape victim is a skill which is appropriate at any time, regardless of the direction, i.e. towards self, others, or the RCI.

In the following two examples, the RCI is asked to choose the feeling or reflective response by placing an X in the correct blank.

Example 1:

Client: "So, I'm wondering if you can help me find a counselor ... (Pause) ... I guess if I did find a new one, she wouldn't understand either."

RCI: ___ a. "Are you sure you want to change counselors?"

___ b. "You feel it would be pretty futile to try again."

___ c. "What qualities do you want in a new counselor?"

Example 2:

Client: "After the assault, my father calls me every other night and demands a detailed description of what I did and who I did it with. He treats me like a child and I've had it up to here with that."

RCI: ___ a. "Do you really mean every other night?"

___ b. "He certainly keeps a pretty close check on you.

___ c. "I'm hearing a lot of anger and frustration coming from you as a result of your father's lack of trust in you."

Answers: Example 1: Response a. and c. seek more information from the woman, whereas response b. accurately responds to the feelings being expressed.

Example 2: Responses a. and b. neither seek more information nor confirm present information. Response c. accurately responds to the feelings of anger and frustration being expressed.

PARAPHRASING-REFLECTION OF FEELINGS — COMMONALITIES: As both paraphrasing and reflective responses are two of the most important responses in the helping process, a summary of characteristics they share in common is appropriate.

They are both:

1. A tentative statement — There is an implied "period" in the RCI's voice.
2. A feeding back, rephrasing in fresh new words the essence of what the client has just said.

They are both used for:

1. Letting the rape victim know that the RCI is "with" her, that the RCI is trying to understand what the woman is saying. This offers the victim much needed support.
2. Keeping the woman actively involved in the helping process. This conveys the message that helping is an interaction in which both client and RCI are responsible active

participants.
3. Getting out all the data in order to define the woman's situation. (Data as used here means pertinent, affective, intrapersonal, and interpersonal material, as well as factual material.)
4. Allowing the victim to assume the lead in the process and run her own story as she chooses. This is accomplished by the RCI's paraphrasing or reflecting the essence, theme, or general idea of the woman's dialogue.
5. Allowing the woman to "hear" herself, hear what she is saying.
6. Tying recent comments together.
7. Clarifying confusion in the message.
8. Making sure the RCI is always understanding the victim by using these perception checkers.

Bringing It Together

The three responses of open-ended questions, paraphrases, and reflection are the core of the helping process. They may be used at any time in the rape crisis, from the actual crisis to the point of successful resolution of the aftermath, perhaps months or years later.

It is important to see how they all tie together in a helping interaction. Perhaps the illustration below will help.

Phone rings.

RCI: "Rape Crisis Center. May speaking. *How* may I help you?" (open-ended response)

Client: "I've been raped!"

RCI: *"Please tell me more about* what happened." (open-ended)

Client: ... silence ...

RCI: "It's pretty hard for you to talk about right now." (paraphrasing response)

"Just take your time and when you're ready to talk then we can begin. I'm in no hurry." (offering acceptance and support)

Client: "This happened two days ago ... I haven't talked to anybody about it but I've just got to talk to someone."

RCI: "It's been too difficult to talk about, but now you need to share the experience with someone." (paraphrasing)

Client: "It's really been unreal. I've been so lost the last couple of days, I don't know what to do."

RCI: "You've been feeling pretty confused since the assault, and kind of helpless." (reflection of feeling)

Client: "Yeah. It's the not knowing what to do or even if I should do something."

Perhaps from this short exchange you can see how the three core responses interrelate and help the process flow smoothly. The RCI first asks an open-ended question, then, depending on whether the victim responds with content or feelings, the RCI next responds with a paraphrasing or reflective response, which then serves to reward the woman for talking and she continues or the RCI asks another open-ended question.

SECONDARY HELPING RESPONSES

There are any number of helping responses the RCI may have to use at particular times or under special circumstances during the helping process. A list and brief description of some are on the following pages.

CLARIFICATION: Often a person will use a word, such as love, hate, them, dirty, depressed, which may have many different meanings. As the RCI may be uncertain as to what the victim means by using a particular word, it is important that the RCI knows her particular meaning. The RCI's clarifying response then takes the form of an implied or stated:

"When you say ... , do you mean ... or ... ?"

PROBING: When coupled with *tentativeness*, a probing response is aimed at gently getting the woman to talk more concretely about a feeling or thought. The RCI is asking the woman to focus on the *who, when, where, how,* and *what* of the message. A RCI's probing response can take the form of:

"I think I understand what you mean, but please tell me about the last time *when* you had this feeling."

REFOCUSING: Frequently, as the RCI begins to probe the specific emotionally laden feelings of the rape victim, she will change topics or begin to speak in an abstract way about her concerns. It then becomes the RCI's task to *gently* help her again focus on the specific aspects of the original concern, and the refocusing response might take the form of:

"I think I now hear us talking about people in general. A couple of minutes ago, you were describing how your friends have seemed to shun you. Please tell me more about what happens."

OWNERSHIP: A fairly good rule of thumb you can use to help the woman move from an abstract intellectualized level to a level of specificity and concreteness, is by helping her use personal pronouns to describe herself in relation to the concern. The RCI can ask the woman who continually describes her problem in the second person, i.e. *"They* say," *"You* have to," *"One* must," *"People* are," etc., to *own* her thoughts or feelings by using an ownership response such as:

"I'm interested in how it is for *you.*"

ADVISING: This is a directive response in which the RCI tells the woman what to do. The RCI draws upon her own knowledge and experience to assist in resolving a concern. If done *tentatively,* it may be compared to suggestion, which is a less authoritative manner of presenting ideas for the woman to consider. A major drawback of advising is that it makes it difficult for the woman to reject any idea without the RCI inferring rejection of her too. Any advice is also value and opinion laden with the RCI's values and opinions as to what would be best for another person.

Client: "Should I report the assault?"

RCI: "I think you should go to the police right now, so he

(the rapist) gets what he deserves."

APPROVAL: This is a response of the RCI in which s/he expresses her/his approval of some particular thing the client has said or done. This response is used in the hope that the RCI's approval will influence the appropriate behavior of the woman. It does have some drawbacks if used indiscriminately or too often, but it can be effective if the RCI is an authority on the subject being discussed.

Client: "Although it will be hard, I think I'll tell my husband about the experience."
RCI: "Good! That seems to be a wise decision for you."

PROVIDING FEEDBACK ABOUT THE HELPING RELATIONSHIP: This is a response by the RCI in which s/he provides feedback to the client about the RCI's perceptions of her in the helping interview. It is used to attempt to move the helping relationship to a more meaningful level.

Client: "I don't really know."
RCI: "You don't know or you don't want to talk about it?"
Client: "What more is there to talk about?"
RCI: "During our time together today, I feel like you've been treading water and I'm trying to help you swim. How does it seem to you?"

INCOMPLETE THOUGHT: This is a technique in which the RCI deliberately pauses in the middle of a sentence to see if the client will finish the thought. This RCI behavior may be used to draw out the thinking which the victim may be doing about a particular point which seems important to the RCI.

Client: "I'm just not being myself and I can't understand it."
RCI: "When you say you're not yourself, you mean
_____ ."

INFORMING: This RCI response is used as a lead in order to convey to the client information with which the woman may be unfamiliar and which may have an impact on her immediate concern. Informing involves supplying information or material that is not known to or not readily available to the client.

Client: "I'm not really sure I should report the rape. What reasons do other women have for deciding to report it?"

RCI: "I can appreciate your uncertainty. I guess most women decide to report the rape because they want the man caught so it doesn't happen to another woman, or because they feel the strong need to do *something* and to talk with *someone* about the incident."

POINTING OUT CONTRADICTIONS: This RCI response is most generally used after a series of statements is made by the woman, some of which seem to be contradictory. The purpose is to understand the client more accurately by having her reflect upon her seeming inconsistencies.

"You (the victim) say that Barbara is your best friend and that she alone understands how you feel. On the other hand, you sometimes don't see her for weeks because you'd rather be alone. I don't get this. It seems like you are contradicting yourself by not doing what you know would help."

STRUCTURING: This is a technique used by the RCI in which s/he and the client share their expectations about the nature of the relationship itself. It is the process by which the nature, limits, and goals of the relationship are delineated. This response provides both the RCI and the client with a framework or orientation for their encounter. It should be minimal however, nonpunitive, and well defined so as to provide a basis of mutuality or a sense of "commonness of purpose." A structuring RCI response might take the form of:

"It's not really my role in either asking, suggesting, or telling you to do something which you may not fundamentally want to do. I am interested however, in talking and thinking these things through with *you* so *you* feel what *you* are doing is what *you* want to do. By talking these things over in the time we have, *you* may be able to find some new ways of coping with these things. Feel free to begin anywhere and talk about anything *you* like."

SPECIAL HELPING SKILLS

There are two other skills which the RCI may use and which there are often a number of questions about during the training program. These two skills are the use of silence by the RCI and the appropriateness of self-disclosure by the RCI in speaking with a client.

Volunteers' concerns about these two skills are usually brought out during the training by the trainees' remarks similar to ... , "I didn't know what to say so I just kept quiet. Is it OK not to always say something to the woman after she has stopped talking?" or "I really wanted to let her know that I understood what she was saying and how she was feeling because I have been raped too, but I didn't know whether I should."

Silence

This is a response by the RCI used to cause or "force" another person to verbally interact. It may be used to give the client "thinking time" to gather her thoughts together before saying something, or allow the client a chance to get in touch with her feelings at that moment.

Perhaps the reason there are so many questions regarding the appropriateness of silence is because the conventions of social conversation in our culture discourage silence. Thus, we have learned to become uneasy or defensive with silences and regard long pauses in communication as tantamount to a social vacuum.

INFERENCES FROM SILENCE IN A RELATIONSHIP:

1. There are basically two types of silences;
    a. *negative or rejecting silence:* We have often used the "silent treatment" as a form of rejection, defiance, or condemnation. When we argue with another person, we are saying we respect the person enough to want to

change them, but negative silence says coldly and harshly that the other person is not even worth talking to.

b. *positive or accepting silence:* This involves the non-verbal rapport-building and acceptance behaviors which communicate a positive message of acceptance to another person, e.g. facial expression, distance, posture, and courtesy.

2. Another meaning of silence is that the person has reached the end of a thought and is merely wondering what to say. A longer pause may mean that both people are confused and have lost track of their way in the interaction.

3. A third meaning of silence is conveying a passive-resistant, hostility-motivated message or anxiety-motivated embarrassment.

4. Fourthly, silence may mean the individual (client) is experiencing some particularly painful feelings which she is unable to verbalize at the moment.

5. A fifth meaning might be called "anticipatory" in that the person pauses verbally, expecting something verbal from the other person — reassurance, acceptance, information. This is often common in one-to-one relationships.

6. Finally, a silent pause may mean the person is merely regaining from the fatigue of a previous emotional expression. Here again, quiet acceptance of the silence is probably the appropriate approach.

USES OF SILENCE AS A RELATIONSHIP SKILL:

1. Positive and accepting silence forces the other person to talk and can focus the responsibility for verbal interaction on the other person involved in the helping relationship.

2. Silence can help the less articulate person feel accepted, and hopefully experience this same attitude toward herself and accept herself for what she is.

3. Another use of silence is that after remaining silent for a long time following a significant expression of feelings, the client is allowed to think and come up with a new insight or awareness to the expressed feeling. Silence in

this case focuses depth on one's penetration into the client's own feelings.

4. Finally, silence can be used to slow down the pace of an interview. Often the amount or the pace of the verbal exchange within an interview is directly related to anxiety levels of the participants.

Don't be afraid of silences or using them constructively in the helping interview. An often stated reason a RCI will not use appropriate silences is because s/he is uptight about it, but this may be just what the victim needs at a particular moment.

Self-Disclosure

If used at the appropriate times and not over done, the RCI's self-disclosures can facilitate the development of a close personal relationship with the woman.

Self-disclosure may be defined as revealing how the RCI is reacting to the present situation and giving any information about the past which is relevant to understanding how you are reacting in the present. To be self-disclosing is to share with the woman your feelings about something she has done or said, or how the RCI feels about the events having just taken place in the client's life. Self-disclosing is not revealing intimate details of your past but sharing your reactions and feelings to events both of you have experienced.

Self-disclosure is appropriate when:

1. It is not a random or isolated act, but rather is part of an on-going relationship.
2. It is offered in the hope of reciprocation by the other participant.
3. It concerns what is going on within and between persons in the present.
4. It creates a reasonable chance of facilitating growth in the relationship.
5. Account is taken of its probable impact upon the other person.
6. The RCI senses that the woman feels very alone now and

feels no one else has experienced her feelings.

7. The RCI senses a great deal of guilt in the woman as the result of thinking, "I'm the only one who has these terrible thoughts of wanting to kill the bastard or wanting to kill myself."

8. It facilitates movement to a deeper level of understanding.

The willingness to be self-disclosing is characteristic of a person who is genuine, open, honest, and who feels a strong need to be "with" others. The self-disclosing person is likely to be flexible, adaptive, and generally views other people as good rather than evil.

So, while deeper understanding can be built through self-disclosure, you may want to hide reactions where the other person is clearly untrustworthy and is likely to misinterpret or overreact to your self-disclosures, e.g. "You've been raped too, well, how can you understand me; you're probably still as mixed-up as I am."

Conclusion

We have moved down the first half of the helping process, i.e. we have put the woman at ease, conveyed empathy and acceptance, helped her explore her concerns, and have developed a meaningful relationship based on mutual understanding.

In the next section, we will discuss the problem-solving process which is the the upward half of the helping model. Here the rape victim is assisted in considering various alternatives, deciding on the one having the best chance of success, and formulating a plan of action so she leaves the helping interview knowing what she is going to do, at least in the immediate future.

PROBLEM SOLVING

Prior to beginning the actual process of problem solving, it is important to ask the crisis victim three questions. These questions will provide the RCI with a base from which to move into the problem-solving phase. These three questions are focused on the past, present, and future.

First: How has it been?
(Past)   What was going on?
            How did you feel before this happened?
Second: How is it now?
(Present)   What's going on now?
            How do you feel now?
Third: How would you like it to be?
(Future)   What would you like to have happening?
            How would you like to feel?

By asking these kinds of questions, the RCI can get a complete overview of the woman's concern. The last question, pertaining to how the crisis victim would like it to be in the future, tells the RCI what the goal of the helping process is to be or what problem will be focused upon.

If the woman presents a number of concerns or problems needing attention, then it will be necessary to ask another question: "Of the concerns we've talked about today, what is the most important one for you now? Which one needs immediate attention or is most pressing?" This will help the crisis victim focus her energies on one task. This has advantages in that: The problems won't seem impossible to overcome; her energies will not be dissipated in attempting to work on too much at the same time; she will see the interconnections between various concerns; the likelihood of success is increased; and the RCI will be teaching the crisis victim a process which she can use in solving future problems without having to rely on the helping person, thereby avoiding a dependency on the RCI.

The next step is to find out what alternatives the woman has already tried. If the RCI were to offer her alternatives prior to this, the RCI may find that the crisis victim has already attempted many alternatives suggested. With each response by the crisis victim saying "I tried that and it didn't work," the RCI's prestige and potency as an effective helper is lessened in the mind of the victim.

Also, don't be too eager to dismiss alternatives the crisis

victim has attempted and said they didn't work. Often the reason they didn't work was that the woman wasn't convinced of their appropriateness, it was too big a step for her, she didn't have the necessary skills to be successful with the alternative, she attempted the alternative under inappropriate circumstances, or the nitty-gritty (when, where, how, with whom) of the alternatives were not discussed fully. Be sure the past alternatives were really inappropriate in the first place or were given a fair chance of succeeding.

One possible model of the problem-solving process consists of asking the woman to think very specifically and concretely about the alternatives she wishes to attempt. After the RCI has asked the crisis victim what alternatives she has already tried, the RCI then asks her:

1. "What might be some other ways of solving your concern?"

    It is important for the RCI and the crisis victim not to rule out or prejudge any of the possible alternatives at this point. They are just brainstorming now. Then, after three or four alternatives have been suggested, perhaps with the RCI suggesting one or two, the RCI now asks:

2. "Which two of the alternatives or choices we have talked about do you think you could carry out or would have the best chance of success?"

    Here again, it is important to reassure the crisis victim that the RCI will consider the specifics of each choice later, right now the RCI is only interested in having two "good" choices to really think about. At this moment, the RCI says, "Now let's see if these two choices can be expressed more clearly, so you know what you will have to do to succeed."

3. The RCI then asks the crisis victim the following questions, first about one alternative, then the other:

    "What would you be doing if you were trying choice # ___ ?"

    "What specific things would you be saying while carrying out choice # ___ ?"

    "Who, if anybody, would this choice depend upon for having their support or playing a part in it?"

    a. "What role would this person play?"

b. "What might happen if this person doesn't offer her/his support?"

"When will you be carrying out choice # ___ ?"

"Where will you be when carrying out choice # ___ ?"

"How will you know the alternative has worked or the problem has been solved?"

4. After both alternatives have been specified in detail, the RCI then asks the crisis victim:

"Of the two choices we have talked about, which one do you think has the greatest possibility of success in the shortest time period?"

After the woman has chosen one alternative, she now has a plan of action clearly in mind. It is wise to have the RCI suggest the crisis victim contact the center again so she can receive support and any assistance in the process which may be necessary when the alternative is being carried out in reality.

This model of problem solving does much to alleviate many of the feelings which are typical of the woman experiencing a crisis.

Confusion is lessened because the RCI has asked the crisis victim to be specific and detailed in her responses to the questions. Feelings of anger are channeled into productive ends and are lessened by expending this energy concentrating on choices. Feelings of hopelessness, helplessness, and worthlessness are replaced with hope and increased self-esteem because the crisis victim has taken an active and important part in resolving her crisis. Feelings of unrealness and being lost are replaced as the result of now having a plan of action which has come about by taking realities into consideration. Finally, feelings of frustration or defeat will be circumvented because the RCI has assisted the victim in choosing the alternative which has the highest probability of success.

When the author presents this model during training programs, he often hears, "My God! That is a lot to accomplish in one phone call or contact. Do you really expect us to do all that? What happens if we don't?" These remarks and questions show a real concern for the client, concern in which they're afraid the client will crumble or go to pieces if the model is not completed.

The client won't come apart or be frustrated if the RCI doesn't complete the model. In fact, she'll probably thank you for giving her a feeling that not all is hopeless, that there is somebody who can help her. Even if you don't move through the entire process, the woman has been helped by your focusing on the beginnings of successful resolution. Perhaps that is all she needed, a beginning and some support for a beginning. You don't want the crisis victim to become dependent on you but to rely instead on her own strengths and resources. If you know the call or contact will be short, just present the model. In this way you have begun to teach her a skill she can use at any time in the future when a problem arises. The helping process is very much a teacher-learner relationship with the advantages of it being individualized, person-centered, success-oriented, and relevant to the victim's future life.

Another model to help your volunteers learn some problem-solving skills is provided on the following pages.

Problem Solving Training Manual[11]

The Problem Solving Process

Another part of the helping relationship deals with problem solving. This process involves helping the caller identify alternative ways she can solve her problem. This does not mean giving advice or solving her problem for her, but rather helping her to think through *her own* solutions and to explore associated feelings. It is important to remember that empathy is still very much a part of the problem-solving process.

The Steps to Problem Solving

(1) Helping the caller clearly state and summarize her problem and how she feels about it.

---

[11]Reproduced by permission of the Women's Crisis Center, Ann Arbor, Michigan.

(2) Helping the caller identify alternative ways she can solve her problem.
(3) Helping the caller explore the pros and cons and her feelings about each alternative.
(4) Helping the caller choose and carry out an alternative.

These steps are merely guidelines which need not be followed in exact order or in their entirety. In some cases, completion of step number 1, particularly if it required considerable work, is sufficient for one phone call. In other cases, completion through step # 2 or # 3 is sufficient.

Clues to When the Caller Might be Ready for Problem Solving

Not all phone calls will involve problem solving. Many calls are simply requests for information and/or referral. In other calls, the person may only want empathy and a chance to ventilate. Still others involve combinations of referral, empathy, and problem solving. Being tuned in to how the caller presents herself, feelings you pick up, and feelings she expresses will help you decide what kind of help she may be ready for. (TRAINERS: See tape section for examples of problem-solving vignettes.)

(1) When the caller is already very much in touch with her feelings about her problem or reaches this point after talking with the RCI for a time.
(2) Having the caller tell you she wishes to *do* something about her situation or problem. That is, her emphasis is on *action* or *doing*.
(3) Circular discussions: the lengthy phone call where empathy doesn't seem to be working and the phone call seems to be going nowhere.
(4) Chronic caller: These are callers who frequently call the RCC, but who, for whatever reason, are not able to make any progress with their problem and simply try to draw in another helping person who feels used in the end. Many times, neither empathy nor problem solving is effective. Moving into the problem solving phase will return the

responsibility for solving the problem back to the caller, and may enable the RCI to terminate the call.

STEP #1: HELPING THE CALLER CLEARLY STATE AND SUMMARIZE HER PROBLEM AND HOW SHE FEELS ABOUT IT

Before you can begin the problem-solving process, *you and the caller* must have a mutual understanding of exactly what the problem is. It must be restated once again that empathic listening is essential to problem solving; that is, using empathy to establish rapport and gain the caller's trust so that she will feel comfortable in revealing more of the problem to you. In many cases, if your empathy is effective, you will have a pretty good understanding of the caller's problem already. You should then *sum up your understanding of the problem and ask the caller if your summary is accurate.* Until she says "Yes," you are not ready to move on to the next step in the problem-solving process.

Example of RCI summary response:

"O.K. Let me see if I'm understanding you correctly. Your husband just came home and told you there's a job he plans to take in _____ . You're angry and resentful because you have a job here in _____ that is very important to you and you want to keep it. You're feeling torn about the whole question of your dual careers, particularly since your husband seems to want to move to _____ . Do I have it right?"

In some cases, you (the RCI) may feel the need for more information than can be obtained through the use of empathy techniques. In seeking more information, try to avoid direct and closed questions; they tend to back the caller into a corner. Questions which require simply a "Yes" or "No" answer are particularly ineffective because they have you doing all the work with little input from the caller. Much more effective than closed direct questions are statements that imply a question.

Example of implied questions:

Instead of asking — "Why don't you want your husband to take the job in _____ ?"

It is better to say — "It sounds like your husband taking the job in _____ is going to create some problems for you."

One additional note before moving on to step #2: in some cases, a caller will overwhelm you with a multitude of problems. You can help her by:

1) empathizing about how overwhelmed she must feel.
2) stating your desire to help but also pointing out your limitations. You can only deal with one problem at a time.
3) asking the client to choose one problem she would like to work on during the call. If another problem continues to resurface during the call, she may have chosen the wrong one to work on; you should point this out and redirect your activity to the second problem.

STEP #2: HELPING THE CALLER IDENTIFY ALTERNATIVES SO SHE CAN SOLVE HER PROBLEM

It is during this step that the RCI peer counselor can determine if the caller really wants to work on finding a solution to her problem. A good lead is:

RCI: "I was wondering if you could think of some ways you could solve your problem."

Caller Response #1: "No, there's no solution, nothing will work."

Here the caller is not ready for problem solving but should be offered empathy for her trapped and helpless feelings. In addition, the RCI might explore with her what alternatives she has thought of even though she feels "they won't work."

Caller Response #2: "Not really. I just wanted a chance to talk about this with someone."

The caller has told the RCI that she has no desire to proceed with problem solving; the RCI should praise her for her accomplishments in getting in touch with her feelings and encourage her to call back if she should wish to work on solutions at another time.

Caller Response #3: Silence ... "No, I can't seem to think of anything."

This can mean that the caller *is* interested in finding a solution, but can't seem to get started. The RCI can help by encouraging her, maybe commenting that it is sometimes hard to get started. Only after exhausting all means of getting the caller to think of solutions should the RCI take a more active role in suggesting one or more broad alternatives: "Well, you could keep both your jobs, and one of you could commute." This may be enough to get the caller thinking of other alternatives. If the suggested alternative does not stimulate any discussion or involvement from the caller, perhaps she is not ready for problem solving. The RCI can terminate the call by stating that it would be helpful if the caller gave her problem some further thought and called back at a later time — do this gently however, so the caller doesn't perceive the termination as rejection.

Caller Response #4: "Well, let's see. We could stay in _____ and my husband could commute, or we can move to _____ and I'd have to commute."

Here, two alternatives have been mentioned, but a third has been left out. If, after the RCI encourages her, the caller still cannot think of other solutions, the RCI can say, "Yes, those are certainly two possibilities to consider. I was wondering if maybe there was another as well. You could move to somewhere in between."

In mentioning additional alternatives to the caller, the RCI will want to remember to keep them within bounds that are realistic and feasible for the caller. For example, if the caller and her husband have limited funds, it would be impractical to suggest that they maintain two separate apartments.

STEP #3: HELPING THE CALLER EXPLORE THE PROS
AND CONS AND HER FEELINGS ABOUT EACH
ALTERNATIVE

After some alternatives have been defined, it would be helpful to explore the pros and cons of each of them. Both the practical aspects and the feelings associated with each of them need to be examined. The RCI could lead into this with something like:

RCI: "Now that we've thought of some possible solutions, let's talk about the pros and cons of each of them. Let's imagine what it would be like if both of you lived in _____ ."

Caller Response #1: "Well, then he would be able to get to his job pretty easily but I'd have to commute. Then too, we'd really rather live in _____ since we both like it pretty well."

The RCI could comment on the practical aspects of her commuting — how it could be done, is the expense feasible, etc., — and how she'd feel about leaving _____

Caller Response #2: "Why should I have to drive sixty or seventy miles twice a day so he can be near his job? After all, I've had my job here for several years and I don't want to leave it right now."

Here the RCI needs to comment on the caller's anger and encourage her to explore this before discussing the practical matters. At this point, the RCI will be using empathy within the problem-solving model.

While discussing practical points such as expenses and availability of facilities and services, referral sources can be used to help the person understand how each alternative might work out.

Feelings of other persons involved in the situation may also need to be discussed. The caller's feelings about this other person's reaction should also be explored.

RCI: "I was wondering if you've asked your husband how he

feels about living here and commuting to _____ ?"
Caller Response #1: "I guess we really haven't talked about
it. I really don't know."

The RCI might explore why she hasn't brought this up to
her husband, preparing her for possible reactions of her husband, and talking about how she might support her position.

Caller Response #2: "He really doesn't like all that com-
    muting, but he'd do that rather than live apart all week."

The RCI should explore how the caller feels about her husband resenting his having to commute and that it is important to him to be with his wife.

Exploration of this should be done in relation to each of the
alternatives which have been defined in step #2.

STEP #4: HELPING THE CALLER CHOOSE AND CARRY
        OUT AN ALTERNATIVE

Now that you've explored the possible alternatives and the
consequences and the feelings surrounding each alternative,
have the woman choose the one with which she feels most
comfortable. At times, a brief summary of your discussion thus
far may be helpful.

RCI: "We've been discussing having you both move to
    _____ with you commuting, having both of you live in
    _____ and both commute, and having you both live in
    _____ with your husband commuting. I was wondering
    which one of these choices you feel most comfortable with
    trying?"
Caller Response #1: "I really can't make up my mind right
    now."

At times, a woman may not be ready to make a choice and
may be content to think about the alternatives you've discussed. This is fine. Don't feel that a call is only complete
when the woman has a definite plan of action. If she wants

to think about what you've talked about, encourage her in these efforts and reinforce her for all the work she did with you on the phone.

Caller Response #2: "I feel it would be best for both of us to remain in _____ ."

At other times, the woman may be ready to choose an alternative. If she makes a choice and if it hasn't been covered in previous steps, you'll need to explore the woman's feelings, both positive and negative, about her choice. Remember your empathy training.

Caller Response #3: "Well ... long pause ... , I guess the best thing would be for us both to live in _____ (sigh)."

When the woman sounds uncertain about her choice, it will be especially important for you to explore her conflicting feelings. Her uncertainty can show both in what she says and how she says it. If you detect this uncertainty, you might say something like: "You sound uncomfortable with your decision." Giving the woman the chance to express her discomfort with her choice may decrease the amount of her discomfort.

Next discuss with the woman how she intends to implement her decision.

RCI: "Let's think of some things you might do to get your decision to work."

Caller Response: The woman might mention or might be encouraged to mention checking with other people who drive to _____ , checking the bus schedule, telling her husband that this is what she prefers and being supportive of her husband in his commuting.

Focusing on the first step the woman needs to take will help her gain confidence in her ability to carry through and implement her decision.

RCI: "It sounds like the first thing you need to do is to check to find other people who commute to _____ ."

When appropriate, discuss the possible difficulties she might have in carrying out this first step. If the woman does not know what to do to implement the first step, you can offer concrete suggestions or refer her to an appropriate resource.

RCI: "You might check the (local newspaper) as well as the University of _____ and _____ University Unions."

. End with a word of encouragement and suggest she call back to let you know how it all turned out, that you are interested in the outcome.

RCI: "It sounds like you've figured out very well what you want to do. Let me know how things come out."

Practicing The Model

For every training session, it is suggested there be two trainers and six trainees. The following is the outline of the training session:

I. Reviewing the steps of problem solving and discussing possible caller responses.

II. Warm-up exercise.

III. Sample role-play by trainers (taping optional).

IV. Six taped role-plays with trainer as speaker and each trainee as listener (straight problem solving).

V. Tape section and discussion.

VI. Six taped role-plays with trainer as speaker and each trainee as listener (problem solving, with speakers taking on various caller postures).

VII. Evaluation.

Warm-up Exercise

To get you thinking in terms of possible solutions to problems, the following exercise is suggested. The trainees will each present a brief problem (not ones that are heavy or unresolved) and the other trainees will think of as many different ways of dealing with the problem as possible. Here's an example:

The Problem: "My roommate and I are having serious personality clashes and I just don't know what to do."

Possible Solutions: Confront the roommate and try to work it out; spend less time at home; find other living arrangements.

Role-Playing

In order to keep the training session within reasonable time limits (about eight hours) and to insure that the problems presented will be conducive to problem solving, the trainers will always assume the role of caller or speaker. While much can be said for use of personal problems in empathy training, preset problems are preferable for the problem-solving training since this avoids duplication of the intensity of the empathy training.

Role-plays should begin with the speaker giving to the listener a summary of the problem, including feelings (see example under step #1). The trainee should then feed back to the speaker her understanding of the problem. Trainees not involved in the role-play should be directed to the section entitled "The Steps to Problem Solving" at the beginning of this mini-manual, so they can follow along.

Following the completion of each role-play, the tape is played back. The trainers should guide the discussion of what occurred. Feedback from the trainees as a group is encouraged, with trainees taking over more of the discussion with each role-play.

The following is a list of suggested role-play situations. Column 1 lists various types of situations from which trainers can choose the initial six role-plays. Trainers should feel free to use other situations. Column 2 lists various postures in which the caller might present herself. That is, a divorced woman who is having difficulty meeting people may present herself in any one of a number of ways: She may overwhelm the listener with a multitude of problems, she may respond in a "Yes ... but ... " fashion to the listener's suggestions, she may be unable to think of alternatives herself. For the second set of role-plays, the trainers should choose a type of problem and a manner in which it can be presented. These can be combined in any way the trainers see fit. Because of the special knowledge needed to handle some calls, it is suggested the trainers begin with a problem having no need for special knowledge. Trainers are cautioned not to get carried away with the role-plays and to concentrate on trying to teach the problem-solving model.

Column 1

A divorced woman who is having difficulty meeting people.
A woman who is afraid of being physically harmed.

A woman who is trying to decide whether to leave her husband.
A woman who is experiencing sexual feelings toward another woman.

A woman who is considering moving out of her parent's home.

A woman who needs a place to stay immediately.

A woman needing a ride to the hospital following a rape.
A minor reporting a possible case of child molestation.
A parent of a sexually abused child calls wanting to know how to handle the daughter's/sons reactions.

Column 2

A woman who overwhelms the listener with a multitude of problems.
A women who says, "Yes ... but ..." to every suggestion the listener trys.
A woman who can't think of any alternatives herself.

A woman who, during the problem solving process, continually returns to a back log of unresolved feelings.
A woman who wants you to solve her problem for her. She could present herself as helpless, dependent, etc.
A woman who sees only one alternative and is uncomfortable with it.
A woman who is not ready to choose an alternative.

A woman who just wants to ventilate her feelings.

Tape Section

To help the trainees to differentiate among types of calls and to feel more confident about working on the phone, a tape of nine sample phone calls should be prepared. The calls should be listened to and discussed individually. The following can be used to guide this discussion.

CALL #1: Informational call — Second party
1. Do you think the caller is really calling for a friend, or perhaps for herself? How should this be handled?
2. How could this woman help her friend?
3. What kind of information would you give the caller? Where would you refer her?

CALL #2: Problem solving and empathy with a need for immediate action
1. What practical issues need to be dealt with immediately?
2. What feelings need to be picked up on?

CALL #3: Caller asking to do problem solving but her basic need is empathy
1. What is the overwhelming feeling coming from the caller?
2. Is her request for help realistic?

CALL #4: Empathy plus problem solving — Lover's coolness towards caller
1. What feelings need to be explored?
2. What problem-solving steps has the caller already done? What needs to be done next?

CALL #5: Informational call with a need for empathy
1. How would you answer her?

CALL #6: Problem-solving call — Involving third party
1. What alternatives does the caller have for helping her roommate?
2. What would some of the pros and cons of each alternative be?
3. Which of the caller's feelings might need to be sensed?

CALL #7: Empathy leading to problem solving — Problem pregnancy
1. What feelings need to be explored?
2. How does this call fit into the problem-solving model?
3. What are your thoughts about referring this caller to a problem pregnancy counselor?

CALL #8: Empathy plus problem solving — Rape Case
1. What feelings do you (the RCI) have about this call?
2. What feelings does the caller express? Suppress?
3. What is the problem-solving task here? What alternatives

can you think of for the caller?
CALL #9: A special type of problem call — Suicidal caller
  1. What is your (the RCI) assessment of the dangerousness of this situation?
  2. What are some of the possible reasons that this woman sounds the way she does?
  3. Might direct questions be appropriate here?
  4. Who might assist you in handling this call?

Evaluation of Trainees

While the problem-solving training should be mandatory for all new phone counselors, a pass-fail system is not recommended. Since empathy is probably the more difficult skill to learn and problem-solving expertise is more likely to be acquired through practice, those volunteers having difficulty with the latter should not be restricted from working the phones, but should be encouraged to practice the model on their own. Strengths and weaknesses of each trainee with regard to the model should be discussed.

Use this worksheet to try the model on a personal problem of your own.

  I. Summarize the problem and your feelings about it.
  II. Think of some alternatives for solving the problem.
  III. Consider the pros and cons of each of these alternatives. How do you feel about each of them?
  IV. Select the alternative you feel most comfortable with trying and think of ways to implement it.

*   *   *

PROCESSING THE CONTACT[12]

After each call or interview with a crisis victim, the RCI may wish to recall the interaction which took place. This will help the RCI become more effective in future interactions, provide her/him with an overview of the helping relationship just concluded, provide material for case conferences to discuss par-

[12]Reproduced by permission of the Chester County Rape Crisis Council, West Chester, Pennsylvania.

ticular feelings or blocks which arose, and to provide information to the training staff to be included in future training programs.

The following questions will assist you in recalling each contact with a crisis victim.

1. What do you (the RCI) think she (crisis victim) was trying to say?
2. How do you think she was feeling at that point?
3. What clues did you pick up from her nonverbal behavior to support your impressions?
4. What was running through your mind when she said that?
5. What were some of the feelings you were having then?
6. If you had another chance, what would you have done or said differently?
7. What feelings or thoughts prevented you from doing or saying that?
8. What, if anything, prevented you from sharing (self-disclosing) some of your feelings and concerns about the person?
9. What were you afraid of risking if you said or did what you really wanted to say or do?
10. What kind of person do you want her to see you as being in the interaction?
11. What do you think her perceptions are of you?
12. How do you feel now?

COUNSELING A RAPE VICTIM[13]

The following pages are examples of the steps involved in the helping process with a rape victim. Generally, these steps are primarily applicable for the RCI helping a woman who has just experienced the rape and is now involved in the rape crisis. Some of this information involves material which will be discussed in greater detail in later chapters.

As a RCI, you will encounter a wide variety of situations and

---

[13]Reproduced by permission of the Rape Relief Program, Olympia, Washington.

requests for services, but you will certainly be called upon to perform one or more of the following functions in helping any rape victim, by telephone or in person:

1. LISTEN IN A WAY WHICH SUPPORTS AND VALIDATES THE WOMAN'S FEELINGS, encouraging her to express these feelings freely.
2. HELP THE WOMAN TO CLARIFY THE PROBLEM(S) AND TO FOCUS ON ACTION which needs to be taken in regard to medical treatment, reporting the rape to the police or any problems that may have developed as a result of the rape.
3. GIVE INFORMATION on medical, police, and court procedures and on what the woman may expect as a consequence of specific actions.
4. ACCOMPANY THE WOMAN AND ACT AS ADVOCATE with doctor, police, attorney, or other persons.
5. IF THE WOMAN IS INTERESTED IN CONTRIBUTING INFORMATION, take a "third party" report.

Your first contact with the rape victim will probably be by telephone. You will have been called by the RCC (in the case of your being an advocate/companion, not listener on the phones) and the RCC will give you the victim's number. In some cases, the victim will call you directly; in this case the RCC should notify you and let you know to expect a call after they give out your number. Identify yourself as a RCI and by your first name. The rape victim is likely to respond in one of three ways:

1. She will tell you what happened and what problems she has that were caused or exacerbated by the rape. Her story may be incoherent at first and she may be crying or even (rarely) sound out of touch with reality.
2. She will ask for fairly specific information only.
3. She may make a *very* brief statement to the effect that she has been raped, or just that some vaguely terrible thing has happened to her. This may be followed by a long silence.

Whatever her response is, the following guidelines should

help you help her:

I. Listen in a way which supports and validates the woman's feelings, encouraging her to express them freely.

Let the woman talk or cry or express her feelings in whatever way she wants to.

The victim may view herself as being in a state of crisis or stress or merely as having a problem to solve. Her attitude will not necessarily reflect the severity of her immediate physical or social condition. It will be based on her perception of the event in its social context plus her life experience in coping with other stressful events, as well as attitudes (towards men, sexuality, violence, self-esteem) which you may only guess at on a brief contact. DO NOT ATTEMPT TO REDEFINE THE SITUATION AS BEING EITHER MORE OR LESS CRITICAL THAN SHE SEES IT. THE VICTIM IS THE ONLY ONE WHO CAN DETERMINE HOW CRITICAL THE SITUATION IS, SINCE IT MUST BE DONE IN TERMS OF HER OWN VALUES.

If the woman is crying and/or sounds very distressed, it is not essential that you understand precisely what she is saying, nor that you convey information at the moment. There is not too much point in trying to get across a clear verbal message, because the woman is not likely to hear what you have to say. If you make supportive comments from time to time, your empathic *tone* will be heard and eventually her comprehension that you have some understanding of her *feelings* will make it possible for her to listen to you.

Let the woman know that you understand something horrible has happened to her, (if that is the way she views it) and that it will probably help if she can express her feelings about it. It may be helpful to reflect back to her what feelings she is conveying, or to summarize what she is saying:

Victim: (crying) "I've hardly left the house since my divorce and I *never* picked up anyone in a tavern before. If my ex-husband finds out I was raped, I don't know what he'll do."

RCI: "It seems like you have a lot of regrets for having met someone at the tavern. If you feel up to it, please tell me more about it."

You may have a very strong feeling in this case that the woman blames herself for what has happened, and if you are right, it is important to help her recognize and cope with that feeling. However, you need to be careful not to plant the idea of guilt where it doesn't exist, and not to reinforce it where it is present to some extent. The above response lets the woman know you are really listening, it gives her the opportunity to correct your impressions if appropriate, and encourages her to express more of her feelings.

Fairly soon, the woman is likely to slow down and become more calm, or she may again repeat herself or ask questions about the RCC's services. In rare instances, her emotional state may begin to escalate to a degree that is becoming disfunctional. When any of these things occur, you may have to shift from primarily a listening role, to a more active role of intervention.

THE WOMAN WHO WON'T TALK OR IS UNABLE TO TALK CAN BE DIFFICULT TO DEAL WITH ON THE TELEPHONE. Ask her if she would like to tell you about the rape, and if she feels comfortable talking where she is now. If she gives only a cursory response, tell her you would find it much easier to talk if you were with her, or that if she would let you, you would just sit quietly with her. In any case, ask to see her in person.

If the woman declines to have you go directly to her, ask a few specific questions that can be answered in a few words, like, "Have you seen a doctor?", "Is it likely you may be pregnant?" If she responds at all, try to get her to continue talking about any subject. She may be in a mild (or not so mild) state of shock, and talking about a nonthreatening subject may help her come out of it; if she is in shock, *you* are her reality. Let her talk for a while about things only peripherally related to the rape and then gradually bring her back to thinking about her specific problems.

If you begin to feel after a while that you don't know what she wants or what to do, the best way to handle it is to say, "I really want to help you, but I'm not sure what you would like me to do." Explain the RCC's services. If she doesn't say what she wants, tell her you are glad to just listen if that helps. Another thing that may help is to talk, yourself, about the RCC, or the general rape situation, with an emphasis on the idea that anyone can be a victim, that it is the rapist who should be held accountable, not the victim, and that to some extent, all women are vulnerable and need to work together to change the situation. This talk will serve the purpose of giving her time to begin to recover from the shock of rape, and if you leave lots of openings as you are talking, she may pick up on one of the things you have said.

When you feel it is time to move into a more active phase of counseling, ask the woman if she would like you to go to her home, or wherever she is. If you think she is ready to hear you, this can be asked early in the interview. Explain that it is one of the functions of the RCC to go directly to the woman. It's all right to say that you would find it easier to talk in person or that you feel you can be of more help in person, and you need to be enthusiastic about the offer because many women are afraid of asking too much of the RCI. However, some women prefer to be anonymous. If the woman says she would rather just talk on the telephone, assure her that it is perfectly acceptable to you. Check with her if she feels comfortable talking where she is now. Does she have the privacy she needs? Is she safe?

II. Help the woman to clarify the problem(s) and to focus on action which needs to be taken in regard to medical treatment, reporting to the police or any problems she may have developed as a result of the rape.

If the woman is hysterical or extremely upset, she is probably feeling overwhelmed by what appear to be massive but ill-defined problems. Even if there are many problems, separating each from the other will help the woman see that they are

specific and concrete enough to cope with one at a time.
THIS DIFFERENTIATION AND CLARIFICATION IS
THE FIRST STEP TOWARD HELPING THE WOMAN
LOWER HER ANXIETY LEVEL BY REGAINING A SENSE
OF CONTROL OVER HER LIFE.

> Victim: "I can hardly walk and my children are going to be
> upset and my mother won't let ... and my husband, my ex-
> husband oh, I don't know why this had to happen or what
> to do and even the landlord ... why do people have to act
> ... I know I probably should not have been in that tavern
> ... I never in my whole life ... "
>
> RCI: "You have quite a few separate problems. Let me see if
> I understand at least some of them. You're concerned about
> the reactions of the landlord, and of several family mem-
> bers, you're having regrets about having gone to the
> tavern, and you have a physical problem ... "

At this point or earlier, the woman is likely to interrupt,
either to explain one of the problems or to express more of her
feelings. *Don't rush* her into getting organized, but you might
say something like this:

> RCI: "I think we can find a way to handle each one of these
> problems separately, but let's start with your physical con-
> dition. Please tell me more about your physical problem
> and whether you've seen a doctor."

In most situations, you may want to ask the woman to say
which of her problems is the most pressing for her, but if the
woman is quite upset and incoherent and you have reason to
think she has a physical problem that needs attention, that is a
good place to begin.

A. Medical Treatment and Safety

YOUR FIRST CONSIDERATION SHOULD BE THE
PHYSICAL AND EMOTIONAL WELL-BEING OF THE
WOMAN. YOU SHOULD NOT INITIATE A DISCUSSION
OF POLICE AND COURT PROCEDURES UNTIL YOU
HAVE A PRETTY CLEAR IDEA OF WHAT THE OTHER

PROBLEMS MIGHT BE. However, if the victim decides immediately to have a medical examination, you should ask if there is any possibility of her reporting the rape to the police. If she says no or is uncertain, explain that it is very difficult to decide important questions when she is upset, and that quite a few rape victims don't want to report at first, but in a day or so they change their minds. If there is any chance at all that the woman may decide to report, it will be best to go to the hospital or a doctor so that the evidence can be obtained in case of prosecution. All this can be explained on the way to the hospital if you accompany her, but BE SURE TO TELL HER BEFORE YOU HANG UP THAT IF THERE IS A CHANCE SHE WILL REPORT THE RAPE, SHE SHOULD NOT WASH OR DOUCHE, AND SHOULD KEEP CLOTHING THAT WAS WORN AT THE TIME OF THE RAPE.

Ask if she has received medical treatment, and if appropriate, explain the best times for an examination for bruises, internal injuries, VD check, morning after treatment or menstrual extraction. Offer to accompany her to the doctor.

The rape victim may be reluctant to see a doctor. REMEMBER, THE DECISION IS HERS AND DO NOT INSIST SHE BE EXAMINED. A woman who is adamant about not seeing a doctor at first may be willing to reconsider her position a few minutes later or in a few days, when her judgment is not clouded by her critical emotional condition. Try to get a telephone number before you hang up, so that you can remind her of the dangers of VD a few days later, when she will probably be more calm.

Even when it seems clear to you that medical attention is needed, the woman may still not be ready to cope with that situation, and you may have to help her deal with her feelings first.

B. Feelings of Guilt

The rape victim's feelings of guilt are often as difficult for her to deal with as are the medical and police problems.

Many women have internalized the prevalent mythology

which emphasized the idea that the woman is to blame for having been raped, i.e. "She must have asked for it" or "Well, what was she doing there in the first place?"

> Victim: "Why did I ever go there? I must have done something to make him think ... my darned mother was right after all, it is my own fault! If only ... "
>
> RCI: "It sounds like you're really getting down on yourself for having been raped. Your mother thinks that you must be to blame. What is it you think you may have done that would make it your fault?"

No matter how strongly you feel that it was *not* the woman's fault, it is important to let her talk and try to help her define in precise terms, what she might have done "wrong" and what she might have done differently. She may need to talk about it a *number of times* before she is willing to consider the possibility that it was not her fault, but the rapist's. Let her come to that conclusion herself rather than you coming right out and saying she isn't to blame. She should, at the very least, be able to view the rape as a crime committed against her, for which the rapist is to blame, even though it may be true that she didn't exercise very "good" judgment in the circumstances surrounding the rape. This may be the only acceptable conclusion the woman can arrive at, if she was intoxicated for instance.

You may believe that the woman is feeling guilty, even though she hasn't said so. If you are certain of spending a fair amount of time with her, you can give her conversational openings and sooner or later she will introduce the topic herself.

Often however, you will have only a brief conversation, with no opportunity to see the victim a second time. In this case, mention or talk to her about the mythology of rape, contrasting it with our ideas that the rapist must be accountable, not the victim. Thus, you plant the idea which she may later draw upon. However, you need to be sure she understands that you are expressing *your* opinion (shared by others who have had a lot of experience with dealing with rapes), and that *you are not trying to invalidate her feelings.*

Ask the woman if she has friends or relatives who will help

her feel better about herself, and who will not contribute to her guilt feelings. Suggest that she might want to tell only *those* people about the rape. If there are no people of that sensitivity in her life, suggest she keep in touch with you.

If the woman is being blamed for the rape by someone close to her, ask if she would like you to talk to him or her about rape. If not, suggest that you and she role-play ways of handling blaming remarks or any other threatening situation.

C. Fear

Fear is another very frequent reaction to rape. It may, of course, be quite rational, and specific to a threatening situation or person; often the rapist has threatened to kill the woman, especially if he suspects she will report it to the police.

Help the woman express and specify her fear. Encourage her to list all the things she could do to protect herself, including those actions which are unacceptable to her. The range of ideas may be from triple-locking all doors and windows and never going out at night, to not hitch-hiking alone or not becoming intoxicated alone or in the company of men. This is another area in which it will help to point out that there *is* a range of choices. Awareness of choice gives a sense of control, which in turn reduces fear.

The woman may need help in acting upon the self-protective ideas that are acceptable to her. She may need to discuss better locks with the landlord, in which case you might act as an advocate. You might help her find temporary housing, or explore self-defense classes.

Remember though, *the more the woman can do for herself, the better she will be, each independent action adding to her sense of control over her own life.*

D. Deciding Whether To Report To The Police

KEEP IN MIND THAT ONLY THE RAPE VICTIM IS GOING TO LIVE WITH THE GUILT OR FEAR THAT MAY BE THE RESULT OF FAILING TO REPORT THE

RAPE TO THE POLICE OR REPORTING IT; THERE-
FORE, EVEN IF THE WOMAN WANTS YOU TO TELL
HER WHAT TO DO, YOU CAN ONLY GIVE HER INFOR-
MATION THAT WILL HELP *HER* TO MAKE THE DECI-
SION, AND SUPPORT WHATEVER DECISION THAT
IS.

You can explain to the woman what is *likely* to happen,
given the particular circumstances of her rape. However, be
sure to point out that there are few guarantees of how she will
be treated, but if she has an advocate with her, treatment will
probably be fairly good. You can make some guesses about the
victim's chances in court — chances of being humiliated on the
witness stand, and of the rapist being convicted. But, be very
sure that the victim understands these are *only* guesses and be
careful you don't move into the area of giving legal advice. Not
all defense attorneys try to humiliate the victim, and there have
been many surprising jury verdicts — the surprise being sometimes welcome, and other times not.

In making her decision to prosecute or not, it is important
for the woman to evaluate how supportive her social environment is, how prone she is to guilt feelings or fear, whether the
rapist was serious if he threatened to kill her if she reported the
incident, whether he will be able to find her, how stable her
self-esteem is and how she withstands pressure.

*The woman should also realize that she need not make an
irrevocable decision immediately,* although it is true that the
sooner the assault is reported, the better for her case if she
thinks she might follow through and prosecute. It is also
helpful to have an early medical examination and to give the
RCC a "Third Party" report, if she is not ready to go to the
police. There is always the chance that any time, up to the last
minute, the rapist may plea-bargain to a lesser charge, so that
she may not have to go through the superior court trial. She
should also be aware that the whole process may take many
months, during which time she will have to be constantly reminded of the rape, when perhaps the only thing she wants is
to forget about it.

E. Counseling

There is no way you can anticipate all situations. *Try to be aware of your own strengths and weaknesses,* the types of people and situations that make you uncomfortable (e.g. Are you embarrassed to ask questions about sexuality? Do you disapprove of women who have a glamorous style?) If you are aware of your feelings, the chances are that you can overcome them or use these feelings in a constructive manner.

If you are feeling anxious or confused, usually the best way to cope is to state how you feel, which will probably help to relieve feelings, as well as to clarify the situation for the victim.

Try hard not to make assumptions about what the woman wants or how she feels. When you *think* you know, check it out by using a paraphrasing or reflective response, before acting on your hunches.

F. Denial of Feelings

Some "experts" believe that rape victims rather quickly move from a very emotional reaction, to a phase of denial, which may last days or weeks and then may be followed by depression. Although this may or may not be true, the possibility of this occurring is one reason for obtaining the victim's permission to call her in a day or so, and then to keep in touch for a week or two. Find out the best time and place to call which will assure her of privacy.

If the woman does become depressed, it will be useful for her to express some of the feelings she has been denying, e.g. fear, shame, guilt, rage. If you are comfortable in helping her express these feelings do so. Be sure you will have time to allow her full expression so as not to cut her short and also time to then help her regain control so the emotional expression doesn't become "unfinished business," adding to her difficulties. If you as a RCI are not comfortable in the face of strong emotions, this may be the time to refer her for professional help.

G. Confidentiality

Remember, some women are ashamed and embarrassed as the result of having been raped. *Never* talk about the victim outside of the RCC, unless you have her written permission to do so or you can change the facts that might identify the woman, such as address, age, name, marital status, etc. In discussing the case, always state that you have changed the facts, so that people will know the RCC staff doesn't talk about the women you try to help, except where we can educate the public about rape while protecting the woman's anonymity.

If someone else has made the original contact with you, and told you the woman's "story" or "problem," let the woman know what things you already know about her, so that she will realize that you are going to be honest, and also so she can make any corrections or reinterpretations. You should try to cut off anything a third party tries to tell you unless it is essential. Just say you don't want to hear anything that the victim doesn't know is being said. You might ask the person to double-check the woman's permission, before continuing the conversation.

IF SOMEONE TELLS YOU ABOUT A FRIEND OR REL-ATIVE WHO HAS BEEN RAPED, WHO NEEDS HELP AND WANTS YOU TO CALL THE WOMAN, *DO NOT CALL.* Explain that the RCC would be glad to help the woman, but that many rape victims are very sensitive regarding personal privacy and the RCC doesn't want to intrude on the woman's privacy. Ask to have the rape victim call the RCC herself. Again, this will provide the victim with a sense of control over her own affairs.

III. Give information on medical, police, and court procedures as well as financial help and other aid available to her and on what the woman may expect as a consequence of specific actions.

A number of women do not need a great deal of help in coping with emotions or in getting mobilized. Many women call for specific information, and want nothing more from the RCC. It is all right to state what our services are and to offer information on subjects that are not specifically asked for, but assume that the woman knows what she wants from us, unless she indicates otherwise. A suggestion is to make a statement such as, "You sound really together now," to give the victim room to open up about her feelings if she chooses.

Much of the specific information you will be asked for can be found in other sections of this material.

IV. Accompany the woman and act as an advocate with doctor, police, attorney, or other persons.

This is a very important part of the RCC's services. Most women are very hesitant about asking people to accompany them, so it is important to offer the service enthusiastically and to explain that "authorities" usually treat victims better when an advocate accompanies the victim. It is for this type of service that many RCCs have been funded, so the victim is really doing the RCC a favor by letting the advocate go along. She should not feel she is asking too much of the RCI.

A. Your Role As An Advocate

Prepare the woman as best you can for the things that are going to happen to her. Include the questions that the doctor and police will probably ask, and the reason for them. Explain which questions she is obliged to answer (if she wants certain results), and which questions she may reasonably refuse. Find out how she feels about answering both types of questions and whether she will be comfortable asserting her right not to answer, or if she would like you to help her out.

B. Encourage The Woman To Handle The Situations Herself, But Also Be Sensitive To What Things She's Embarrassed To Ask.

For instance, the policeman may begin examining the woman in a very public place and she may be very reluctant to answer his questions, but also too hesitant or upset to say so.

The doctor may want to know what neighborhood the rape occurred in, whether the man was a stranger, etc, things which are not related to the medical examination. Some women would just as soon talk about it and may use the opportunity as a catharsis. If you have determined beforehand what the woman wants and is likely to be able to take care of, then you will know whether it is appropriate to intervene.

If you feel you must intervene, be as polite and unobtrusive as possible. A question may be less threatening than a statement, e.g. "I think Ms. _____ is uncomfortable here. Do you have a more private room we could move to?" Better yet, ask the woman how she feels about what is happening, e.g. "How do you feel about answering all these questions?" Thus, you remind the woman of your previous discussion, her expressed desire then, and that she has the right to control the interview to a large extent. She will then probably feel free to express her wishes, which is much better for her than for you to do it.

C. Before You Leave

Be sure the victim realizes that the RCC is very eager to act as advocate. Be sure she has the opportunity to give, if appropriate, a third party report.

LET THE WOMAN KNOW YOU WOULD LIKE TO CALL BACK THE NEXT DAY. Find out when the best time is to call. Without being pushy, try to get her number, rather than having her call you. If there is anything you will not be able to follow through on, let her know that another advocate will take over for you and be sure you find someone to do so.

The woman may be very wary of records being kept on her. Be perfectly honest and explain the RCC's system of confidentiality. Show her the contact sheet and explain why the RCC keeps records.

If you haven't already obtained adequate information to complete the contact sheet, ask the victim if she is willing to answer a few questions so that the RCC can learn more about rape. MOST WOMEN ARE GLAD TO GIVE INFORMATION SO DON'T DEPRIVE THEM OF THE OPPORTU-

NITY OF SAYING YES OR NO.

D. After You Leave

Make out contact sheets immediately, while your memory is fresh. Arrange for any necessary follow-up.

Check with yourself and your partner as to whether you remembered to encourage the woman to act, rather than taking over where it wasn't necessary; whether you were able to keep from making assumptions about her values, what she should do, etc. If you goofed, give some thought as to how you can be more effective next time. Try to share both goofs and things that went well with the contact with your RCC staff.

* * *

When the Victim Calls More Than 72 Hours After The Rape[14]

As was said at the beginning of the previous material, most of that information is primarily applicable to women who have called to report a rape within the past 72 hours. The material presented below deals with the RCI's responses in contacts where the contact comes more than seventy-two hours after the rape.

A. Victim's Emotional State
  1. Listen for signs that the victim is experiencing denial of her feelings or that her true feelings are buried under guilt.
  2. Apparent adjustment may be present. The victim may have resumed her usual activities. She may deny feelings which are typically expressed early after a rape, such as anger, rage, guilt, shame. She may deny that she has any feelings about the rape at all or state that she has become less interested in talking about it. This is a rationalized and intellectualized response which serves to be self-protective. If the RCI allows her to remain at this stage,

[14]Reproduced by permission of the Kalamazoo Women's Centre, Kalamazoo, Michigan.

the victim may never really "finish" the experience. Here, the RCI can offer the victim strong emotional support, not challenging her coping behaviors or defenses, but helping her regain control by taking action on her own behalf.

3. The RCI can gently encourage the victim to talk about the experience by describing the feelings other rape victims typically experience. In this tentative way the rape victim will be given an opportunity to admit and accept her own feelings.

B. Physical Safety
   1. Especially attend to her current ability to defend herself.
   2. What precautions is the victim taking for her own sense of security?

C. Medical Aid
   1. Examinations and tests will not show evidence of penetration. However, medical treatment is important to her health, especially in cases of possible VD or pregnancy.

D. Family And Friends
   1. The victim may have been urged by a friend to seek help; try to talk to the friend also so as to provide the friend or relative an idea of predictable future reactions of the victim and a chance to discuss the friend's or family's own reactions.

E. Legal Action
   1. Little legal action is possible now. If a description of the rape and rapist has been given to the police and another woman does charge him, the first victim may wish or be able to testify.
   2. If the victim can identify the rapist, knows where he lives, etc., a civil suit may still be possible. Consult a feminist lawyer.

Essentially, the RCI will be helping the rape victim integrate the experience so it can become part of the past and will not continue to have an effect on the woman's emotional health.

CHAPTER 6

MEDICAL PROCEDURES

AN excellent reference in assisting your area hospitals and physicians in developing sensible and sensitive procedures in the emergency medical treatment of rape victims is *Medical Protocol for Emergency Room Treatment of Rape Victims*.[1] The author highly recommends it become part of your training manual. Also, press for changes in your locale's hospital procedures if they are not up to the "Protocol's" standard.

If the rape victim is not interested in pressing charges against the rapist, it is still necessary that she consult a physician to receive treatment for any wounds or bruises, and prophylactic information and follow-up treatment for VD or other vaginal infections and pregnancy. Be aware of the possibility that if the woman has not reported the assault, many hospitals are obligated by law to do so. This does not mean the victim must prosecute however, only that the police are notified.

It is also true that many hospitals will not treat rape victims unless they are brought to the hospital under the authority of the police or by a police officer. The woman will usually have to sign a consent form before the medical examination may be conducted and for release of materials to authorities. If the victim is a minor, consent of parents, guardians, or juvenile authority may be necessary.

Depending on the affiliation of the hospital (private, city, county) the victim may have to pay for the emergency treatment, so be sure she has cash or medical benefits coverage on hand. Depending upon the size of the hospital, a resident, staff physician, or intern may conduct the examination in the presence of a nurse. Some states also require that the police officer observe the entire process so the chain of evidence is intact. The

---

[1]Bay Area Women Against Rape, P. O. Box 240, Berkeley, California 94701, November, 1974.

rape victim can request that a female physician conduct the examination and that a policewoman rather than a policeman be present, if these people are available.

It is advisable to have the rape victim call a friend to accompany her to the hospital emergency room if the RCC doesn't have a companion program. In general and of primary importance, the friend can provide the strength and support which might not be available from the hospital staff. The length of time spent waiting to be examined will depend upon the condition of the victim, the seriousness of other cases, waiting for admittance, and on the availability of the resident or staff physicians. It would be wise to press the hospital to establish priority treatment policies for rape victims, so that the long wait can be reduced. You may try to establish a system with the hospital whereby sexual assault victims can be taken to the hospital's gynecological clinic (which is typically a more secure and less chaotic environment than the emergency room) during the daytime hours. Whenever the gynecological clinic is not open, the victim can then be taken to the emergency room. Such a system has worked well for the Women's Crisis Center in Ann Arbor.

Many hospitals are supplied with "rape kits" by the police departments which the hospital *must* use in examining a rape victim. Each "rape kit" typically contains: instructions to the examining physician; one test tube containing a swab and labeled "vaginal"; one test tube containing a swab and marked "other" for samples taken from the rectum or mouth of the victim; microscopic slides for unstained smears from the vaginal swab; two small cardboard boxes or plastic bags — one for standard pubic hair from the victim, the other for possible foreign hair; and one comb. It is important to note that all swabs and slides used for taking and analyzing specimens *must be air-dried* before they are stored, if they are to be of any use to the police crime lab. *Do not* store any evidence, including clothing, when it is wet.

SUGGESTED PHYSICIAN AND NURSE PROCEDURE
FOR TREATMENT OF ALLEGED SEXUAL ABUSE

It should be noted that some of the following procedures may not be true for your area hospitals. Consult your needs assessment survey to be sure what procedures are in effect.

If a standard medical protocol is approved and followed completely and the evidence is sealed and handed to the police to allow a continuous chain, the doctor and hospital staff *may not* have to testify later on. The protocol may be sufficient evidence in court without the doctor's testimony. This can be a good selling point in getting the hospital and physicians to adopt the protocol. The medical protocol to be followed by examining physicians in sexual assault cases *must* be approved by the district or States attorney and police department, as well as the hospital staff.[2]

1. *Purpose*

The purpose of this material is to suggest proper procedures for the protection of patient and medical personnel, as well as for the interest of justice in cases of alleged rape or sexual molestation.

2. *Care of the Patient*

The protection of the patient is an important duty of the physician and nurse. Psychosexual trauma must be recognized and minimized. Emotional support and empathic understanding of both the patient and family are very important. The family should be given understanding and guidance. They should be warned specifically against magnifying the situation. They should be told to avoid such terms as "ruined, violated, dirty, or lost her innocence," lest the patient develop severe guilt feelings and anxiety. It has been shown that the patient's emotional reaction to sexual molestation is far less damaging than that arising from the imposition of society's values upon the episode.

Many times the alleged sexual abuse will be the first sexual contact the patient has had. In addition, the patient may have had no experience with a gynecological examination. Physicians should carefully explain the procedure to be used in the gynecological exam, and should be as considerate as possible. A child victim may or may not desire the family be

[2]Reproduced by permission of the Miami/Dade County Rape Task Force, c/o 427 Bargello Avenue, Coral Gables, Florida 33146; prepared for the training manual of the Rape Treatment and Trauma Center, Jackson Memorial Hospital, Miami, Florida.

present during the exam. The physician should ask the patient, when they are alone, if she prefers the family member be present or absent, and should relay this information to the family.

Clinical concerns for the protection of the patient are treatment of physical trauma, external and internal, such as lacerations, and the prevention of venereal disease and pregnancy. The attacker may have a venereal disease, and for this reason, with the written consent of the patient, physicians customarily give prophylactic antibotic therapy. A test for venereal disease already present in the patient should also be administered. Similarly, a pregnancy test should be administered and the probability of the patient's becoming pregnant from the incident evaluated. The possibility of pregnancy should be discussed with the victim, and the means of preventing pregnancy suggested. Estrogen therapy, either oral or by injection, and endometrial aspiration are appropriate measures, separately or in combination.

Follow-up care for the rape/sexual abuse patient is important in order to be certain that the patient does not become pregnant or develop a venereal disease despite the immediate preventive measures taken. The importance of a follow-up examination and tests should be explained to the patient and family, and help given them in arranging for such care. The possibility of delayed psychological effects on both patient and family must be remembered, and allowed for in suggestions for care in the future.

3. *The Medical Record*

The record should contain the patient's statement. It should give descriptions of what the physician did and of the physician's findings. It should contain information as to what specimens were taken and *to whom* they were delivered. The physician and nurse should express no nonmedical conclusions, opinions, or diagnoses to the patient or to anyone else, including the police, and none should be written into the record. The phrases, "suspected rape" or "suspected sexual molestation" may be used when necessary.

Because the medical record may be used in investigation of

a case of rape or sexual molestation, and may become evidence in a court of law, full information should be given in it. All information should be exact and detailed to avoid any misinterpretation. Negative findings are as important as positive ones, and may assist in the protection of an alleged assailant who has been falsely accused.

4. *Specimens*

Often the evidence needed to establish guilt or innocence in a court case of alleged sexual abuse has been thoughtlessly destroyed by well-intentioned medical personnel. Laboratory specimens should be obtained by the responsible physician or nurse and personally handed to the pathologist, technician, or police officer. They should not be sent to the laboratory by routine messenger service. All slides should be clearly labeled with the patient's name, preferably etched with a diamond pencil. Unless specimens can be positively identified, the prosecuting attorney may have difficulty in submitting the reports into evidence.

Any potential evidence, including clothing worn at the time of the alleged assault, should be retained and personally turned over to the proper police authorities in return for a detailed receipt. In cases where the police are not immediately involved, specimens should be retained. This is essential should the patient later wish to prosecute.

5. *Cautions*

Physicians and nurses must protect the interests of the patient, of justice, and of themselves. Every instance of sexual abuse is a potential court case, and physicians should expect to be subpoened to justify their statements on the medical record. Whether rape or sexual molestation occurred is a legal matter for the court to decide and is *not* a medical diagnosis.

The principle cautions to be observed are:

a. Verify consent
b. Obtain a history in the patient's *own words*
c. Report the general physical and mental condition of the patient and the findings of the examination. The examination should include inspection of the external and in-

ternal genitalia for evidence of trauma, the presence of sperm, combing the pubic hair for the purpose of identifying alien hair, and obtaining scrapings from under the patient's fingernails when applicable.

d. Get the necessary specimens and order any indicated laboratory work.

e. Save all necessary specimens and clothing.

f. Inform the patient of the possibility of pregnancy, venereal disease, and psychic trauma, and the options available.

g. MAKE NO DIAGNOSIS AS TO SEXUAL ABUSE TO THE PATIENT, HER FAMILY, OR TO THE POLICE.

After the above considerations, we will discuss the medical procedures in more detail.

MEDICAL PROTOCOL:

The physician on call will be notified that a rape patient is in the hospital. The physician will respond immediately or will refuse the assignment.

A. The initial contacts for the patient/victim will be the emergency room nurse and a RCI from the RCC. The RCI may have obtained a history (in cases where the RCC is in the hospital), but the physician may obtain it directly from the patient.

1. A good history is essential and should be written using the patient's words. The time, place, and circumstances of the alleged assault should be recorded. The emotional state should be noted. Whether or not a bath and/or douche has been taken since the assault should be documented. Ask if clothing has been changed.

2. If at all possible, written consent (witnessed) should be obtained for the following procedures:

   a. Examination

   b. Collection of specimens

   c. Photographs in cases which include assault and battery

3. The time of the examination should be written.
4. The name of the detective and the police department involved should be documented.
5. It may be helpful to obtain a past history of the patient's:
   a. Menstrual pattern
   b. Possible use of contraceptives
   c. Coital experience
   d. Psychological behavior
6. Examination of the patient should be extensive enough to include all necessary areas. When possible, a complete pelvic should be done.
7. A female attendant, either R.N. or L.P.N., must be present during this examination.
8. The general appearance of the patient should be described and the emotional state and behavior recorded.
9. Signs of external trauma should be documented:
   a. A drawing may be helpful
   b. The oral and anal as well as genital areas should be included when indicated.
   c. The Woods light (ultraviolet) is useful because semen will fluoresce and may identify areas needing specific attention: skin, clothing, etc. Adaptation to the dark is necessary for successful use of this light.

B. The following procedures must be done: *(All evidential material will be given to the proper police department if applicable. In cases where the patient does not wish to have police intervention, hold specimens for twenty-four hours — she may change her mind.)
   *1. All specimens should be labeled properly so that they are clearly identifiable as being from this patient. Ideally, they should be handed to the police so that the "Chain of Evidence" is not broken.
   *2. Semen specimens should be collected from the cervical canal and the vaginal pool and examined for:
      a. presence and activity of sperm
      b. acid-phosphatase — a phosphatase active in an acid medium; such enzymes are found in prostatic epithelium of males.

3. Culture any involved body orifices (openings) for gonorrhea, such as the endocervix, pharynx, and rectum. Slant chocolate agar, CO_2 bottles should be used.
4. Pregnancy test if indicated.
5. Venereal Disease Research Laboratory (VDRL) — a thorough test for the presence of venereal disease.
*6. Venous blood from patient for type and Rh.
7. Pap test if indicated.
*8. Comb pubic hair for foreign body (i.e. assailant's hair, lice) and place combings in a clean envelope or box provided. Label it appropriately.
*9. Take scrapings from under the fingernails and place in a clean envelope or box and label appropriately.
*10. Original clothes are evidence and should be saved for the police.

C. After the above have been accomplished, the following should be done:
1. The patient should be calmed and reassured. If necessary, sedatives or tranquilizers should be prescribed.
2. The patient should then be apprised of the possibility of having contacted a venereal disease and the possibility of becoming pregnant. Her options as to treatment should be explained clearly.

D. VD prophylaxis: (this may vary from physician to physician and hospital to hospital)
1. If the patient is not allergic to penicillin:
   a. Syphilis — Bicillin® 2.4 mill. U. IM STAT. (brand of penicillin in the amount shown to be given intramuscularly immediately)
   b. Gonorrhea — 1 gm. probenecid orally followed in 30 minutes by 1 gm. ampicillin. The 1 gm. ampicillin orally in 5 hours.
2. If the patient is allergic to penicillin:
   a. Spectinomycin 4 gm. IM
3. Lacerations should be repaired when indicated. Tetanus toxoid may be given in some instances.
4. Pregnancy prophylaxis:
   a. Stilbestrol — 25 mgm. bid x 5 days, p.o. The patient

may wish a prescription for Bendectin® or Tigan® to combat the nausea which is often the result of administering stilbestrol.

   b. Menstrual extraction — The patient should be assured that this is available to her if she misses a period or fails to have withdrawal bleeding after the stilbestrol.

5. A cleansing douche may be given:
   a. 4 T Betadine® douche solution in 2 quarts of warm tap water.
6. The patient should be impressed with the fact that a FOLLOW-UP VISIT TO HER PHYSICIAN OR THE CLINIC IS ABSOLUTELY NECESSARY. At this time, the VDRL and cervical culture should be repeated, and the patient examined to make sure she has not conceived.

CONCLUSION:

1. "Rape" and "Sexual Assault" are legal and not medical diagnoses. Use the terms "History of Alleged" rape or sexual assault.
2. Specifically indicate the trauma: "contusion," "laceration," "avulsion," etc.
3. Document the presence or absence of sperm; its motility.
4. Remember that the chart may become a piece of legal evidence. Be sure all statements are objective and accurate. Keep a copy for yourself so you can recall the case when required.
5. Send a report to the RCC, Emergency Department.
6. Leave a prescription (℞) for all medications used so that replacement can be procured.

Sexual Assault Patient's Bill of Rights

1. You are entitled to good quality medical care by counselors, doctors, and nurses.

MEDICAL REPORT   JACKSON MEMORIAL HOSPITAL
Alleged Sexual Assault   (Reproduced by permission)   Date _____

Brought By _____

Birthdate _____ Age _____

Name of Patient _____ Date & Time of Alleged Rape _____

Time Arrived _____

Address _____ Time of Exam _____

MEDICAL REPORT
HISTORY (as related to physician)

Physical Examination (Include ALL signs of external evidence of trauma)

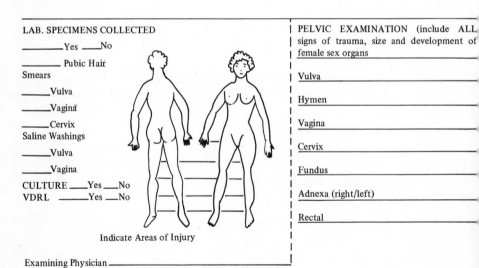

LAB. SPECIMENS COLLECTED

_____ Yes _____ No

_____ Pubic Hair
Smears

_____ Vulva

_____ Vagina

_____ Cervix
Saline Washings

_____ Vulva

_____ Vagina

CULTURE _____ Yes _____ No
VDRL _____ Yes _____ No

Indicate Areas of Injury

Examining Physician _____

PELVIC EXAMINATION (include ALL signs of trauma, size and development of female sex organs _____

Vulva _____

Hymen _____

Vagina _____

Cervix _____

Fundus _____

Adnexa (right/left) _____

Rectal _____

ASSAULT FORM
RAPE TREATMENT CENTER
JACKSON MEMORIAL HOSPITAL
(Reproduced by permission)

Date-Time Report _____ Date-Time Occurrence _____

Location Occurrence _____

Victim's Name-Address _____

Age   Race   Occupation _____ Married _____ Live Alone ____

Sober   HBD   Intox   Injuries _____

Result Sperm Test _____ Result AP Test _____

If Break-In, Where, How _____

Property Taken _____

Offender If Known _____ Address _____

Age   Race   Ht.   Wt. _____ Complexion _____ Hair _____

Eyes   Build   Scars   Tattoos _____ Other Descrip. _____

Sober   HBD   Intox   Force Used _____

Does Victim
Know Offender? _____ How Long? _____

Occupation _____ Employment _____

Auto Description _____

Clothes Description _____

Language Used (Accent) _____ Statements _____

_____

If more than one offender, use extra form for each offender. Use this space for
a brief narrative of what occurred before, during and after the assault. Include
any additional descriptions, statements, and other circumstances.

Pubic Hair Specimen _____

Preserved Evidence, Clothing, etc. _____

CONSENT FORM FOR TREATMENT
OF VICTIMS OF ALLEGED SEXUAL ABUSE
RAPE TREATMENT CENTER-JACKSON MEMORIAL HOSPITAL
(Reproduced by permission)

I know that the practice of medicine is not an exact science, and that, as a
result of this understanding, reputable practitioners cannot guarantee results.
I acknowledge that no guarantee has been made by anyone regarding the procedures
I have read and understood, and I hereby request and authorize the appropriate
treatments and services.

Witness_____Patient's Name-Printed

Witness_____

Date_____Time_____AM/PM   Patient's or Guardian's Signature

_____

. . . .
CHECKLIST ON TREATMENT RECEIVED AT THE RAPE TREATMENT CENTER

_____I provided the examining physician with all the facts pertinent to my history.

_____I had a physical examination to determine the extent of any bruises, lacera-
tions, or other detrimental physical conditions from which I might be suffering.

_____I was given a routine pelvic examination, including examination of my ex-
ternal genitalia, cervix and vagina, and rectum.

_____Aspiration of the contents of my vagina was performed for laboratory tests,
and microscopic examination of this specimen was performed to determine the
presence or lack of sperm.

_____Smears were taken for the purpose of finding possible infectious or other
organisms to which I may have been exposed.

I also had all of the following done for the purpose of collecting possible
evidence:

_____Scrapings were taken from under my fingernails.

_____My pubic hair was combed to determine if any hair other than my own was pre-
sent.

_____I relinquished my clothing to the examining physician for possible evidence
and I did receive a receipt for the clothing.

_____I was made aware of the fact that I may have been exposed to venereal disease
of some type. I was administered appropriate antibiotic therapy to prevent
the development of such a disease in my body. I was informed that I should
have a check up in six (6) weeks to ascertain that no disease has developed,
and I was informed that such antibiotics will not kill any venereal disease
that I may already have.

_____I was told that there may be a possibility of an unwanted pregnancy occur-
ring. In order to prevent this, the examining physician prescribed for me a
synthetic estrogen, diethylstilbesterol (DES), to be taken by me or administered at the physician's discretion. I was told that requesting this drug
indicates that I do not wish to become pregnant, and I was advised that if I
do not have a menstrual period within ten (10) days of my last dosage of this

drug, some form of uterine extraction is indicated, as this drug may have long term harmful effects on the child. I was also told of possible side-effects from taking DES.

____I was informed that whether or not I choose the above DES treatment at this time, if I should not begin my menstrual cycle within (10) days after its usual onset, a simple, inexpensive out-patient procedure called menstrual regulation or uterine evacuation is available as an alternative to an un-wanted pregnancy.

____I was told that, in addition to these alternatives for the prevention or termination of pregnancy, a safe, legal, and inexpensive abortion by vac-uum aspiration is available in my locale.

(This checklist will be filled out by the examining physician, a copy attached to the chart, and a copy given to the patient.)

* * * * * * * * * *

2. You are entitled to full information about your present condition, the treatment you may receive and the reaction your body may have to medication that may be given.
3. You have the right to personal dignity, to be treated without discrimination.
4. You have the right to considerate and respectful care.
5. You have the right to privacy and confidentiality, for your-self and your personal records.
6. You have the right to refuse and/or choose treatment, to be told of the medical consequences of your actions, and the right to leave the hospital when you wish.
7. You have the right to refuse and/or choose to have this event reported to police officials.
8. You have the right to take issue regarding your personal and/or medical treatment in this hospital.
9. You have the right to full information about treatment, including information about any charges made and your hospital records.
10. You have the right to continuity of care, including a timely response to your future related needs.

* * *

MEDICAL INFORMATION FOR THE RCI

Some of this material will be repetitious, but it tends to

provide supporting information for the RCI, explaining why
some of the procedures are used, tends to be less clinical, and
more clearly delineates the RCI's role during the medical process.[3]

A rape victim's personal dignity and self-respect may have
been destroyed by the assault. A gentle, considerate, and respectful postrape medical examination may do much to help
restore the victim's personal dignity.

Privacy is a major factor. Try to arrange questioning by
hospital or police personnel in a private room or area.

Good medical advocacy requires a little knowledge and a lot
of presence of mind. Before going to the medical facility,
remind the woman not to shower or douche if she has not
already. If the victim feels like talking about the rape, let her.
Also, talking to you (RCI) may help the woman feel less anxious about explaining the incident, especially the more embarrassing details about the sexual act(s), which are important for
the doctor to know to do proper testing. However, you may
wish to discuss with the woman the fact that she is not required
to answer questions. Certainly a doctor or other medical person
who asks, " ... and why were you at the tavern alone?" is doing
more than obtaining medical history.

Before you reach the hospital or clinic, it is important to
ascertain if the woman wants you to be with her during the
exam. "Would you feel more comfortable if I came with you
during the exam?" or "I'll be glad to come in with you, if you
wish me to," presumably gives the victim a chance to say either
yes *or* no.

Sometimes, advocates are confused about the role they should
play in the exam. Mainly, you're there to *support* the woman.
Suppose she says, "Ouch. That hurts!" and the doctor gives
some nonvalidating response, such as, "Oh, this shouldn't hurt
much." If she seems intimidated (most of us are by those white-
coated imposing figures), you could direct some question to her
such as, "Where does it hurt?" or "What kind of pain is it?" By
directing such questions to the woman, you are giving her the

---

[3]Reproduced by permission of Rape Relief Program, Olympia, Washington.

responsibility for expressing her feelings. Such an opportunity would obviously not have been provided by your screaming at the doctor, "You insensitive clod! If she says it hurts, then it *hurts*!!" Also, to assist in getting into the examining room more easily you can say, "I'm _____ from the RCC and Mary has asked me to be with her during the exam," rather than saying, "I'm _____ from RCC and I'm going to be with Mary during the exam!"

Another awkward situation may develop if the doctor starts addressing all points to you and referring to the woman in the third person. Again, the best response is to try to find some way to direct the conversation to the woman, even if you only turn to her and say, "Is that clear?" The general rule is simple: KEEP IN MIND THAT IT IS THE WOMAN, NOT THE RCI OR THE DOCTOR, WHO IS THE FOCAL PERSON IN THE MEDICAL VISIT.

1. General Physical Exam:

General bodily injuries may be in the form of lacerations, stab wounds, bruises, etc. Surgical care, X rays, dressings, and medication may be necessary. If so, the woman can expect to be seen by a number of hospital personnel, and she can expect to spend time waiting.

The doctor or paramedic will ask about the woman's menstrual periods, contraceptive and VD history, as well as questioning her about the rape itself. Her blood pressure will probably be taken and blood may be drawn from her arm for a VDRL. The doctor should examine the woman for cuts, bruises, broken bones, and internal injuries. Detailed notation of bruises or marks including drawings may be helpful in establishing that force was used.

Clothing should be inspected for tears, blood, and sperm stains. The doctor, victim, RCI, or police can request to keep an item of clothing as evidence.

2. Pelvic Exam:

There are two reasons for having a gynecologist examine her

soon after the rape: (1) to determine if she has been injured internally; and (2) to obtain possible evidence of sperm in the vagina for the police if she should prosecute.

The examining doctor is at all times urged to be as objective and nonjudgmental as possible, since both the doctor and medical records can very well be subpoenaed in court. In any case, the victim will be able to tell by her treatment whether any judgments have been made.

This part of the exam is particularly distasteful to the victim. If the RCI is allowed into the exam room as an aid to the victim, she should stand and stay at the victim's head.

In a pelvic exam, the woman lies on her back in the examining table with her legs apart and feet supported in "stirrups." It is extremely important for a woman who is considering prosecution not to douche or shower away medical evidence such as sperm and semen. A thorough pelvic exam consists of several parts. The doctor may first examine the external genitalia (clitoris, major and minor lips, vaginal orifice, hymen, meatus, perineum, and anus) for irritation or injury. If the woman was a virgin, she may have questions about her anatomy, particularly her hymen. Since hymens vary considerably in their thickness and elasticity, tearing and/or bleeding may or may not have occurred.

The doctor may also be able to "estimate" if the victim was pregnant before the rape.

The doctor may do a rectal gonorrhea test during this phase of the exam in cases of anal intercourse by the assailant, and a throat culture should also be done in cases where the woman was forced to perform fellatio — the penis being forced into the woman's mouth.

The second part of a pelvic exam consists of visualizing those internal organs which can be seen with the use of a speculum, a metal instrument with two round-edged blades. The speculum is inserted into the vagina and opened to hold the vaginal walls apart. The doctor can then check for injuries to the vagina and cervix and perform several tests. If the woman plans to prosecute, there are several important tests which need to be done to establish sexual contact. With the speculum in place, a sample can be taken from the posterior fornix of the vagina to check for the presence of sperm. This sample will then be examined under the microscope and the number of sperm noted as well as the proportion of motile (moving) to nonmotile, and degree of motility of sperm. The reason for noting motility is to attempt to estimate, from a predetermined or known die-off rate, how long ago the sperm was deposited in the body, thus corroborating the woman's statement.

There is another, more complicated test for the presence of semen rather than sperm, called an "acid-phosphatase" test. A sample for this test can be obtained in several ways. Either another sample besides the sperm test sample can be obtained from the posterior fornix or a sample can be obtained from anywhere on the body using the Woods lamp. With the lights turned off in the examining room, this small ultraviolet light will cause semen on the external genitalia, face, clothing, etc., to fluoresce and a sample for the acid-phosphatase test can then be obtained from these flourescent areas.

A gonorrhea test will be performed during the speculum exam (see VD section). A test for Trichomonas is not routinely done immediately after a rape, but if the woman develops symptoms of this vaginal infection, she should be tested. Doctors may also do a pap test for cervical cancer on a woman who has not had one within a year, but this is not necessarily a routine part of the postrape exam.

The third part of the pelvic exam is called the "bimanual." After the speculum is removed, the doctor places two fingers of the gloved hand into the vagina and presses down on the woman's lower abdomen with the other hand. In this way, the size, shape, and texture of internal organs (uterus, fallopian tubes, and ovaries) can be felt and internal injuries may be detected. Further confirmation of normality or abnormality is obtained by performing a rectal exam — one finger inserted into the rectum, one finger inserted into the vagina, the other hand again on the abdomen, pressing the organs down to the fingers.

3. Pregnancy Test:

If a woman was not using any birth control, it is possible she may have become pregnant as a result of the rape. To determine the likelihood of pregnancy, it is necessary to know some details about the woman's menstrual cycle.

If there is a possibility that she was pregnant before the rape, this should be noted to all the hospital personnel so treatment can be adjusted accordingly.

There are three possible alternatives to avoid pregnancy from the rape. Although most of the rape victims will prefer to terminate a pregnancy, not all victims may have this preference. The three methods of termination are the Morning After Treatment (MAT), menstrual extraction, and abortion.

A. MORNING AFTER TREATMENT (MAT, DES, or Morning After Pill)

Author's Note: A statistically significant association has been reported between the maternal ingestion during pregnancy of diethylstilbesterol (DES) and the occurrence of vaginal cancer in the female offspring. There have also been reports by the Ralph Nader Health Research Group of sterility and abnormalities in the reproductive organs of male offspring of women who have taken DES. The woman contemplating the use of DES should be clearly forwarned of the potential risks involved. Many RCC personnel do not consider the DES treatment a viable or realistic alternative for the rape victim to be offered.

Also, the severe nausea which accompanies the use of DES over the five days of treatment which it entails, occurs at the most inappropriate time and may even enhance the risk of psychological harm for the rape victim. The victim is extremely sensitive to pain and hurt following the assault and is in need of support, encouragement, and comfort at a time when she is trying to feel better. To subject her to the suffering accompanying the administration of DES may be totally inexcusable and only enhance the sexual assault victim's trauma while retarding future adjustment.

Diethylstilbesterol is *contraindicated* (should not be taken) if the woman is already pregnant, if she is using birth control pills, if she has ever had any problems with using birth control pills and her physician took her off of them, or if she has ever had cancer, diabetes, heart disease, circulation problems and blood clotting problems.

The MAT is a short-term high dosage of synthetic estrogen which prevents implantation of a fertilized egg in the uterus. The treatment must be started within seventy-two hours after unprotected intercourse and continued for five days. The closer to the unprotected intercourse the woman starts treatment, the more effective it is.

Common short-term side-effects are severe nausea, vomiting and dizziness. Besides the unpleasantness of nausea, the effectiveness of the treatment is lowered if the woman vomits up any of the pills. If a pill is vomited up, another pill *must* be taken to replace it. It is recommended that Bendectin be taken to prevent nausea, and that the woman begin taking it at the beginning of the MAT because if she waits until she feels nauseated, the Bendectin may not work. Other side-effects may be vaginal spotting, diarrhea, breast tenderness, insomnia, and skin rash.

If the victim may have been pregnant before the rape, have a pregnancy test done to be sure she doesn't take DES after pregnancy has begun. It won't stop that pregnancy. This test may be done routinely. Remind the victim that this test is only for a prior pregnancy.

There is no conclusive evidence of any long-term side-effects of the MAT. However, because of the possibility of damage to the fetus, it is recommended an abortion be performed if the MAT fails, i.e. if no period results. The possibility of increased risk of long-term side-effects makes repeated use of the MAT a decision to be made deliberately.

It is possible that after the "morning after treatment," the victim will have increased fertility. Therefore, it is necessary to have the woman consider contraception.

REMEMBER — THE CHOICE IS THE VICTIM'S — SHE CAN REFUSE ANY MEDICATION FROM ANYONE. MAKE HER AWARE OF THIS CHOICE.

B. MENSTRUAL EXTRACTION (ABORTION)

Author's Note: Menstrual extraction (B) and vacuum suction (C) are both forms of abortion. As such, the RCI presenting the woman with the alternative of obtaining an abortion following a sexual assult should approach this alternative just as deliberately as in the case of considering the use of DES. Although there are conflicting views on whether pre- and postabortion counseling is a valid requirement for a woman seeking an abortion or is even necessary except for medical follow-up, a suggestion is that the woman contemplating having an abortion receive at least one to four hours of counseling. This seems to be just good helping behavior and is another indication of the RCI's sensitivity and caring. The RCI should also become aware of any restrictions in her state regarding *when* an abortion may be performed; no restrictions are typically stated during the first trimester (3 months) of pregnancy.

Menstrual extraction is a method used up to six weeks after a woman's last menstrual period. Since it is performed *before* the results of a pregnancy test are considered reliable, the woman cannot be sure she is pregnant. Some women may have symptoms of pregnancy, such as breast tenderness, fatigue, frequency of urination, but many do not. A late period may be a result of the emotional stress following an assault, but a woman may prefer to have a menstrual extraction rather than wait the necessary weeks to have a positive pregnancy test and then having a vacuum aspiration (suction) abortion performed. Menstrual extraction is medically simpler to perform and the cost is usually less than a vacuum aspiration. A canula (suction tube) is inserted into the uterus and attached to a suction syringe. There is no need for anesthetics or dilation of the cervical os (opening). The contents of the uterus, that is, the whole month's period plus the fertilized egg if there is one, is removed. The woman may experience cramping during this part of the procedure similar to severe menstrual cramps, but the whole procedure is very short. The woman should observe the same postoperative precautions as following a vacuum suction abortion discussed next.

C. VACUUM SUCTION ABORTION

This manner of abortion is used up to the twelfth week of

pregnancy (counting from the last menstrual period). An anesthetic similar to Novocain® is injected in several places along the back walls of the vagina, next to the cervix. This technique of local anesthetic is commonly used for abortions and is called the paracervical block, which blocks pain coming from the cervical canal and uterus. Another means of administering the anesthetic is to inject it directly into the cervix itself. Either way, at the physician's discretion, is effective. Dilators (metal rods of increasing size) are then inserted in the cervical os (opening) to enlarge it so the doctor can insert the necessary surgical instruments. The canula is inserted and attached to a small machine which then sucks out the contents of the uterus. A curette (a spoonlike instrument) may be then inserted to scrape the linings of the uterus, making sure all the contents have been removed. The woman will probably experience cramping starting with the introduction of the dilators, but the entire procedure is over quickly, usually in five to eight minutes.

As the cervical os remains slightly dilated after the abortion, the woman should be careful not to douche or tub bathe as these may force water or air into the uterus, potentially causing infection. The woman may take a shower, which does not force water into the vagina or uterus. Some physicians routinely administer antibiotics such as penicillin to all women following an abortion in attempts to prevent postabortion infections, but the woman herself should be careful to avoid the possibility of uterine infection. She should also make an appointment for a postabortion check, two to four weeks following the procedure, preferably with the doctor who performed the abortion.

4. Venereal Disease:

As with the pregnancy testing, the VD test at the hospital can only determine if the victim had VD at the time of the rape. A vaginal culture (cotton swab into cervix) for gonorrhea and a blood test (sample being taken from the arm) for syphillis would be involved.

It is essential for the victim's own welfare that she does get such diagnostic tests for VD at some point after the rape. It is recommended that this be done six weeks following the rape because:

(1) the gonorrhea culture can be taken one week to three months after contact.

(2) the syphillis blood test can be taken as soon as three weeks after contact.

A negative VD result six weeks after exposure does not mean it won't be positive at a later date. In other words, regular VD testing at six month intervals is essential. Many VD clinics perform these tests free of charge.

Women on birth control pills are said to have an increased susceptibility to gonorrhea.

TREATMENT

Penicillin G is the drug of choice for treatment of gonorrhea. It is most effective if administered by injection in the buttocks, but can also be taken orally. For those women who are allergic to penicillin, tetracycline can be given orally, but it should not be taken during pregnancy. A woman should be rechecked a week after treatment as there is some possibility of treatment failure, especially if tetracycline was used. For a recheck, a rectal as well as cervical culture should be taken, as rectal gonorrhea is more difficult to treat than vaginal gonorrhea.

Treatment for syphillis basically involves the same drugs as treatment for gonorrhea — penicillin G, erythromycin, and tetracycline — but the aim of syphillis treatment is to maintain a constant level of the antibiotic in the woman's body for at least two weeks. Follow-up is also more extensive than for gonorrhea; the woman may be rechecked at intervals up to two years.

Allergic reactions to penicillin are rare, but do occur. Most of the allergic reactions to penicillin are called "delayed" and may occur five to fourteen days after treatment, usually appearing as a red skin rash or blisterlike wheals (a smooth, slightly elevated area on the body surface). Such delayed reactions are usually harmless and disappear by themselves in a few days; however they must be reported to the prescribing doctor. An even more rare reaction to penicillin is called anaphylactic shock, but this is much more serious, and symptoms typically occur within one to fifteen minutes after the injection. This requires immediate medical attention, as death is a possible result unless treatment is received.

People with a known allergy to penicillin receive tetracycline in oral form every six hours for about four days. It should be taken with the same precautions as for penicillin. Side effects most commonly experienced are heartburn, nausea, vomiting, and diarrhea. The only antacid you should take for heartburn in this case is sodium bicarbonate. Report the symptoms of diarrhea to a physician.

One fact women should be made aware of with any antibiotic therapy is that it may disrupt normal existing vaginal bacterial organisms by allowing an organism foreign to the area to grow. The result can be a new vaginal (nonvenereal) infection with accompanying symptoms of unusual and/or increased discharge. Other minor vaginal infections may also be transmitted or some may occur after treatment.

5. *Emotional Needs:*

That a rape victim is very upset is one important aspect of rape which is often unrecognized or even denied by hospital personnel, both female and male. In this crisis a woman will need support from someone she knows will be empathic. The most desirable person to have would be a close friend. Another alternative is·a woman who will come just because the victim talked with her on the phone after the rape, such as a RCI. The point is that the woman needs and must receive support. Support means strength and with strength the victim can insist on the sensitive humane medical treatment she deserves. Support also means that the victim can better recognize her rage. It means she may better deal with the guilt that society and she may impose on her.

Concerning medical treatment, a sympathetic physician may

prescribe a sedative for short-term use. The victim should not be hesitant to ask for it.

6. *Follow-Up Tests:*

A. Venereal Disease — six weeks following the sexual assault.
B. Pregnancy — six weeks following last menstrual cycle.
C. Psychotherapy Referral — as needed.
D. Medical Referrals — for postabortion or post-menstrual extraction and effectiveness of VD treatment.
E. If MAT (DES) was prescribed, a pap smear every six months to screen out possibility of cancer. Also indicated is the Schiller Iodine Test (Lugols Test) which can detect any changes occurring in vaginal wall cells following administration of DES.

Note: Two excellent resources for information on VD, birth control, pregnancy, and abortions are provided by Montreal Health Press, entitled *VD Handbook* and *Birth Control Handbook.*

A book which is also an excellent guide to other health related topics for women is *Our Bodies Ourselves* (1973) by the Boston Women's Health Book Collective.

CHAPTER 7

LEGAL PROCEDURES

AS rape is primarily a ~~~~~ess, it becomes necessary to discuss some of the pr~~~~~ law enforcement personnel. *In th~~~~~ assume that the policies or pr~~~~~ for your locale and state. *

~~~~~ or your police ~~~~~ ds assessment, ~~~~~ ou should also k~~~~~ depending on wheth~~~~~ the city police department ~~~~~ nt. A handbook entitled *Medica~~~~~ an excellent resource for RCCs.~~~~~ nay be repetitious, the legal a~~~~~ vide a beginning point for w~~~~~ e.

The~~~~~ Women Against Rape, Chica~~~~~ of the legal machinery. Ev~~~~~ art based on their own

~~~~~ the police can be sensi-~~~~~ at at the same time con-duct ~~~~~ vestigation.

POLICE G~~~~~ DELINES:
INVESTIGATING A SEX OFFENSE[2]

There are two basic problems with which a police officer

---

[1]Women Organized Against Rape, Trineb Bldg., 420 Service Dr., Philadelphia, Pennsylvania 19104.
[2]Reproduced by permission of the Rape Counseling Center, Minneapolis, Minnesota. The guidelines were prepared by Ann L. Alton, Assistant County Attorney, and Richard Hansey, Lt., Minneapolis Police Department.

169

STEPS IN THE LEGAL PROCESS
(Reproduced by permission)

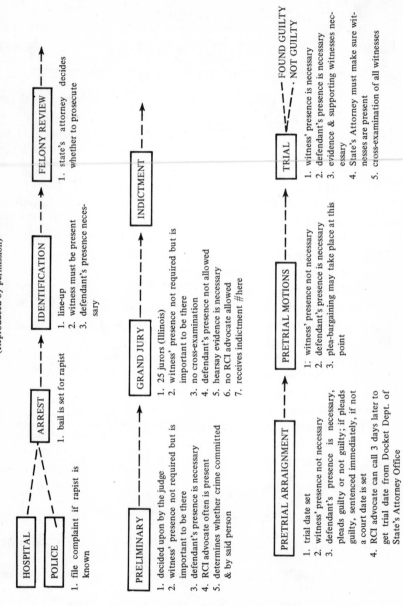

HOSPITAL

POLICE

1. file complaint if rapist is known

ARREST

1. bail is set for rapist

IDENTIFICATION

1. line-up
2. witness must be present
3. defendant's presence necessary

FELONY REVIEW

1. state's attorney decides whether to prosecute

PRELIMINARY

1. decided upon by the judge
2. witness' presence not required but is important to be there
3. defendant's presence is necessary
4. RCI advocate often is present
5. determines whether crime committed & by said person

GRAND JURY

1. 25 jurors (Illinois)
2. witness' presence not required but is important to be there
3. no cross-examination
4. defendant's presence not allowed
5. hearsay evidence is necessary
6. no RCI advocate allowed
7. receives indictment #here

INDICTMENT

PRETRIAL ARRAIGNMENT

1. trial date set
2. witness' presence not necessary
3. defendant's presence is necessary; if pleads guilty or not guilty; if pleads guilty, sentenced immediately, if not a court date is set
4. RCI advocate can call 3 days later to get trial date from Docket Dept. of State's Attorney Office

PRETRIAL MOTIONS

1. witness' presence not necessary
2. defendant's presence is necessary
3. plea-bargaining may take place at this point

TRIAL

FOUND GUILTY

NOT GUILTY

1. witness' presence is necessary
2. defendant's presence is necessary
3. evidence & supporting witnesses necessary
4. State's Attorney must make sure witnesses are present
5. cross-examination of all witnesses

must be concerned when investigating a sex offense or any incident where the victim has been subjected to severe emotional trauma.

The first problem confronting the officer is to deal appropriately with the emotional distress of the victim and her family. The second problem is to properly investigate the case and preserve the evidence for possible prosecution.

The following guidelines suggest ways in which the police officer can most effectively satisfy both the needs of the victim and the needs of the prosecution, which need not be inconsistent. A victim who is treated with kindness and patience and who understands what the officer is doing and why, will be of far more assistance in the investigation and will usually be a more cooperative witness for the prosecution. At the same time, a thorough initial investigation will also result in a stronger case for trial than the situation where the initial investigation is sketchy and a detective must later attempt to reconstruct evidence that has disappeared or has been destroyed.

The guidelines here should be of particular use to the patrolperson or sergeant who responds to the victim's complaint, and whose initial investigation often provides the bulk of the prosecution's evidence at trial.

I. Important Principles To Remember:
   A. In the crisis situation, whether it is a car accident or a rape case, the police officer is both a social worker providing human services and a trained investigator. Each of these roles is equally important.
   B. The victim of a sex offense is always humiliated, defensive and distrustful, and may also be angered, afraid, or hysterical. She may also be in shock and appear absolutely calm and collected as a result, or manifest equally strong reactions.
      1. In dealing with the victim of a sex offense, have patience and explain what you are doing and why you are doing it so that she understands the need for each step in the investigation procedure. Offer her some alternatives, such as, "Would you like to tell me what happened here or would you like to si

down first?" This will help her feel she is in some control of the situation. She will be far more willing to cooperate with you and will be able to offer real assistance to your investigation only when she understands what you need and why you need it. You are more likely to obtain a full and accurate report of the details from the victim when she fully understands what you are doing than you will if she feels further victimized by the police investigation. A successful prosecution can only result if the entire truth is known.

C. The victim's family is likely to evidence emotions ranging from silence to hysteria to vicious anger. The victim's parents, spouse, or lover may react with anger because they feel helpless to correct the situation, and that anger may be turned against the victim by blaming her for whatever happened.

1. Do not interview the victim in the presence of her family or friends unless you are dealing with a very small child, in which case you should ask the parent to encourage the child to tell the story herself without permitting the parent to tell it for the child. The victim usually will not be as candid with you if her family or friends are present. She may not want her family to hear the details at all, so the officer should briefly inform the family generally what happened and suggest that they should not inquire into details unless the victim volunteers them, as it could lead to confusion and problems with the investigation.

2. The officer should contact a relative or close friend for the victim if she wants this done, and request this person meet the officer and the victim either at the hospital after the medical examination or some place else that is convenient at a time that will not interfere with the initial investigation. You should make sure that someone is present to comfort and be with the victim once your work with her has been

completed, but be careful not to let family or friends interfere in any way with your investigation.

D. Ordinarily, the only witnesses to a sex offense are the victim and the assailant. Corroborating evidence (in most states), which is evidence tending to prove the crime ultimately charged, is necessary to achieve a conviction. As a practical matter, a jury will rarely convict a defendant unless there is some corroborating evidence in addition to the victim's testimony.

1. There is rarely much corroborating evidence available in a rape case and that available evidence is most often subject to rapid destruction, such as sperm, blood stains, dirty or messy clothing or hair, minor abrasions or scratches, physical evidence to identify the scene, or evidence of a struggle. Even minor details, such as the victim's recollection that there was a red light bulb in the ceiling of the room to which the defendant took her, if proven, will provide very important corroborating evidence. It is therefore essential that every bit of possible evidence be preserved and gathered immediately.

II. In a sex offense, statements made by the victim concerning what happened and the identity and description of her assailant as soon as possible after the offense occurs, are admissible in court to corroborate her testimony. Such statements made by the victim as soon as possible after the offense are called "res gestae" statements under the law. They are admissible basically because of the principle that an immediate statement made under the influence of an exciting or traumatic event before the individual has an opportunity to reflect or to fabricate a story is most likely to be reliable and should be admitted on that basis. Frequently, a police officer is the first person to whom the victim tells her story in any detail and if the police officer's interview with her occurs reasonably soon after the crime or reasonably soon after she was able to reach safety, the officer will be able to testify at trial about what she related to him/her and that testimony will not be inadmissible as heresay. It is therefore important for a police officer initially interviewing the victim to make a complete report of her story to him/her, but the officer should make it in her own words rather than attempt to recall quotations that might be later used to embarrass the victim, who will not remember the exact words she used when she testifies.

III. The officer who initially interviews the victim should do the best to report the details of what she informs him/her, but the officer should not attempt to question the victim about minute details that she does not volunteer. If the officer does, the victim is likely either to clam up or to tell the officer a partial story which will later cause problems in any trial. The initial investigating officer, under that stressful situation, will not have the time to establish the same kind of rapport with her that the investigating detective will later be able to establish, so the inquiry concerning details should be left to the detective and the prosecutor.

IV. The detective must ascertain the entire story and the complete truth about the incident. The victim will usually withhold important intimate details about the offense because of embarrassment or because some aspect of it, such as sodomy, was very repugnant to her. Furthermore, evidence of her prior chastity (previous acts of sexual intercourse or sodomy committed with someone not then her husband) may be admissible at trial if the defendant admits the act charged but claims that it was consentual. Therefore, the detective will have to know about such things as whether or not she was a virgin or is living with a man to whom she is not married, her marital status, and whether she has ever had an illegitimate child. Any previous contact, social or sexual, with the defendant is relevant evidence of a prior relationship with the defendant and will be admissible. The initial investigating officer needs to achieve sufficient rapport with the victim so that when the officer leaves her, the officer is personally convinced as to whether or not a crime occurred, is confident she has given an accurate description of the suspect, and has gathered or preserved and turned over to detectives, all available physical evidence and the names of any potential witnesses. The detective, on the other hand, must develop a rapport with the victim to enable the detective to be convinced that he/she knows *everything* about the offense and *everything* about the victim which is relevant to the case.

V. Sex offenses generally are the hardest crimes to prosecute. *Some* corroboration of the victim's testimony, such as her immediate complaint, medical evidence, torn clothing, or bruises is helpful to obtain a conviction. In a sex case, a defendant will virtually always demand a jury trial. Juries understand that rape is easy to claim and they require substantial evidence in addition to the victim's testimony before they will render a guilty verdict. Furthermore, if the jury believes that a woman put herself in a compromising position, they may well feel (incorrectly) that she deserved what happened to her and use that as an excuse for a nonguilty verdict. Middle-aged jurors, particularly women, are very difficult because they were raised in the belief that a woman would not be raped unless she did something to ask for it. Where a victim has been hitch-hiking, met the defendant in a bar, has been drinking, or has been smoking marijuana, the case will be much harder to prove. In a sense, the victim of a sex offense is on trial herself. She must tell her embarrassing story in complete detail and reveal many personal matters about her private life. She is subjected to extensive and often grueling cross-examination and if she cries, the jury may reject her. At the same time, the defendant has an absolute right to be silent under the Fifth Amendment and may use a double-barrelled defense through his defense attorney that, "I wasn't there and didn't do it, but if I did, she consented."

* * *

The following procedures are generally followed by police, but may not be followed by your police department, and may not be followed in every case where generally used.[3]

---

[3]Adapted from the San Bernardino Rape Crisis Service, San Bernardino, California. Used by permission.

The Report

When a report of rape is made to the police, either by the victim or someone calling for the victim ("Third Party"), usually a uniformed police officer in a marked police car will respond. As there are typically few policewomen in any police department, there will be a great chance that the investigating officer will be a man.

The officer will typically question the victim very briefly. If she is still at the site of the attack, the officer will begin a preliminary examination of the area for evidence, i.e. stains, spots, hairs on floor or furniture, and objects the attacker may have handled.

Medical Care

Transportation will usually be arranged or provided by the police to the hospital for the medical examination and necessary treatment. The victim may choose to be seen by her private physician or go to a specific hospital in the area. If she has no preference, she will most likely be taken to a city or county hospital emergency room. When the victim is accompanied by a police officer, she will probably be seen by the emergency room physician more quickly.

If the woman has not already called the police and goes directly to the hospital, the hospital is usually required by law to notify the police, especially if the victim is a minor. She may have to wait for the police to arrive before being examined.

The police officer may or may not be present during the physical exam; in some states his/her presence is necessary to preserve the "chain of evidence." All evidence is collected at the site and from the medical examination, then taken to the crime laboratory for analysis.

Depending on the emotional state of the victim, the police officer may continue the initial interview at the emergency room or upon the victims return home.

Second Interview

The second interview may take place within twenty-four to forty-eight hours after the assault if the woman wishes to press charges and if the suspect is known or apprehended. If there is no known suspect, a long interval may pass until the victim is interviewed a second time.

The second interview will usually be conducted by a plain clothes detective with the investigative division of the department. In some cases, this detective may be from a "Sex Crimes" or "Sex Offense Unit" where such units exist or a squad dealing with crimes against persons. This detective will probably remain with the case throughout, unless he/she had reason to believe another one of the detectives might relate better with the victim or if individual case load requirements dictate reassignment.

The detective will contact the victim and see her either at her home or ask her to come down to the police department, the latter being more likely. This interview, in addition to going over facts covered by the investigating officer, will be much more detailed. The interview will most likely be audio recorded, especially if there is a known suspect in the case. This second interview is often where most of the criticism of police procedures occurs in their dealings with rape victims, as the woman is often drilled for very specific facts, almost as though she were reliving the rape.

The detective will probably ask for the following information from the victim:

1. Suspect's(s') Description: The woman must be careful not to let the police put words in her mouth, as police often already have a person in mind.
2. Activities of Victim Prior to Assault: "What was she doing? Where was she? With whom?"
3. Suspect's Relationship to Victim: "Had you ever seen him (them) before — family member, friend, relative, stranger?"
4. Resisting the Attack: "Did the rapist threaten you physi-

cally, verbally? What did you do to resist the attack?" In some states, the victim's fear resulting from a verbal threat is legally reason not to physically resist — scratching, kicking, etc.

5. Victim's Clothing: The woman will be asked to identify the clothing she was wearing at the time of the assault. The police will probably keep the clothing as evidence.

6. Suspect's Exact Words: "Did he use obscene words while raping you — describe? Did he ask you to perform unnatural acts — describe?" If the woman does not remember the exact wording, she should state she remembers only *approximate* wording and it is so recorded.

7. Victim's Statement: This may be taken prior to the detailed questioning of the victim. It is a long, thorough, subjective account of exactly what happened, in the victim's own words.

Follow-Up

There may be many more interviews with the detective, particularly in cases where new information becomes available or for further identification purposes. Usually, the victim will be asked to identify the suspect through photos and mug shots and she will probably have to identify the rapist at least once in a police line-up.

The victim may request that news media not disclose any information which may identify her. Sometimes they may cooperate, other times not. Many states now have laws forbidding the release of this information.

Reported rapes, where the victim wishes to press charges, will be turned over to the prosecuting attorney only when and if a suspect is known or is in custody.

Victims reporting rape may refuse to be interviewed or to give detailed information. The police will try to encourage her and perhaps understand her reluctance. When the victim decides not to cooperate, the case will be terminated.

* * *

FUNCTIONS OF RAPE CRISIS CENTERS
DURING THE LEGAL PROCESS

Ideally, at some point early in the initial police interview the victim will be informed of the RCC. If the victim requests it, the police should call the RCC or allow the victim to do so.

Many police departments are beginning to allow a RCI to accompany the victim during the initial and subsequent interviews. This is done if the victim requests such assistance and as long as the RCI's presence absolutely does not disrupt or distort the interview nor distress or embarrass the victim.

In calls in which the RCC outreach team is requested to go to the victim, the question of safety arises. The RCC should call the police department and inquire about the safety of entering a particular area or neighborhood. If it is necessary, ask the victim if the police could accompany the RCI team to the questionable neighborhood.

When the RCI team arrives at the victim's place, they should be on guard against destroying, distorting, or rearranging any evidence, physical or otherwise. The following "Do's" and "Don't's" may also assist the RCI in what behavior is appropriate and inappropriate during the crisis and initial contact.

1. Do not handle nor disturb the victim's purse, clothing, bedclothes, or any item which might have been touched by the rapist.
2. Don't ask any specific questions about facts of the assault, as you may then be subpoenaed to appear in court as a witness.
3. Do encourage the woman to talk about her reactions and feelings to the assault.
4. Do encourage prosecution of the crime and cooperation with law enforcement people, but respect her wishes as well.
5. Don't become too intimately involved in the crisis, as this will lessen your objectivity in assessing her strengths and weaknesses and needs for support.

6. Don't argue with professionals involved at this point. If any mistreatment occurs, make a note of it so it can be taken up at an appropriate time.
7. Do not talk to any representative of the news media, as all material you have about a case is confidential and in some states this is guaranteed by law.
8. Do realize that your function is to assist the victim, not conduct the investigation.

THIRD PARTY REPORTING

Third party reporting was developed by the Rape Relief Program in Olympia, Washington with the cooperation of their police department. Basically, a "third party report" is the compilation of information, in anonymous form, from a victim or "third party" who does not wish to report the incident to the police, but who wishes that something be done about the assault.

Third party reporting serves a valuable function for the victim in relieving some of the possible guilt resulting from not doing "anything" about getting the rapist who assaulted her "off the street," although she has decided not to go through the process of making a formal police report. This method provides her the opportunity to assist the police without causing her further emotional stress involved in the legal process. Although the information is not admissible as evidence, the material can be included in the "pre-sentence report" prepared for the judge (in Washington state at least), if it clearly indicates the defendant.

Some other very important uses of the material for police departments are that these reports can be included in statistics so the police may obtain a more accurate assessment of the rape rate. It may also provide the police the additional information needed to locate a multiple rapist who has assaulted a woman who has formally reported the assault to the police.

A possible third party information form follows.

THIRD PARTY REPORT [4]

PD REPORT #	CRIME	DATE REPORTED	TIME REPORTED	RCI CONTACT

AREA OF OFFENSE (block & street #)	DATE	TIME	DAY OF WEEK

LOCATION OF OFFENSE (Park, street victim's home, car)	#OF SUSPECTS	TYPE OF WEAPON

SUSPECT # 1: NAME:

AGE	RACE	BIRTH	WT	HT	BUILD	COMPL.	HAIR	EYES	OCCUP.

CLOTHING:

OTHER IDENTIFYING MARKS OR OUTSTANDING FEATURES (Speech, glasses, scars, facial hair, tattoos):

SUSPECT # 2: NAME:

AGE	RACE	BIRTH	WT	HT	BUILD	COMPL.	HAIR	EYES	OCCUP.

CLOTHING:

OTHER IDENTIFYING MARKS OR OUTSTANDING FEATURES (Speech, glasses, scars, facial hair, tattoos):

VEHICLE USED:
Victim/suspect own

YR.	MAKE	MODEL	COLOR	LICENSE #& STATE

IDENT. MARKS (dents, equip., ornaments, etc. on suspect's car):

HOW WAS WEAPON USED & THREATS MADE:

WHAT DID SUSPECT SAY? (exact/approx. statements, repeated phrases):

FORCE USED: Threats _____ Held by suspect _____ Tied _____ Struck _____

Held by other(s) _____ Other force (specify): _____

ACTS FORCED ON VICTIM:

WERE OTHERS PRESENT? ADULTS _____ #WITH VICTIM _____ #WITH SUSPECT _____

CHILD _____ #WITH VICTIM _____ #WITH SUSPECT _____

HOW WAS FIRST CONTACT MADE WITH VICTIM? (break-in, on street, party, offered or accepted a ride):

VICTIM:

AGE	RACE	MARITAL STATUS	LIVING WITH	TYPES OF PREMISES

BRIEF ACCOUNT OF HOW INCIDENT OCCURRED (Use reverse side)

[4]Reproduced by permission of Rape Relief Program, Olympia, Washington.

SPECIAL PROBLEMS IN THE COURTS

This material comes from the Chicago Women Against Rape in Chicago, Illinois and is provided so RCIs, as lay advocates, will be aware of some problems they will face. These problems will often be frustrating and time consuming.

1. No translators are provided for women who do not speak English.
2. Most defendants in the courts are blacks.
3. Rape victims are usually alone in the court. Often the States attorney does not review her case in advance and she is in no way prepared for the ordeal of testifying.
4. Most courtrooms are male-identified in that the proceedings are run by men, and rules and laws are set by men.
5. Women are *always* the victim in rape cases.
6. Rape is considered a sexual offense rather than an act of aggression.
7. Minority women receive less preferential treatment than white women.
8. White middle-class women receive the best treatment, but are still treated as property — just more valuable property.
9. Court proceedings are long and drawn out and do not take into account the psychological duress of the victim.
10. Juries are not composed of the defendant's peers as specified by law.
11. The courts are run and controlled by white people — often making decisions about black people.

SUGGESTIONS FOR THE VICTIM TO CONSIDER

It might be valuable to go over some of the important points the RCI will want to discuss at an appropriate time with the rape victim.

For some women, a call to the police station has provided quick and needed protection. For many others, however, the police questioning and subsequent legal proceedings have made the women feel that they have been raped twice, first by a violent assailant, and second by a system of justice that is supposed to offer support and protection but offers instead unsympathetic policemen and attorneys, who make implicit or explicit accusations that the victim invited the rape and got what she deserved.

There may be many situations in which a woman's only recourse is to contact the police as soon as possible. If she wants to have the time to make a choice and feels that she wants to think things through, suggest she go to the hospital for treatment before she goes to the police station. Even if the victim has no serious injury, her medical needs demand primary attention. While she is being treated, she can decide whether or not to formally report the incident to the police. Later, she can decide whether or not to bring charges against the rapist, when and if he is arrested.

It is suggested that the victim at least report the crime to the police via a third party report, to insure the greatest accuracy possible in documenting the incidence of rape. The FBI calls rape the least reported of all crimes; as a result, it is also one of the least understood. On the other hand, it may be too emotionally trying to the woman to deal with the police. She must make her own decisions.

Formally reporting a rape may not mean she must prosecute, but a real likelihood exists in which the authorities will pressure her into doing so. Largen[5] noted " ... though the cases are few, women who wish only to report the crime and not prosecute, may be forced to do so (prosecute) at a later date by threat of subpoena as a material witness ..." This possible action by the authorities thus negates the woman's ability to exercise her freedom of choice and as Largen goes on to state " ... the major goal of the crisis worker is to return the victim to her precrisis state. Therefore, it is ESSENTIAL that the victim be allowed to make her own decision in regard to reporting. Her self-determination has been denied her through the act of rape. To make decisions for her further denies her that self-determination."

In those cases where the woman has made the decision to

---

[5]Largen, M. A., Personal Communication, November 18, 1975.

prefer charges against her assailant, she should report this to the police soon. The slower she is in reporting the crime, the less likely it is that the assailant will ever be convicted. Any delay, even a few hours, gives the defense a strong argument against the victim's credibility at the time of the trial.

Going to the police is her prerogative, but that does not mean that her charges are automatically accepted. The police may not believe the story. Such questions as, "Why were you there?" need not be answered, but she must remember the police have discretionary power to accept or not accept the charges. She may find it more useful to be as cooperative as she possibly can with the police, helping to ensure that they take and investigate her complaint. The victim may refuse to answer a personal question by indicating that she will speak to a physician about it; the physician's statement can then be used as evidence.

The statement given to the police can and most likely will be used as evidence at the trial. The woman may feel some confusion immediately after the incident regarding the details of time, place, or identity. She should try to be as absolutely accurate in her description as she can be. For her own use and the later use of the prosecution, it is advisable to keep a record of details as she remembers them.

A woman who has been raped and wishes to press charges against her assailant should realize from the time that she goes to the hospital, that a conviction of the rapist rests upon her testimony. Therefore, the victim will want to obtain as much accurate evidence as possible.

First, the hospital report is crucial. The examining physician's report will state penetration, if any, and the presence of semen, if any, in and on the woman's body. If injuries were received during the rape, they too should be reported and treated. Photographs from the scene of the incident may be helpful if they show cut phone cords, broken windows, etc. Follow-up medical reports are very important. Also, if the rapist contacts her to talk, apologize, or threaten, this may be used as evidence. It is suggested that the victim try to bring forward corroborating evidence of force used, attempts at intercourse, as well as identity of the assailant.

Pretrial preparation of testimony and familiarization with lines of questioning and the types of evidence the court is looking for will be invaluable to her. The responsibility of proof is on the victim, and she should talk as long as possible to the district attorney who will handle the case. Often the DA has very little time to prepare for the trial, while the defense attorney prepares extensively. She can seek additional counsel (a private attorney) if she is confused. It should be noted, however, that a private attorney cannot represent the victim in criminal proceedings.

The trial will be before a judge and a jury, unless the defendant waives his right to a jury trial. At the end of the trial, the judge directs the jury to determine the guilt of the defendant beyond a reasonable doubt. Therefore, the role of the jury is crucial. The men and women of the jury tend to be older and conservative; it is wise to be cautious about the terms the victim uses in her testimony. Have her try to decide for herself what terminology the jury would fully understand. Don't use language they might find offensive.

Since identification in a rape case seems to be less difficult than in some other violent crimes, the defense usually centers on whether the victim "invited" the rape. Questions along this line usually involve, "What was she wearing? Was she hitchhiking? Was it dark? Was she drinking with the defendant?"

Another line of questioning may seek to discredit her by proving that she had a "bad" or promiscuous reputation in the community. The defense will attempt to discover whether she is "loose," whether she lives a rather "free" lifestyle, for example, does she live in a communal situation, or have a "suspect" occupation like that of a stewardess or waitress in a tavern.

Also, she has to be careful to differentiate in her testimony and in later questioning that she did consent to intercourse, but that she was forced to submit, by threats or fear of physical injury. "Submit" is a crucial word. If the defense asks her, "Did you in fact consent?", "No, I was forced to submit."

LAY ADVOCACY TERMS TO KNOW

This material is provided to clear up some of the confusing legal terminology connected with a legal proceeding regarding rape.[6]

A. PEOPLE:

1. *Plaintiff* — the complaining party in all lawsuits. In criminal cases, the State is the plaintiff. The State represents the rape victim. The victim's attorney is the States attorney. The victim in a criminal case is the "complainant," and is also the complaining witness. The woman is the state's most important witness and usually the only witness.

2. *Defendant* — the person who is accused of harming the victim. He then has to defend himself in court against the charges.

3. *Judge* — often called "the Court" or "Court" and always "your honor" by anyone addressing her/him. The judge rules on issues of law. Even in a jury trial, the judge can be vital, for it is s/he who shall decide what is admissible as evidence, both physical (such as clothing) and testimony of the concerned parties.

4. *States Attorney* — s/he is also called the prosecuting attorney or district attorney. Her/his job is to represent the State when they prosecute the case against the accused.

5. *Defense Attorney* — s/he who represents and defends the accused defendant. Her/his job is to get as favorable a verdict as possible for the accused client. The defense attorney may be the public defender or a lawyer hired privately by the defendant.

B. CHARGES:

1. *Misdemeanor* — any offense for which a sentence to a term of imprisonment in other than a penitentiary for less than one year may be imposed.

2. *Felony* — a much more serious offense for which a sen-

---

[6]Reprinted by permission of the Chicago Women Against Rape, Chicago, Illinois.

tence of death to a term of imprisonment in a penitentiary for one or more years is provided.

3. *Complaint* — a document signed by the plaintiff accusing the defendant of one specific crime. Each crime is charged in separate complaints. Every crime is either a misdemeanor or a felony. The initial complaint is filled out and signed in the police station. Additional complaints can be filled out and signed in court. Incorrect complaints can often be amended later.

4. *Indictment* — means the same as a complaint, but is given this term after the grand jury has found cause for charging a person with a criminal offense. It relates only to felonies.

C. COURTROOM TACTICS:

1. *Proceedings* — all appearances and hearings held in the court at which the defendant is present. The complaining witness need not be present at each and every proceeding, e.g. motions relating to questions of law, presentation of the indictment.

2. *Pleadings* — all written documents pertaining to this particular case, i.e. the complaint, motion to dismiss, motion to suppress, discovery motion.

3. *Subpoena* — notice to a witness to appear in court on a certain date and time. Complaining witnesses do not usually receive a subpoena in time for court hearings so a victim should not rely upon this as sufficient notification. All subpoenas received too late should be brought to the attention of the States attorney.

4. *Continuance* — a delay (usually one month), which is granted easily for the barest of reasons. Sometimes, it is granted by the court's (judge's) own motion, but usually by one side or the other because their case is not ready. This is a strong weapon used by the defense attorney to discourage the victim from continuing the prosecution.

5. *Plea-Bargaining* — is usually begun after any pretrial hearing. The two opposing attorneys get together after having evaluated the evidence for both sides. If the defense attorney is being paid well, s/he will get the best

deal s/he can, but will still be willing to go to trial for her/his client. If it is a public defender, s/he will settle for a worse deal for the client because public defenders typically have more work than time and must settle some cases out of court. The States attorney always has too many cases (too few are hired), and s/he tries to settle all but the most heinous crimes. At the end of the plea-bargaining, the court allows the defendant to plead guilty to a lesser offense than he was charged with and to receive a lighter sentence. The charge is usually reduced from a felony to a misdemeanor. The states attorney will also agree to a recommended sentence, which is usually followed by the judge. Examples are aggravated assault, assault, battery, aggravated battery. The victim is not consulted in plea-bargaining.

D. COURT HEARINGS:
  MISDEMEANOR OR FELONY
  1. *Motions* — usually must be written; requests by either attorney for the court to do or not to do something. These are then argued before the court, and the court will make a decision on that motion. Motions that the victim will see include but are not limited to motions for continuance (delay) and suppression of evidence (blood test, torn clothing, confession taken improperly).
  2. *Hearing* — any matter heard by a judge and involving the attorneys for both sides. It can be on just one issue. Usually occurs some time before the trial. (Also see Pretrial.) Evidence may be presented.
  3. *Pretrial Hearing* — anything that happens before a trial in the nature of a legal proceeding. It could be a conference involving both attorneys (and the judge). It may be a preliminary hearing in which each side has the opportunity to evaluate the evidence that the other side has. Motions may be filed at the pretrial hearing.
  FELONY ONLY
  4. *Preliminary Hearing* — a minitrial where the court hears the evidence from both sides to determine whether there is probable cause for the case to be sent to the grand jury.

At the end of this hearing, the court can either dismiss the charges against the defendant or have the case "held over" to the grand jury.

5. *Grand Jury* — takes place after the preliminary hearing. A special group of citizens that decides whether to charge someone with a criminal offense. The States attorney presents evidence before this group (with *no one* from the defense to challenge in any way). If the grand jury thinks the evidence is sufficient, they vote to indict; otherwise the case is dropped (terminated).

6. *Presentation of Indictment* — court hearing before chief judge of the criminal court when the indictment is presented to the defendant. The case is then assigned to a trial judge with a court date.

E. PUBLIC TRIAL:

1. *Bench Trial* — a trial in which the judge decides issues of fact *and* law. No jury is involved.

2. *Jury Trial* — a trial held in front of a jury of six to twelve persons. The jury's job is to decide the questions of fact, not questions of law. Usually the jury decides which side they believe and which side they don't.

3. *Usual Steps In Any Trial* —

   a. Voir dire: an oath administered to a person by which that person swears to answer truthfully in an examination to determine the person's competence as a witness or juror — This only occurs in a jury trial where the jury must be selected.

   b. Jury selection.

   c. Opening statement by the State.

   d. Opening statement by the defense attorney.

   e. Presentation of evidence by the State. Each witness can always be cross-examined by the defense attorney.

   f. Presentation of evidence by defense attorney. Each witness can be cross-examined by the state.

   g. Rebuttal by State. The States attorney can only bring up information that has not been already presented by the State in the trial. The purpose is to contradict something the defense has said.

h. Closing statement by the State.

i. Closing statement by the defense attorney.

j. Instructions to the jury by the judge. Submitted in writing by each attorney and delivered orally by the judge, dealing with law only. This can be important because of wording and the tone in which it is delivered.

k. Verdict.

l. Sentencing. If the defendant is found guilty at the trial, then a date is set for sentencing — usually one month later. A pre-sentence investigation is made of the defendant's background. A hearing in aggravation and mitigation is held. The States attorney tells the court the reason why the sentence should be maximum (in aggravation), and the defense attorney gives arguments why the sentence should be minimal (mitigation). "Third Party" reports can have a bearing here.

F. EVIDENCE AT A HEARING OR TRIAL:

1. *Inadmissible Evidence* — evidence which is not permitted to be used at the trial, either because of the method in which it was obtained or because it violates one of the many rules of evidence, e.g. hearsay evidence or confession obtained inappropriately.

2. *Hearsay* — inadmissible evidence which is not from the personal knowledge or observation of the person giving the testimony. Instead, it is a repetition of what the witness has heard others say.

3. *Chain of Evidence* — the links of circumstantial evidence that are tied together logically to prove a point.

4. *Earshot Witness* — one who hears something; this is relevant evidence.

5. *Objections to Evidence* —

   a. *Objection* — made by one attorney; asks the judge to keep out testimony or evidence.

   b. *Sustained* — decision by the judge to agree with objecting attorney and thereby keep out evidence objected to.

c. *Overruled or denied* — decision by the judge to disagree with the objecting attorney and thereby allow evidence to be admitted or testimony to be given.

6. *Burden of Proof* — the State has the responsibility of presenting enough evidence to prove that the defendant committed the crime as charged.

   a. *Motion for a directed verdict* — after the State presents its case, the defense can ask for a directed verdict (dismissal of charges) on the grounds that the State did not prove its charges.

7. *Primary Techniques Used By Defense Attorney* —

   a. *Consent* — If the victim gave her "consent," it is not the crime of rape. Consent can be shown by conduct of the victim and lack of force or coercion by the defendant in committing the act. Usually used against black, Latino, American Indian, oriental, and other minority complainants. This is effective because the racist belief that minority women have low moral character. This is a prime example of overt racism in the court system.

   b. *Identification of defendant as assailant* — This is used where the complaining witness is injured, i.e. obviously assaulted and usually needing special treatment at a hospital for injuries. The defense attorney says, "Yes, she has been raped, but not by my client." The amount of light, eyesight, ability to view, and description given to the police are emphasized.

G. POSTTRIAL PROCEEDINGS:

1. *Posttrial Hearing* — If the defendant has been found guilty, his attorney may present a posttrial motion to reverse the verdict for certain reasons, such as the evidence was insufficient to convict, and new evidence is available.

2. *Sentencing* — (See E.3.1.)

Note: An excellent article discussing criminal proceedings against suspected rapists is entitled, "Judicial Attitudes Toward Rape Victims," by Carol Bohmer.

Another excellent resource discussing not only legalities regarding rape, but also other issues important to women, such as divorce and abortion laws, is entitled *State-by-State Guide to Women's Legal Rights,* by Shana Alexander.

CHAPTER 8

REFERRAL PROCESS

AS you now realize, the process of effectively helping the rape victim is a very complex process. It involves the areas of psychology, medicine, and law. All these areas require many years of training to be proficient in their practice, and the RCI should not be expected to be as knowledgeable as are the professionals.

It is very necessary that the RCI understands her/his limits of expertise, knows when s/he can no longer effectively assist the rape victim with long-term or complex concerns. This necessitates involving a third party, either at the victim's request or the RCI's urging.

The following material on the referral process comes from two crisis centers, the Listening Post in Salt Lake City, Utah and the Crisis Clinic in Bellingham, Washington. The material is also contained in the *Crisis Intervention Resource Manual* published by the author when he was the Coordinator of the Vermillion Hotline in South Dakota.

Definition

The referral of a woman from one service to another is a process (interaction) rather than a procedure. It constitutes a transaction between two people to involve a third party. At best, the woman referred will have *mixed* feelings.

Feelings of the Rape Victim

A combination of a number of feelings on the part of the victim about being referred for special help may be important, whether these are expressed or unexpressed. Unless her feelings are taken into account, the referral will not be successful. The following feelings are most commonly encountered:

Rejection

The rape victim may interpret the suggestion of referral else-where as a rejection by the RCI. The woman might then feel a loss of interest by the RCI, unaccepted, and "pushed away." She might increase her efforts to "please" the RCI and regain interest; she might react with anger and reject the idea; or she might not follow through on the referral but also feel less inclined to call the RCC in the future.

Guilt

The rape victim may interpret the reason for the referral as the result of feelings she has exposed in talking with the RCI, such as anger, aggressiveness, sexuality, which the victim may already feel guilty about herself. Referral would then have a special meaning to her. If she is frightened by her own im-pulses, she might also feel she has upset the RCI, who out of anxiety recommends that she seek professional help as a control of impulses or to "cleanse" herself. The victim may feel her trust in the RCI was misplaced or regret her exposure of her-self. If she follows through on a referral at all, she would then be less inclined to expose herself once again.

Anxiety

A rape victim appropriately would have some fear about being referred to a strange person or unfamiliar setting. It is usually helpful to provide her with a name, a telephone number, and to alert the referral resource that the woman has been referred and the reasons for this action.

Special Fears

The rape victim may have special fears related to referral to a psychiatric service or psychological agency. Such a referral may mean to her that she is unbalanced, in need of hospitalization, special control, or is crazy. Referrals to an employment service may suggest that she *should* work, which may remind her of a previous traumatic experience in looking for employment. Referral for public assistance may also reinforce her fears about investigation or helplessness and inadequacy. With all referrals of minors, parental involvement is necessary, which could involve all kinds of unique problems and fears.

A fear not to be minimized is the fear related to the separation from the RCI. This can be present even after a relatively short relationship, but particularly after a period of time during which the rape victim has obviously formed a close alliance with the RCI.

The Basics in Making a Referral

1. Before making any referral, find out if the victim is in active treatment already. If so, refer her back to the current helping person. Remember, very often clients will insist that the current helping relationship is worthless when, in fact, they are commenting upon their own fear of impending change and decision. If you refer this client to somebody else, you may be helping her to avoid change.

2. Don't be afraid to take time out from the call to think about a referral. Not every call has to end with a referral. You can end a call short of making a referral by telling the woman that you need time to think about it or to discuss it with someone else and that you'll call her right back or have her call you back within a reasonable time period.

3. Expect some cases where it seems obvious to you that the woman will not be able to call on her own behalf. Gently encourage the woman to contact the referral agency herself, or she may be unsure of the referral.

4. Never discuss another agency's fee policy except in the most general terms. Encourage the woman, if she asks questions about cost, to raise these with the agency to which she is being referred. (The RCC's referrals should not charge outrageous fees however.)

5. Do not confuse the victim by referring her to three or four

places at the same time. Establish priorities for the need and make one or two referrals for that concern. The woman can always call back should the initial referrals not work, and encourage her to do so.

6. Even when referring to private practitioners, don't give three or more referrals. That's a waste of time and an artificial sensitivity to being accused of loading up and favoring one private practitioner over another. Put yourself in the victim's shoes. If you called for help and somebody gave you three names and didn't clearly indicate to you which of the three s/he preferred — how would you feel?

7. Be sure the woman clearly understands information given her. Repeat it or ask her to write it down and then repeat it to you.

8. If possible, develop and carry out a follow-up procedure for all referrals and contacts. Inform the client that you will call back or someone else will call back. This provides continuity, it expresses your concern, and it will also give you valuable information regarding how effective your referral has been, and what is happening at agencies you most often refer people to.

Principles To Keep in Mind

1. Expect the woman to be anxious.
2. Expect the woman to have mixed feelings.
3. Don't expect the referral to be accomplished when first discussed. Three times with intervals in between the suggestions would be more typical. Avoid the sense of urgency unless it is real.
4. Encourage thinking about the referral in between discussions.
5. Emphasize freedom of choice.
6. Encourage the rape victim to express what she would like and what kind of help she expects.
7. Don't be discouraged if referral takes a long time. Be willing to proceed at whatever pace the woman can proceed.

8. Don't measure your success in helping the woman by whether or not referral is accomplished. Sometimes many problems are alleviated by the referral process alone.
9. Don't abandon the woman during the period of referral — even after the victim has been seen by the referral resource. Encourage the woman to report back. The initial contact may be a disappointment. Airing the feelings related to the experience may make a difference in the woman by following through with later appointments.
10. Encourage the rape victim to take as much initiative as she can. Don't underestimate her ability to do this. As a RCI, don't be too willing to "carry the ball" beyond a reasonable "clearing of the way."
11. Inform the woman realistically about the limitations as well as potential help to be available by way of the referral.

Problems of the RCI Making the Referral

1. Be willing to examine your reasons for deciding that referral is indicated:
    a. Is there something about the relationship that is troubling you? Has the rape victim been too demanding or upsetting for other reasons?
    b. Are you more concerned about solving the woman's problem(s) than she is, but have the feeling you are not experienced enough?
    c. Do you feel guilty for some reason about the rape victim? Do you dislike her or wish to "unload her" for your own comfort?
    d. Does the discussion of her rape bring back suppressed material you have been hiding and don't want to face?
2. A referral based more on the readiness of the referring person's needs rather than those of the rape victim's welfare, is doomed to failure. If you are in doubt or conflict about what action to take, discuss the idea with your supervisor or consultant first. Refer to the material on when to move into problem solving discussed in Chapter 5 to assist you in making this decision.

CHAPTER 9

EVALUATION MATERIALS

MOST of the material in Chapters 4 to 8 contains information you will want to use in some form in your training program. It might now be appropriate to give some examples of various forms RCCs have developed to assess the effectiveness of their volunteers, the effectiveness of the training program, and the effectiveness of the RCC in meeting its goals and population for which it was intended.

This may also be an appropriate time for you to readminister any pretesting devices such as the Index of Discrimination and the Information and Attitude Survey, which were discussed in Chapter 5. You will or should be able to see the growth which has taken place in your volunteers as the result of your training program.

This chapter will conclude this section of the resource manual. In later chapters, material less directly related to the effectiveness of your volunteers will be discussed, such as hints on self-protection, facilitating group cohesiveness, and problems confronting RCCs. This material is still important to the overall effectiveness of the RCC.

VOLUNTARY AGREEMENT WITH RAPE CRISIS CENTER[1]

Many volunteers in many volunteer service organizations sometimes have difficulty in developing a sense of committment to the service, as a result of not knowing what is really expected of them. This form, a kind of contractual arrangement, may help in providing them with a sense of belonging.

I, _____, am willing to serve as a volunteer for the Rape Crisis Center. I understand and agree to the following responsibilities as a volunteer:

1. I will attend at least one volunteer meeting each month at the Rape Crisis Center. If I am unable to attend, I will notify one of the officers.

---

[1]Reproduced by permission of the Oklahoma City Rape Crisis Center of Oklahoma City, Oklahoma.

2. I will verify once each month my availability for scheduling with the volunteer responsible for scheduling.

3. If I am unable to be at the Center when I am scheduled and also unable to take calls at home, I will arrange for another trained volunteer to take my place.

4. To the best of my ability, I will keep up-to-date on policies and procedures relevant to the Rape Crisis Center.

5. I will respect and maintain the confidentiality of all information pertaining to individuals who seek help from our Center.

6. I will keep accurate records of all calls, cases, and my volunteer hours and see that they are in the office by the date specified each month.

7. If I decide to discontinue my volunteer activities, or if I am unable to fulfill the responsibilities outlined in this agreement, I will notify one of the officers.

_____   _____
Date   Volunteer's Signature

* * * * * * * * * *

RAPE CRISIS COUNCIL
LISTENING SKILLS PROGRAM
EVALUATION FORM[2]

This form, completed by one or more trainers at the completion of the training program during which the trainee was observed, may be helpful in assessing those interpersonal qualities which are important to have in an effective volunteer. These qualities, it will be remembered, are separate from communication skills, but can do much to increase the effectiveness of the communication skills.

Name:_____

1. Awareness of her own values:

1	2	3	4	5
no awareness	below average	average	above average	very aware

2. Awareness of her limitations as a counselor or helper:

1	2	3	4	5
no awareness	below average	average	above average	very aware

[2]Reproduced by permission of the Chester County Rape Crisis Council of West Chester, Pennsylvania.

3. Level of active involvement and committment to the RCC:

1	2	3	4	5
no committment	below average	average	above average	very active & committed

4. Level of sensitivity and insightfulness the person exhibits in understanding the thoughts, feelings, and needs of others:

1	2	3	4	5
lacking insight & sensitivity	below average	average	above average	very insightful & sensitive

5. Degree of flexibility the person exhibits in adjusting to new ideas, relationships, and situations; readiness to accept change, novelty, or uncertainty:

1	2	3	4	5
inflexible & rigid	below average	average	above average	very flexible & accepting

6. The woman projects herself or comes across to others conveying:
   a. Sincerity, honesty, genuineness

1	2	3	4	5
Not sincere at all	below average	average	above average	very sincere

   b. Interest

1	2	3	4	5
no interest	below average	average	above average	very interested

   c. Calmness

1	2	3	4	5
uptight	below average	average	above average	very calm

Total score:_____

The higher the score, the more potential the volunteer has to be an effective RCI.

* * * * * * * * * *

On the following pages are presented forms to assess the effectiveness of the training program from the volunteer's point of view. This information can then assist the trainers in developing a more effective training format which will meet the needs of the potential RCIs.

TRAINING PROGRAM EVALUATION[3]

This questionnaire is designed to evaluate the training program and the information involved. We would like some feedback so we can adjust the program where
necessary and make it more effective. This is in no way a determination of your
competency as a crisis person. Please be frank and feel free to share with us
any feelings you have. Thank you.

Please Rank

Low   High
/1 /2 /3 /4 /5 /

1. Were the training sessions held at convenient
   locations?   / / / / / /

2. To what degree do you feel you learned about
   the following:
   A. Basic communication skills   / / / / / /

   B. Interviewing skills   / / / / / /

   C. Telephone counseling techniques   / / / / / /

   D. Referral procedures   / / / / / /

   E. Police procedures as related to assault
      and rape victims   / / / / / /

   F. Hospital procedures as related to assault
      and rape victims   / / / / / /

3. To what extent were the following areas re-
   affirmed for you through the training:
   A. Awareness of one's own limitations   / / / / / /

   B. Willingness to make referrals   / / / / / /

   C. Basic respect for individual uniqueness   / / / / / /

   D. Respect for individual dignity, opinions,
      and privacy   / / / / / /

   E. Continuing growth in awareness of oneself
      as a woman and committment to discover what
      that means to oneself   / / / / / /.

4. How useful were the handouts?   / / / / / /

5. At what level of efficiency do you feel prepared to:
   A. Assist the victim of sexual abuse to put
      the incident into a workable perspective
      for her   / / / / / /

   B. Support the victim in integrating the in-
      cident constructively in her life   / / / / / /

   C. Provide immediate supportive response to
      the victim   / / / / / /

   D. Provide the victim with accurate informa-
      tion relating to community services and
      referrals   / / / / / /

[3]Reproduced by permission of the Center Against Sexual Assault, Phoenix, Arizona.

6. How useful were the small group discussions?   / / / / / /

7. What did you expect to learn in the training sessions that would facilitate your growth and development as an effective crisis person?

8. Were you aware of training goals when the sessions began?

    What were they?

9. Which speakers were most effective?

    Least effective?

10. Would you have preferred more printed material?

    Suggestions?

11. Would more small group discussions have been helpful?

    In what way?

12. What materials in the training program seemed irrelevant or repetitious?

13. What other issues would you like to see included in the training program?

14. What is your reaction to a screening process for volunteers, in the interest of developing the most effective crisis personnel possible?

15. Who should be involved in such a screening procedure, e.g. a panel of interviewers, individual professionals, other experienced crisis personnel - suggestions?

16. Would you be interested in a periodic in-service training program to update knowledge of community procedures?

    If yes, how often do you think it would be necessary?

17. What was the most valuable knowledge gained through this program?

18. At this point, do you think you need more training?

    If yes, please indicate specific areas.

19. In what ways have you become more aware of sexual abuse as a pervasive phenomenon and its place in our culture?

20. Additional comments:

* * * * * * * * * *

EVALUATION OF TRAINING PROGRAM[4]

Name (optional): _____

Intensive Training Program:

Did you think the information you needed to know was adequately covered? Please explain.

---

[4]Reproduced by permission of the Milwaukee Women's Crisis Line of Milwaukee, Wisconsin.

Did you think that two consecutive weekends was too much? Explain.

How did you like the schedule, i.e. was it too cramped with speakers and information, and not enough time for discussion; was there enough time for breaks and for meals?

What do you think of the method of evaluation by the coordinators, i.e. did you feel watched, or afraid of being judged?

What did you think of the speakers? Any comments on a specific one?

How do you feel about the role-playing? Also, was there enough of it or could there have been more?

What do you think could be some basic improvements in this training program? Please continue on the back if needed.

In-service Training Program:

How did you feel working with your supervising operator?

How did the in-service training compliment the intensive training?

Do you think the in-service training is adequate? Should there be more of it?

What are your thoughts and feelings about your preparation to go on the Line by yourself after completing this program?

As a new operator, or as a trainee, do you feel isolated from the rest of the operators on the Line? Please explain.

Any additional comments?

* * * * * * * * * *

INTENSIVE TRAINING PROGRAM
ROLE-PLAYING EVALUATION FORM[5]

Name of Trainee:_____

Name of Evaluator:_____

Date:_____Time of Evaluation:_____

Topics Covered:_____

Role-playing: Trainee participated ( ) as operator, ____# of times
                                    ( ) as caller, ____# of times

Did the trainee participate in the discussions?_____

_____

Additional Comments:_____

_____

_____

_____

* * * * * * * * * *

ON-DUTY EVALUATION FORM[6]

Name of Trainee:_____

Name of Evaluator:_____

Date:_____Time of Shift:_____No. of Hours:_____

Approx. no. of calls taken by trainee:_____

Nature of calls taken by trainee:_____

_____

What, if any, problems came up as a result of how the trainee handled the calls?

_____

_____

What are your comments on how the trainee performed in general?

_____

_____

* * * * * * * * * *

[5]Reproduced by permission of the Milwaukee Women's Crisis Line of Milwaukee, Wisconsin.
[6]Reproduced by permission of the Milwaukee Women's Crisis Line in Milwaukee, Wisconsin.

VOLUNTEER FOLLOW-UP EVALUATION[7]

THIS IS IN NO WAY AN EVALUATION OF YOUR PERFORMANCE AS A VOLUNTEER; ONLY OF THE PREPARATION YOU WERE GIVEN FOR YOUR VOLUNTEER DUTIES.

1. Was scheduling worked out to your satisfaction?

2. How many calls have you taken so far?

3. How many of these were solely informational in nature?

4. How many were hot or crisis calls?

5. How many did you go out on?

6. How well do you think you were prepared for the situations you faced?

7. Now that you are doing the actual work, what if any gaps can you identify in the training program?

8. Did you need immediate consultation at any time when the service did or did not make it available to you?

9. What should be added to the training program?

10. What should be taken out of the training program?

11. Would you be interested in talking informally to orientation groups of new volunteers to share your experiences?

12. How would you feel about going to an office to answer crisis calls?

13. Would you have been better able to attend two eight hour training sessions if child care had been provided?

14. What, if any, difficulty have you had in getting backups?

15. What, if any, communication problems exist with the answering service, other volunteers, etc.?

* * * * * * * * * *

VOLUNTEER'S PERSONAL CRISIS LOG[8]

WE ASK YOU TO KEEP THIS LOG BECAUSE WE REALIZE THAT IT IS YOUR PERSON AND FEEL-INGS WHICH HELP A VICTIM IN TIME OF CRISIS. IN ORDER TO DO THIS EFFECTIVELY, A VOLUNTEER NEEDS TO THINK ABOUT HER EXPERIENCES AND HER BEHAVIOR. IN DOING THIS, YOU WILL BE MORE ABLE TO CONSTRUCTIVELY HELP IN THE SITUATIONS YOU ENCOUNTER. IT IS HOPED THAT KEEPING THIS RECORD OF YOUR EXPERIENCES AND FEELINGS WILL HELP YOU KNOW YOURSELF BETTER IN THE ROLE OF A HELPER.

THE LOG IS FOR YOUR USE AND YOU SHOULD USE IT IN THE MANNER IT PROVES MOST HELP-FUL TO YOU. PLEASE DON'T FEEL THIS LOG IS IN THE ONLY FORM IT CAN TAKE. EXPER-IMENT WITH IT AND ADD YOUR SUGGESTIONS WHEN THEY WORK FOR YOU, SO OTHERS CAN PROF-IT.

What feelings did my initial phone encounter arouse in me? How did these feel-ings change when and if I met the victim?

---

[7]Reproduced by permission of the Center Against Sexual Assault, Phoenix, Arizona.
[8]Reproduced by permission of the Center Against Sexual Assault, Phoenix, Arizona.

How did the victim respond to me? My physical appearance, voice, etc.?

How did we relate physically? Did the victim want to be touched, held, or not?
What were my feelings in the situation?

How did professional personnel relate to me? Police, medical staff, counselors?
How did I deal with hassles? What implications did this have for the Center and
volunteers to come?

In what ways could I have been better prepared in the Center's training for what
occurred in this incident? Is this something that needs to be put into, or left
out of the training?

What do I feel best about, relative to this incident?

What would I do differently?

What, if any, patterns in my behavior, or in that of others towards me, warrant
examination?

Now that it is over, how do I feel about it?

Additional comments?

* * * * * * * * * *

CONFIDENTIAL[9]

To be used *only* for data gathering.

Please read *all* questions and answer those that are applicable in as much detail
as possible. There are *two* sections. Thank you.

SECTION 1

1. Have you or anyone close to you, such as a relative or friend, ever been
    raped or otherwise sexually assaulted? yes___no___

2. Age of victim when assault occurred?_____
    Time of day_____Time of year_____
    Location of assault (alley, home, car, etc.)_____

3. Was the assault reported to the police? yes___no___ If not, why?_____
    _____

    Was assailant apprehended? yes___no___
    Was assailant prosecuted? yes___no___
    Was assailant convicted? yes___no___

4. Did the victim receive medical treatment? yes___no___ If not, why?_____
    _____

    Was any provision made for follow-up care? yes___no___

5. What agency(ies) was most helpful to the victim?_____
    Was any one person most supportive?____ Who?_____
    Do you think that trained men can be as instrumental in supporting rape

[9]Reproduced by permission of the Victim/Witness Division, Montgomery County Prosecutor's Office, Dayton, Ohio.

victims as women? yes___ no___

6. Was any follow-up counseling received? yes___ no___
    If yes, what kind?_____
    If yes, did it help?_____

7. What was not done for the victim that you think could have or should have
    been done?_____
    _____

SECTION 2

1. If you, a relative, or a friend were sexually assaulted today, what would
    you do?_____
    _____
    _____

2. Had you heard of the Victimization Project before today? _____If so,
    through what media? (friend, newspaper, radio, etc.)_____

3. Was this presentation helpful to you and do you have any suggestions for its
    improvement?_____
    _____
    _____

* * * * * * * * * *

DATA FORM[10]

This form is used to compile data on the typology and incidence of rape so the
information can then be analyzed for trends which may be taking place affecting
the services provided by the RCC.

1. Time you saw victim
    0. midnight to 6:59 AM
    1. 7 AM to 11:59 AM
    2. noon to 3:59 PM
    3. 4 PM to 6:59 PM
    4. 7 PM to 11:59 PM

2. Day rape occurred
    0. Monday
    1. Tuesday
    2. Wednesday
    3. Thursday
    4. Friday
    5. Saturday
    6. Sunday

3. Month rape occurred
    0. Jan.   6. Jul.
    1. Feb.   7. Aug.
    2. Mar.   8. Sept.
    3. Apr.   9. Oct.
    4. May   10. Nov.
    5. June   11. Dec.

4. Year rape occurred
    0. '73
    1. '74
    2. '75
    3. '76

5. Victim's age
    0. 0-6   6. 27-35
    1. 7-12   7. 36-50
    2. 13-16   8. 51---
    3. 17-18   9. Don't know-Child
    4. 19-21   10. Don't know-Adult
    5. 22-26

6. Victim's race
    0. Black
    1. White
    2. Latino
    3. Oriental
    4. Am. Indian
    5. Other

[10]Reproduced by permission of Women Organized Against Rape in Philadelphia,
Pennsylvania.

7. Time rape occurred
   0. unknown
   1. midnight to 3:59 AM
   2. 4 AM to 7:59 AM
   3. 8 AM to 11:59 AM
   4. noon to 3:59 PM
   5. 4 PM to 7:59 PM
   6. 8 PM to 11:59 PM

8. Time with police before hosp.
   0. unknown
   1. 0-59 mins.
   2. 1 hr.-119 mins.
   3. 2 hrs.-179 mins.
   4. 3 hrs.-239 mins.
   5. 4 hrs.-299 mins.
   6. 5 hrs. or more
   7. Didn't go to police

9. Did she go to precinct?
   0. unknown
   1. yes, before hosp.
   2. no, after hosp.
   3. no, not going
   4. no, no further info.

10. Precinct_____

11. Did she go to_____
    0. unknown
    1. yes, before hosp.
    2. no, after hosp.
    3. no, not going
    4. made state. at hosp.
    5. no, no further info.

12. Time spent at hosp.
    0. unknown
    1. 0-59 mins.
    2. 1 hr.-119 mins.
    3. 2 hrs.-179 mins.
    4. 3 hrs.-239 mins.
    5. 4 hrs.-299 mins.
    6. 5 hrs. or more

13. She/you thought police
    treatment was
    0. unknown
    1. excellent
    2. good
    3. fair
    4. poor
    5. very bad

14. She/you thought hosp.
    treatment was
    0. unknown
    1. excellent
    2. good
    3. fair
    4. poor
    5. very bad

15. Legal complaint
    0. no
    1. yes

16. Medical complaint
    0. no
    1. yes

17. She was accompanied to
    hosp. by
    0. unknown
    1. no one
    2. relative, F.
    3. relative, M.
    4. friend, F.
    5. friend, M.
    6. other

18. Had she/they heard of RCC?
    0. unknown
    1. no
    2. yes

19. Did she/they call RCC be-
    fore going to hospital?
    0. unknown
    1. no
    2. yes

20. Setting rape occurred in
    0. unknown
    1. victim's home
    2. rapist's home
    3. empty building
    4. park
    5. alley
    6. housing project
    7. car
    8. not at home but ukwn
    9. other

21. Section of city where
    rape occurred
    0. unknown   8. south
    1. west   9. north
    2. southwest   10. suburbs
    3. northwest   11. other
    4. east   12. not in
    5. southeast   this city
    6. northeast
    7. center city

22. Did she know any of the
    attackers?
    0. unknown
    1. well
    2. superficially
    3. not at all

23. Did she accept an offered
    ride?
    0. unknown
    1. no
    2. yes

24. Was she hitchhiking?
    0. unknown
    1. no
    2. yes

25. Was rapist a relative?
    0. unknown
    1. no
    2. yes

26. Number of attackers
    0. unknown 6. 6-10
    1. 1   7. 11 or more
    2. 2   8. more than 1,
    3. 3   but don't
    4. 4   know #
    5. 5

27. Was it gang-related?
    0. unknown
    1. no
    2. yes

28. Was she scratched/bruised?
    0. unknown
    1. no
    2. yes

29. Was she injured more
    seriously?
    0. unknown
    1. no
    2. yes

30. Was she threatened with
    a weapon?
    0. unknown
    1. no
    2. yes, gun
    3. yes, knife
    4. yes, other
    5. yes, don't know what

31. Does she intend to
    prosecute if assailant
    is apprehended?
    0. unknown
    1. no
    2. yes
    3. not sure

CHAPTER 10

FACILITATING GROUP COHESIVENESS

YOUR center is going to be staffed by people of different ages and lifestyles, who have volunteered for a variety of reasons. Within any heterogeneous group such as this, conflicts are bound to arise: conflicts over the goals of the center and conflicts as how to best deal with the rape victim during the crisis. It is OK if these conflicts do arise as this means the volunteers in your center feel comfortable enough to air differences. The important thing is that you have steps or procedures to deal with these conflicts effectively.

There are also bound to be situations which arise where the RCI has just dealt with a particularly frustrating, anger-producing, or painful contact with a rape victim and is in need of group support. It will be at these times of conflicts and frustrations when the sense of group togetherness or cohesiveness will prove its real value and play a very vital role in the success or failure of your center.

What then is group cohesiveness? Group cohesiveness might be defined as that characteristic of a group in which all members pull together for a common purpose and all are ready to take responsibility for group chores and endure frustration in their cooperative efforts (Bennet, 1963). Some signs of a cohesive group are expressions of "we-ness," e.g. "*We* ought to do this" or "*We* need to reach out more." There exists a spirit of friendliness and loyalty to each other within the center.

Some of the factors which can facilitate the development of group "oneness" are: the opportunity to meet together often as a group; having a definite means for and modes of communication with one another; an existing stability within the organization and leadership; and a sense of responsibility of each toward the others — kind of the old Three Musketeer's "all for one and one for all" (Bennet, 1963).

One very important factor in the development of your center

is commitment. People are usually more committed to and care about that which they help create. Where change or decisions regarding goals, policies, or techniques are required, the process will be facilitated if the people involved have a sense of ownership. Thus, there must be active participation in the planning and conduct of change in the center's activities by the staff. You may also want to consider using a personal contract which the volunteers sign such as that contained in Chapter 9. This will quickly convey to the volunteers that the staff wants people who are committed to the center and the personal contract is symbolic of that commitment. However, be cautious to not word the contract so strongly that you scare off potentially excellent volunteers.

Factors which may hinder the development of group oneness are "unpleasant experiences, unattractive activities, group frustration, strongly conflicting goals, differences regarding suitable ways to reach a goal which tend to split the group into factions, rivalry for status, and interpersonal dislikes" (Bennet, 1963).

The leadership of a RCC, be it one person or a collective, will probably set the climate or atmosphere of the center. It has been shown that those who (a) can encourage the group to discuss its policies and reach decisions based on the discussions, (b) try to present alternatives for various techniques and procedures, (c) offer the members the chance to divide the work and select their own working partners, (d) offer praise and criticism objectively regarding group goals, and (e) can make themselves members of the group but not forsake their leadership responsibilities, will set for the center a climate in which growth and productive change can occur.

Problems you will want to watch out for and which are destructive to the center's continued growth are:

1. Condescension on the part of the experienced volunteers toward the new volunteers.
2. Feelings that the leadership does not hear or listen to, and ignores the other staff members.
3. With a large staff especially, the forming of cliques and subgroups which may become independent of the general

membership (Delworth et al., 1972).

Now, what are some ways to put the previous information into practice? To begin with, as the center is growing, it may serve your purposes better if a group will function in leadership roles rather than having one person or director. This will also help facilitate a sense of continuity of your center should a director resign. This group can later be chosen by the members of the staff itself on a regular basis. This will help provide a regular influx of new ideas and thoughts.

The center might also wish to establish various work groups such as record keeping, correspondence, referrals, research, and training and have the staff working in these subgroups rotate to work on other groups at regular intervals. This will aid in insuring that a few people don't get stuck with laborious or boring jobs. Also, try to mix these work groups with new and more experienced staff, those who are young in age and those who are older, etc.

The training program can also have a strong trust-building effect if it is done on a regular basis where there may be at least ten to fifteen people moving through the program. Use some specific group exercises which will facilitate the trust-building and sharing experience within the group. Also, have your in-service training on a regular basis as well, so there will be routine contact between new and more experienced staff.

Provide for regular meetings for purposes of progress reports, case conferences, and human relation's groups. The latter two are especially important as your volunteers are likely to confront situations in which they don't know what they should do, are hurt or frustrated by an encounter with the authorities or family of the rape victim, or are suffering from burn-out.

Also, don't overlook the use of picnics and parties to provide your staff the opportunity to become revitalized, to let go, and to interact on something other than a business level. The use of weekend retreats might also be of value.

Finally, early in the development of your center and depending on its size, it may be helpful to establish a flow chart of lines of communication for the airing of complaints, hassles, etc.

There are many books available containing group exercises to help develop a sense of group cohesiveness, trust, oneness, and "we-ness." The author recommends Lewis and Streitfeld, *Growth Games*; Pfeiffer and Jones, *A Handbook of Structured Experiences for Human Relations Training*; and Johnson, *Reaching Out: Interpersonal Effectiveness and Self-actualization.*

CHAPTER 11

HINTS ON SELF-PROTECTION

THERE has been much advice given lately in popular magazines such as *Reader's Digest* and *Ladies Home Journal*, on what women can do to lessen the probability of their being raped, or, if they are raped, how to lessen the probability of being severely injured by the rapist. Although the intent of these suggestions is to help women protect themselves, the advice at the same time severely restricts the women's personal freedom and implies that women should live in constant fear of rape and view all men as being potential rapists.

The following suggestions are based on material the author has read. Judge these suggestions as valid or invalid for yourself. Decide what you think you can or cannot abide by.

To begin with, an exercise in imagination may help. Using your home as a starting place, how would you attack the woman inside? How would you get in? Would you jimmy the door or climb a tree and get in a bathroom or bedroom window? What time of day would you choose? How would you know a woman lives there and whether she lives alone or with others? How do you know the man at the door is who he represents himself to be? Perhaps now you're getting the idea. Cover the contingencies and use your common sense.

One of the most frequent suggestions made to women is to enroll in self-defense classes in judo, karate, etc. Rather than teaching women the self-defense arts, the author believes their real value lies in instilling a feeling of realistic self-confidence and assurance. To become really proficient in the use of self-defense requires a lot more time, money, and determination than many women are willing or able to commit. Many people have devoted a life-time to becoming skilled in self-defense and then there is still no guarantee that the skills will be of use in a real situation or that the rapist also doesn't know karate. But, in a relatively short period of time, a woman can begin to

214

internalize some of the philosophy of common sense, rationality, judgment, and discipline which also accompany the teaching of self-defense. Many rapists prey more on the psychological weaknesses (shy, retiring, insecure, and unassertive) than the physical weaknesses of women. Potential rapists may think twice before assaulting a self-confident, secure, and assertive woman. Why should the rapist risk this when he can probably find a less formidable victim?

Many women consider carrying knives, guns, mace, or a variety of other weapons. Most state laws prohibit the ownership of weapons sufficient to deter a rapist. Should you decide to disobey any laws restricting their use, it is advised that you become fully aware of the possible punishment you face if you ever use such devices. Without meaning to infringe on any one person, it is suggested that your choice of protection and the way in which you conduct any and all defensive actions be within the limits of the law.

Hatpins, can openers, screw drivers, etc., are sometimes suggested as potential weapons and can be legally carried by anyone. Should a woman choose to carry and use any of these tools or devices, she should remember that they can, just as easily, be turned against her. Plus, they are not effective in a purse, they must be in her hand.

During times of imminent danger, you will hopefully remain rational and use your common sense. Your mind is your best weapon. If you can control your own state of mind and not become immobilized with fear, you have the greatest chance of surviving the experience physically unhurt. Calm, quiet decisions and logic can be a very effective form of resistance. Some rapists might even give up the attack completely when they are unable to terrorize their victim.

In the event all else fails, it has been suggested by some that the victim evacuate her bowels, urinate, or vomit, as this has been used effectively to deter some rapists. As far fetched as these suggestions may sound, this again may be an instance where the end justifies the means.

Many women dress so they will be less appealing to a potential rapist. This is a factor completely under your control. Perhaps, in rare instances, you may wish to wear different clothing if you know in advance you will be spending time late at night in a potentially dangerous area. The majority of rapes occur between 6:00 PM and 3:00 AM and on weekends. Know the statistics so you can play the odds to your advantage. Don't change your style of dress, but temper it under special circumstances. It should be noted however, that in the majority of sexual assaults, the woman is not dressed "provocatively."

No matter what the books say, the rapist is a person with a problem, be it temporary or chronic. He functions in a way which, at the time of the rape, is totally unacceptable. However, don't treat him as a crazy person, but rather use this knowledge of his disregard for your rights to your own advantage. Should you be unlucky enough to find yourself in the position of being confronted with such a person, try to remain rational. If you lose control of your rationality, your last defense is exhausted. A woman, as a potential victim, need not be at the mercy of the rapist, but she can instead think very imaginatively to potentially escape serious harm or better yet, stop an assault before it becomes physical.

The following material offers more sugestions on prevention.[1]

Where You Live

Many rapes and attacks happen in houses and apartments. The landlords of these places don't keep up with security. They should be pressured to do so however.

1. There should be lights in all entrances where you live. All windows must have locks; if you live in a basement or first floor, bars should be put in by the landlord. Curtains and/or blinds should be on every window and pulled down, especially in the evenings. There should be strong locks on every door.
2. Don't open the door for a package, keep the chain on and ask that the package be left by the door.
3. Be aware of places where men might hide; under stairs,

---

[1]Reproduced by permission of Women Organized Against Rape, Philadelphia, Pennsylvania.

between buildings, etc. If you live by yourself or with other women, don't put your full name on the mailbox, use your first initial, e.g. S. Smith. Get to know which neighbors you could trust in an emergency.

4. Don't use the laundry room in an apartment house basement by yourself late at night.
5. Always know who it is knocking at your door before opening. If it is a service man, ask for identification. If you're alone at night and not expecting anyone, respond to a ring or knock with, "I'll get it Bill!"
6. Keep a light on the lawn or backyard, it discourages prowlers.
7. When returning home, have your keys ready before you get to the door so there is a minimum of fumbling. If someone is watching you, don't show them where you live. If there is a suspicious person on the same elevator, push the emergency button and all floor buttons. Get off at the first floor it stops on.
8. Lock your door, even if you are going out for a moment.

On The Street

How you look is important. An attacker always expects a passive victim, so if you walk slowly or in a daze, you will seem not together. Walking at a steady pace, looking confident, and knowing where you are going, *makes a difference!*

1. Know your route home from work, school, or a friend's house. Notice locations of stores, especially those that stay open late, buildings with doormen, and police and fire stations. Also, avoid those areas where men hang out, alleys and unlit parts of the street.
2. Avoid revealing clothing when you are out and about; they may give the wrong impression. Men may infer the wrong thing from your apparel.
3. On the street, wear clothing that allows you to move as freely and quickly as possible. If you find yourself in danger, yell "Fire!" rather than "Help!" or "Rape!". Carry a whistle with you in your hand or dangling from your wrist. Sometimes a whistle can save you when your voice

fails.

4. If you think that someone is following you, do not hesitate to turn around and check. *BE AWARE!* It is neither silly nor cowardly. Try changing your pace or crossing the street. If the other side of the street looks unsafe, walk down the center of the street. Use store or car windows as mirrors.

5. Once you have decided that someone is following you, look for a safe place — any place that is lighted or where there are people. Figure out the distance from where you are to the nearest safe place.

6. Should you shed any clothing in order to run faster? All the while, increase your walking speed. If you decide to run, then do it as fast as you can, all of a sudden, and YELL EVERY STEP OF THE WAY! Remember, if you do make it to a lighted house, that you are not just stopping by for a visit. Ring the bell, bang on the door, and if no one answers immediately, smash the glass. Your life may be at stake!

7. If running is not the wisest tactic, remain calm and controlled. Try to psyche-out your would-be rapist. Is he likely to fall for a sob story? Could he be frightened if you acted very strong and sure of yourself? Would he believe that your roommate, family, or neighbors are expecting you at this time and will try to find you if you're not at home? You can try acting crazy, pretending to faint, or saying that you have VD or some other contagious disease. Such excuses have worked for women before, they *may* work for you.

Weapons

Your other alternative is fighting back. Your attacker will be expecting a passive victim. Any weapon you have can be taken away from you, so *keep a firm grip on your weapon, and keep it in your hand at all times!* Don't worry about winning when your life is being threatened, worry instead about keeping your life and getting away! The following list of WEAPONS SHOULD BE USED ONLY TO STOP AN ATTACK SO YOU CAN GET AWAY!

If faced with a gun or knife, forget about using weapons; the attacker might still be able to shoot after your efforts. Your best defense is to remain calm and try to talk him out of his intentions.

1. Lighted cigarette — smash it out in his eye or in the area around his eye.
2. Pen or pencil — hold it securely, stab at face and neck.
3. Corkscrew — jab quickly and directly, then twist. Particularly effective on face, neck, and abdominal region.
4. Plastic lemon — can squirt juice up to fifteen feet. Aim for the eyes. Replace juice with ammonia or any "caution" liquid.
5. Long, five cell flashlight — use in a jabbing manner to the face, stomach, or bone areas, knees, ankles.
6. Rolled-up magazine or newspaper — ram into the abdominal area or face, directly under the nose or into the throat.
7. Umbrella — place one hand near the center of the umbrella, the other hand behind it; use in quick jabbing fashion with upward thrusts.
8. Stiff hairbrush or steel comb — use in a slashing/raking motion across face or back of hand. Bush combs are good weapons when you're walking alone.
9. Hard-bound book — hold with both hands and smash the flat surface into attacker's face, or hold with one hand and strike with bound edge into side of his nose or throat.
10. Purse — hold in both hands and jab hard into face. Don't swing it as it can easily be grabbed, and gives attacker the chance to duck and you may loose your balance.
11. High heels or shoes — grind heel into attacker's foot, or remove shoe and strike around head and neck area.
12. Keys — with keys sticking out between the fingers, use a fist blow to face and neck, or scrape keys across the back of his hand.
13. Hat pin — carry in your hand, tightly, or pin it in your shirt, dress or pants; with all fingers around it, go for face and neck.

The trouble with suggesting all these potential weapons, is that many women are not psychologically capable of inflicting the injury often necessary to use these devices effectively. Instead the women may make a half-hearted attempt only ending in angering the rapist more. This is why the psychological training from self-defense classes is so important.

Search your kitchen and bathroom shelves for other objects that would make likely weapons. REMEMBER, THESE WEAPONS SHOULD BE USED ONLY TO STOP AN ATTACK SO YOU CAN ESCAPE!

Don't Hitchhike! Avoid Rape!

Hitchhiking is very dangerous! Women who accept rides are not only risking rape, but their lives as well.

Remember, you are seen in a weaker position if you accept a ride from a man, and if anything happens to you and you report it to the police, they will put a lot of blame on you.

Many Rape Crisis Centers take a strong and firm stand against hitchhiking!

Transportation

1. While sitting on the bus or subway, look aware. If you're not sure of where you're going, ask the driver, sit near the front.
2. When driving, keep your car doors locked.
3. If you have a car, check the back seat. Many attackers hide there and wait for the driver to return.
4. If you are ever in an emergency situation and have to jump from a moving car, make sure you can roll to a clear spot away from other moving cars. Throw your shoulders first with your right hand near your body. Tuck head into neck and keep back curved. Let your feet follow.

* * *

lifestyle into a drag. That's not what is being suggested. The hard cold facts are that sometimes to gain one thing you have to give up another. Giving up some personal liberties such as walking home at 2:00 or 3:00 in the morning by yourself, past a section with no street lights, might have to be given up. It's up to you to decide which way to go; and remember you can't have it both ways.

Note: There is an excellent discussion of self-defense tactics in the book *Against Rape*, by Andrea Medea and Kathleen Thompson, 1974, pps. 73-96.

CHAPTER 12

GROUP RAPE

"GROUP rape (or gang rape) is sexual assault perpetrated on one or more victims by more than one person"[1] " ... behaving in accord with well-established principles of collective behavior" (Beis, 1971). Various estimates have group rape accounting for at least 50 percent of the rapes reported (Geis, 1971; MacDonald, 1974). It is also likely that group rape will be on the increase, as the perpetrators of this crime are usually adolescents, those in the age range of thirteen to twenty-one, and the *1973 Uniform Crime Reports* state that the "age groups of males sixteen to twenty-four years of ages, constituted the greatest concentration of arrests ... with arrests for persons under eighteen years of age up 13 percent over 1972."

Group rape is a situation in which the personalities of a group of members blend together to form a group personality markedly different from the majority of the individuals who make up the group. Many studies on group behavior indicate that when people get together in a group, they function differently, i.e. according to the collective psychology. This is especially true with regard to social and moral inhibitions. What some people can do when they are alone is very different from what they are capable of doing within a group. The common feeling of individual members of the group is that the *group* is responsible and the individual members are only a part of what is going on, not individually responsible.

This is particularly true during adolescent years when peer pressure is extremely strong, albeit vital for the development of a healthy personality. Perhaps there is some need for testing individual masculinity by group members and the group psychology allows a greater lessening of social and moral restrictions. To rape a woman in the presence of other males supposedly says something about mutual concepts of mascu-

---

[1]Lombard, Linda. Personal Communication, June 18, 1976.

linity and sexuality of the members, about comaraderie, and about women's place in relation to men (Geis, 1971). The adolescent is struggling in an area of uncertainty about his sexuality between homosexual urges and heterosexual identity and there is a strong desire to belong to a group so that he can prove himself as a man. By sharing the assault with his peers, the group rapist can feel more secure and less anxious in his performance (Sadoff, 1974) and his role within the group receives support (Amir, 1971). Rape by a group may also create a situation in which there is a feeling of common guilt and thus, perhaps a sense of like fate (Geis, 1971).

Amir (1971) observed three types of participants who take part in group rape:

1. The first is what Amir calls the "core." These are those members who immediately join in and totally identify with the group and its aggressive atmosphere. These participants need the gang for expressing personality traits and the maintenance of personal identity. This member will tend to be the most aggressive toward the victim and may even be the initiator of the assault rather than the identified leader stimulating the attack.

2. The second type is called the "reluctant participant." He needs urging as he is waiting for signs that the woman is "magically" turned on by others preceding, him, but after some hesitancy will take part. He may rationalize the committing of the rape to the woman by saying he doesn't want to hurt her but needs to perform or he may be harmed by the other group members.

3. The final type is what Amir calls the "nonparticipant." This person just happens to be present at the time and place of the group assault but wants nothing to do with the rape. He may actually be terrorized by the brutality to the extent that so much anxiety is created within him that he is unable to have an erection. His idea of what it is to be a "good group member," or who is an acceptable victim, is different from that of the larger group.

There are a number of factors playing a role in the commission of the group rape. One of the primary factors most notably cited in the literature is the use of alcohol or marijuana by the offenders, causing their inhibitions to be lowered enough so the aggressive component can be expressed by the attackers. Like single-offender rapes, group rape tends to occur within a racial minority rather than being cross cultural (Amir, 1971). Amir goes on to say that the group offenders usually live in the same neighborhood as that of the victim and the rape is more frequently planned than are single-offender rapes. Automobiles, as the place in which the group rape occurs, are less predominant than in single-offender rapes, although the car is often the means for moving the victim to a more isolated spot. There is a significantly higher occurrence of fellatio being forced on the victim in group rapes (Geis, 1971). Although there is some conflict among the investigators, there appears to be a notable decrease in the number of injuries occurring in group rapes as the offenders have little reason to feel insecure. Amir states however, that the most excessive use of violence occurred in group rapes, and in all types of rape occurring outdoors.

MacDonald (1974) cites five common patterns of group rape:

1. The first is where the victim is picked up outside her home, is persuaded to go in the offenders' car for a ride, after which more male companions are picked up along with beer and wine and they all proceed to some isolated location where the girl is forced to drink alcohol or smoke marijuana and finally raped.
2. The second pattern is where the youths go to the girl's home, one member fakes knowing a brother or relative. Once inside the house, they all take advantage of the absence of other people and rape the girl.
3. The third pattern has a party for a setting. One boy will end a heavy petting session by inviting the other males in.
4. Another pattern takes place where a woman has been drinking in a tavern and as she leaves, she is seized and taken by several men in their car to an isolated area.
5. Finally, a girl will be captured as she is walking on the street alone, is forced into a car and under threats of violence, is driven away and raped.

In the group situation, there is usually a leader who typically suggests the assault and who is typically the first to rape the victim. Often, he is the most brutal assailant but not always; sometimes he may even keep the other members from hurting the woman (MacDonald, 1974). He is the boss and the one who says how things are going to proceed.

The victims of group rape are girls with a reputation for "promiscuity" (Geis, 1971; MacDonald, 1974) and fall between the ages of fifteen and twenty-four (Amir, 1971); the offenders may be younger or older than the victim. Geis goes on to say that there is a second type of group rape victim. This person is one who is involved in the situation because of circumstances (fate), i.e. she is in the wrong place at the wrong time. The victim may be the target of a planned rape, which is typical of group rapes (Amir, 1971) or less likely as an impulse by one of the members, most probably the leader. As in single-offender rapes, group rape occurs most frequently during weekend evenings.

This chapter was included primarily because there is so little written about the subject. As Geis states in a commentary following MacDonald's article, "Unfortunately, we have no *definite* information on its (group rape) character; what kinds of person initiate the idea, which persons fail to participate in the act though they could and how they excuse themselves, and how group status influences the roles played by the different male partners."

There is even less known about the effects the group rape has on the victim, whether the psychological trauma is more or less severe. The seriousness of the group rape's effects on the victim is suggested however in comments by Dr. Goldner (1974) following MacDonald's article when he states, " ... group rape is a particularly terrifying experience for a woman. It well may be that group rapes are reported proportionately less frequently than solo rapes (as suggested by MacDonald) because they are more humiliating to the victim, often accompanied by extraordinary psychological trauma." The author however, has not seen any articles comparing the trauma of group rape victims to that of single-offender rape victims.

CHAPTER 13

PROBLEMS CONFRONTING
RAPE CRISIS CENTERS

THIS chapter will discuss some of the important problems Rape Crisis Centers are facing. The basis for this discussion is based on the results of the author's 1975 RCC Questionnaire. On the questionnaire, the RCCs were asked to rank order thirteen potential problems with one being the foremost problem for the RCCs and thirteen being the least pressing.

FUNDING

Funding was chosen as the number one problem confronting RCCs. During the early 1960's, when the Hotline and suicide prevention center movement was growing, funding was also a primary concern for these services, as it now is for RCCs. The people organizing such services were typically outside of traditional funding circles because these services were seen as bucking the professional helping community.

Most of those RCCs received monies through donations to the Center; an average sum from donations totals approximately $620.00 per year. The next most popular funding sources were universities and colleges for those Centers which were located on the campuses. The annual funds coming to them from this source totalled $3,160.00. Another source of funds for many RCCs were grants. The majority of grants received were from private foundations, which awarded an average grant of $6,225.00; then came federal grants with an average award of $7,790.00, and finally, city grants with money provided them through revenue sharing for an average grant of $5,760.00. Monies received through the United Fund, though few and far between, averaged $7,650.00 per year. So, it would appear that RCCs in this survey are typically doing better financially than were crisis centers at the same stage in their development. As this is only a very limited sample of the more than 200 RCCs in existence, there are undoubtedly many RCCs operating on budgets of less than $2,000, which is very tight if RCCs are expected to perform the many services they have undertaken to offer.

In regard to obtaining a federal grant for funds to operate your center, a resource with which you will want to become familiar is the *Catalog of Federal Domestic Assistance*. This book is a comprehensive and detailed listing of the types of grants which the federal government, often in cooperation with state, county, and city governments, has available for agencies and persons qualifying. Many colleges and local governments have a copy of this book, usually in the office responsible for research and assistance. If you are unable to find the book in your area, it is for sale from the Superintendent of Documents, U.S. Government Printing Office, Washington, D.C. 20402.

Those RCCs receiving federal grants obtained the majority of them through the Law Enforcement Assistance Administration (LEAA) and worked in cooperation with their local law enforcement agencies and city governments to combat the crime of rape. You may want to discuss writing a LEAA grant proposal with your area officials. To receive more information on the grants available and applicable to RCCs, you can write to the Assistant Administrator, Office of National Priority Programs, Law Enforcement Assistance Administration, U.S. Department of Justice, Washington, D.C. 20530.

As the result of federal legislation, specifically the Health Services, Revenue Sharing, and Nurse Training P.L. 94-63, Title III, Part D, there has been established the National Center for the Prevention and Control of Rape within the National Institute of Mental Health. In FY 1976, a total of $3 million had been appropriated for this program to support such projects in the areas of basic and applied research studies, and research-demonstration projects on consultation and education. To find out whether your center may qualify for some of these funds, you may want to write to Dr. Bertram S. Brown,

National Institute of Mental Health, 5600 Fishers Lane, Rockville, MD 20852.

Other areas you will want to investigate in the *Catalog* may be under the headings of Social Services, Mental Health, and Health Care Services. One word of caution about attempting to receive a federal grant or any grant for that matter, is that the process involves a lot of hard work, paper shuffling, red-tape, interagency cooperation, the need for accountability, and at times pressure to redefine the RCC's philosophy and goals so it can qualify for the aid — be careful, don't let your need for money keep your center from offering nontraditional, alternative care for rape victims.

A resource you will want to investigate for information on private grants from foundations is *The Foundation Directory*, Edition 5, by M. O. Lewis (Ed.), 1975.

Another potential information resource on funds for your center is the National Youth Alternatives Office, 1830 Connecticut Avenue, N. W., Washington, D.C. 20009. Also, don't overlook the possibility of state, county, and city grants which might be applicable to your center.

Although some RCCs have succeeded in obtaining monies through grants, most of your funds will probably come from local resources. Some of the many fund-raising ideas which RCCs have used with varying degrees of success are: rummage sales, fees from speaking engagements and workshops, recycling campaigns, membership dues, sale of literature on rape, contributions from churches, service clubs (Lions, Jaycees, etc.), and businesses in your community, rock concerts, walk- or dance-a-thons, and asking that monetary gifts be given to the RCC in wills.

In conclusion, although monies are needed for the successful operation of a center, you might be surprised as to how little it takes to get by. This is especially true if you can get some organization (YWCA, Mental Health Center, Hospital, etc.) to donate space rent free, not having to pay federal taxes on telephone service if you are nonprofit and tax-exempt, and utilize radio, television, and newspapers who typically do public service announcements free of charge.

Whether the center survives or fails depends much more on the commitment, energy, and drive of your staff than on how large your budget is. When the community sees what services you are providing, the money will come.

In any case, when asking for funds, most people will want you to show them:

1. who you are accountable to.
2. a thorough description of the service, including rationale, philosophy, policies, and training of the personnel.
3. the results of your needs assessment survey in the community.
4. evidence of your cooperation with already existing agencies in the community.
5. statistics on the services the RCC provides and who uses the Center.
6. a realistic, flexible, and itemized budget (Fisher, 1972).

Note: Excellent discussions of funding hints are contained in:

Delworth et. al., *Crisis Center/Hotline*, 1972, pps. 46-54.
Fisher, S., *The Voice of Hope ... To People In Crisis*, 1972, pps. 44-45.
McClary et al., *How To Organize A Women's Crisis-Service Center*, 1974, pps. 12-15.

REPORTING THE ASSAULT

The victim's fear of reporting the assault was ranked as the second most important problem confronting RCCs.

Much of the victim's fear arises from publicity given to rape cases by radio, television, and the press, the concern over how her family and friends will react, fact and fiction regarding the treatment given rape victims by medical personnel and law enforcement agencies and officials, and the mythology surrounding rape as a taboo subject.

Where there exists a lack of informed knowledge, many fears will exists. The RCC's primary way to lessen these fears of rape victims in reporting the assault is through community education on the subject and by pressuring officials to change treatment policies. Community education can be accomplished by the use of rape speak-outs, conferences and symposiums, public service programs in the media, printing educational material for distribution at speaking engagements in schools and at service clubs, and letting women know what services are available in the community to help them if raped. Once the community education program is in full swing, the public will pressure agencies and officials to rehumanize their treatment of the victims.

This problem will probably never be conquered but a RCC can attack it and make sure inroads to shedding informed and knowledgeable light on rape are begun.

VOLUNTEER DROP-OUT

Volunteer drop-out was ranked as the third most important problem confronting RCCs. Although there will be exceptions, many of your volunteers will not remain with the RCC more than four to six months, no matter what is done to prevent it.

In those cases where volunteers are leaving earlier than four to six months with the center, most of it is probably the result of their feeling unrewarded, frustrated, burnt-out because of the stresses or the training of RCIs, or the leadership and organization of the center was inadequate, insensitive or bogged down.

For people to continue as volunteers, the work must be challenging, yet personally fulfilling. A number of people volunteer for alternative human care services because they are just that, alternatives to traditional helping services. After many of the hurdles of beginning are overcome, some alternative services become the status quo, establishment, and traditional services which they said they were never going to be. For people who volunteered because they thought they personally could cause change in the system, this is very disheartening.

Signs you may want to watch out for which may be hinting that your center is becoming stagnant are: too much red tape; insensitive policies *telling*, not suggesting, what volunteers do;

more federal money than local money and too much of it (so the struggle which pulls people together is missing); a training program which has not been changed in six months or is primarily run by outsiders; and the lack of seeking out community input and support which was so necessary at the beginning.

For more hints on what may help your volunteers stay, refer to the material in Chapter 10.

LIAISON

Developing and then maintaining cooperative relationships or liaison with the police, hospital, and court officials were ranked as the fourth, sixth, and seventh most difficult problems respectively, which confront RCCs.

The police department, hospital, and court representatives are very integral to your RCC, as they provide certain services which no other agency in your community provides. Let's consider some suggestions to more effectively deal with these people.

The most often suggested means of fostering better relations with these officials is to become acquainted with them early in the development of your center. As you need to interview the police, hospital, and DA personnel for your needs assessment, this can be a good beginning point. A suggestion here is that you meet with the higher ups first, such as the Police Chief, Chief of Detectives, Chief Prosecutor, Hospital Administrator, Chief Resident, or Supervisory Nurse. If these higher-level people can be convinced of the need and validity of a RCC, their attitudes and examples can often have a strong beneficial influence on lower-level people. It may sometimes occur that the key people at the top cannot be convinced of the need for better treatment of rape victims and the need for cooperation with the RCC. Therefore, you will have to work from *within* the agency, organizing the police on the street, the secretaries in the prosecutor's office, and the nurses on the floor, to get the changes and cooperation at the top. This is not to say that you shouldn't also develop good working relationships with the patrol officers, secretaries, and floor nurses. They are just as important, as the RCI will probably be working more closely with these persons anyway. When meeting with these and other people, make your initial approach low key and offer to *help* them with coping with rape crisis.

Make sure both the police and medical personnel are fully aware and knowledgeable about the RCC. Leave a few copies of your program goals and purposes in the officers' duty room and the nurses' lounge, so they can read about your service at their leisure.

To maintain a good working relationship, continue to meet often with these parties. Send them your monthly reports or newsletter, along with suggestions as to how they can serve more effectively. Ask for input at monthly meetings with them and provide *feedback* not condemnation.

Another popular suggestion on developing a good working relationship is to conduct symposiums, conferences, sensitivity training sessions, etc., and invite the police, medical, and court people to take part as participants and as presenters. These people are professionals and they want to provide helpful information if asked; like most people, they also like to feel needed.

Soon after the center has begun operating, you may want to have an open-house and invite all interested people and agencies to attend. The friendly warm atmosphere of a party can do much to develop rapport with the police, medical, and court personnel, more than where the center makes a formal presentation.

Another suggestion for developing rapport is to have a regular duty police officer, floor nurse, or States attorney serve on your Board of Directors. If you can get these people to feel committed and have "ownership" for a part of the RCC by serving on the board, their attitudes will likely be reflected where they work.

As most people like to feel their efforts are appreciated when they do a good job, send letters of commendation or award to police officers, nurses, and attorneys who are exceptionally sensitive and caring towards a rape victim. Make a big deal out of it and be sure their immediate supervisors receive notice of the award; you may even want to announce the award in a short news article.

An innovative suggestion was that the RCC offer to conduct minicourses in medical, nursing, and law schools, and at the police training academy. This might be a particularly relevant suggestion to those RCCs which are located on university and college campuses where such professional schools exist. Perhaps in this way, you will be nipping the problem of dehumanization of the rape victim in the bud.

Other suggestions for developing and maintaining effective liaison with police, hospital, and court representatives are: work with policewomen; ask police, hospital, and court personnel to participate in the RCC training program; speak positively about the agencies the RCC has dealt with and make it known to those involved that you trust them to do their job effectively and sensitively; work through the police and hospital's public relations office; offer immediate feedback to police and medical personnel following an interrogation or medical exam; and work through a recognized social agency so they can act as your intermediary.

HANDLING REACTIONS

Dealing with the reactions of family, relatives, and friends of the victim to the rape was ranked as the fifth most pressing problem for RCCs. This subject has already been dealt with in an earlier chapter. To reiterate, the primary task of the RCI is to cause these third parties to shift their focus from anger and blame towards the victim, themselves, and the rapist to a realization that the girl or woman has just experienced a very painful and traumatic event. It is their behavior towards the victim which will help or hinder the victim's long-term adjustment to the assault. Suggest that they be patient, supportive, and calm, but above all, not to keep the victim from discussing the rape when she is ready.

REMAINING PROBLEMS

The problem of *bad publicity* was ranked as number eight in importance. Again, the quality and kind of publicity the RCC receives will depend to a large measure on the manner in which the RCC has represented itself in the community, quality of services it provides, conduct of its staff, and cooperation the center has developed with police, hospital, and court representatives. An excellent discussion of publicity and public relations for crisis centers is contained in the book *The Voice Of Hope ... To People In Crisis*, by Sheila Fisher, 1972, pps. 59-64.

The ninth most important problem was with the *transfer or referral of victims* to another agency or person. It is very important that the RCC have up-to-date referrals which have a minimum of red-tape and who are willing to work for and with women. Refer to Chapter 8 for a discussion of how to make appropriate and helpful referrals.

Staff hassles were ranked as number ten in importance as a problem confronting RCCs. This issue has already been dealt with earlier, so please refer to that material contained in Chapter 10.

Crank calls were ranked as number eleven, with *false reports* as problem number twelve, and *obscene calls* as the least important or thirteenth problem facing RCCs. An excellent discussion of how to deal with these calls as well as the chronic caller, the silent caller, the masturbating caller, and the "one-counselor" caller is contained in the book *Crisis Intervention and Counseling by Telephone*, by David Lester and Gene Brockopp, 1973, pps. 156-218. This book is a very excellent resource for any crisis service utilizing the telephone as an intervention tool.

RAPE CRISIS CENTERS*

ARIZONA

Center Against Sexual Assault
P.O. Box 3786
Phoenix 85030

CALIFORNIA

Bay Area Women Against Rape
P.O. Box 240
Berkeley 94701

Feminist Women's Health Center
1112 South Crenshaw Blvd.
Los Angeles 90019

Fresno Rape Counseling Service
P.O. Box 708
Clovis 93612

Marin Rape Crisis Center
P.O. Box 823
Kentfield 94904

San Bernardino Rape Crisis Service
c/o Family Service Agency
1669 East Street
San Bernardino 92405

San Francisco Rape Center
P.O. Box 40709
San Francisco 94140

Orange County Women Against Rape
P.O. Box 651
Placentia 92670

COLORADO

Community Crisis and Information Center
202 Edwards Street
Fort Collins 80521

Virginia Neal Blue Resource Centers for Colorado Women
Colorado Women's College
Montview & Quebec
Denver 80220

FLORIDA

Rape Information and Counseling Service, Inc.
P.O. Box 12888
University Station
Gainesville 32604

*The inclusion of any organization's or person's name contained in this section should not be construed by the reader as an endorsement or recommendation of this book. The author only wishes to publicly acknowledge those organizations and persons who assisted him in the development of this book.

Rape Treatment Center
Emergency Department
Jackson Memorial Hospital
1700 N.W. 10th Avenue
Miami 33136

ILLINOIS

Chicago Women Against
    Rape
c/o Loop YWCA
37 South Wabash Avenue
Chicago 60603

Prelude
P.O. Box 1303
Knox College
Galesburg 61401

IOWA

Mid-Iowa Rape Crisis Center
Box 1150
ISU Station
Ames 50010

Rape Crisis Line
c/o Women's Resource and
    Action Center
3 East Market Street
Iowa City 52240

Cedar Rapids Rape Crisis Ser-
    vices
c/o YWCA, Women's Re-
    source Center
Cedar Rapids 52201

KANSAS

The Fone, Inc.
615 Fairchild Terrace
Manhattan 66502

MARYLAND

Baltimore Rape Crisis Center
101 East 25th Street
Baltimore 21218

MASSACHUSETTS

Every Woman's Center
Goodell Hall
Univ. of Massachusetts
Amherst 01002

Springfield Rape Crisis Center
Room 215
292 Worthington Street
Springfield 01103

MICHIGAN

Ann Arbor Women's Crisis
    Center
306 North Division Street
Ann Arbor 48108

Grand Rapids Rape Crisis
    Team
P.O. Box 6161, Station C.
Grand Rapids 49506

Kalamazoo Women's Center/
    Rape Crisis Program
Room 210
211 South Rose Street
Kalamazoo 49006

Oakland Crisis Center for
    Rape and Sexual Abuse
269 West Huron
Pontiac 48058

MINNESOTA

Rape Counseling Center
Neighborhood Involvement Program
2617 Hennipin Avenue
Minneapolis 55408

MISSOURI

Metropolitan Organization to Counter Sexual Assault
P.O. Box 15492
Kansas City 64106

MONTANA

Women's Place
600 Orange Street
Missoula 59801

NEW MEXICO

Albuquerque Rape Crisis Center
c/o The Women's Center
1824 Las Lomas N.E.
Albuquerque 87106

NEW YORK

Oswego Women's Center
286 Washington Boulevard
Oswego 13126

Syracuse Rape Crisis Center
113 Concord Place
Syracuse 13210

Women's Counseling Project
Earl Hall, Room 112
Broadway & 117th Street
New York 10027

Woodstock's Rape Committee
c/o Family of Woodstock
16 Rock City Road
Woodstock 12498

NORTH CAROLINA

Chapel Hill-Carrboro Rape Crisis Center
P.O. Box 871
Chapel Hill 27514

Greensboro Rape Crisis Center
c/o Ms. Donna Smith
P.O. Box 938, Route 7
Greensboro 27407

OHIO

Rape and Assault Crisis Line
750 Livermore Street
Yellow Springs 45387

Toni Goman Feminist Rape Crisis Center
P.O. Box 12313
Tri-village Station
Columbus 43212

Women Against Rape Collective
1309 North Main Street
Dayton 45405

Victim/Witness Division
Montgomery Co. Prosecutor's Ofc.
41 North Perry Street
Dayton 45202

OKLAHOMA

Rape Crisis Center
c/o Oklahoma City Women's
Resource Center
722 Northwest 30th
Oklahoma City 73118

OREGON

Rape Prevention Center
P.O. Box 625
Eugene 97401

PENNSYLVANIA

Rape Crisis Council of
Chester County
P.O. Box 738
West Chester 19380

Women Organized Against
Rape
Trineb Building
420 Service Drive
Philadelphia 19104

RHODE ISLAND

Rhode Island Rape Crisis
Center
c/o YWCA
324 Broad Street
Central Falls 02866

SOUTH DAKOTA

Rape Crisis Team
c/o Ms. Paula Linehan
Student Development and
Counseling
109 West Hall
South Dakota State University
Brookings 57006

TENNESSEE

Chattanooga Rape Prevention
and Crisis Center
c/o YWCA
300 East 8th Street
Chattanooga 37406

Rape Prevention and Crisis
Center
P.O. Box 12531, Acklen Station
1929 21st Avenue South
Nashville 37212

TEXAS

Austin Rape Crisis Center
P.O. Box 2247
Austin 78701

Dallas Rape Crisis Center
c/o Dallas Women Against
Rape, Inc.
P.O. Box 12701
Dallas 75225

San Antonio Rape Crisis Line
c/o Crisis Center of San Antonio Area, Inc.
P.O. Box 28061
San Antonio 78228

VIRGINIA

Rape Crisis & Information
Line
3515 Williamson Road
Roanoke 24012

WASHINGTON

Rape Relief for Thurston County
c/o YWCA
220 East Union
Olympia 98501

WASHINGTON, D.C.

Feminist Alliance Against Rape
P.O. Box 21033
Washington 20009

Rape Crisis Center
P.O. Box 21005
Washington 20009

WISCONSIN

RAPE Crisis Center
P.O. Box 1312
Madison 53701

Women's Crisis Line
2211 East Kenwood Boulevard
Milwaukee 53211

OTHER PERSONS AND ORGANIZATIONS

Chicago Chapter
National Organization for Women (NOW)
5 South Wabash, Suite 1615
Chicago, Illinois 60603

Women's Kempo Karate Class
499 Franklin
Buffalo, New York 14209

Ms. Susan Klemmack
Rape Research Group
Center for Correctional Psychology
P.O. Box 2968
University, Alabama 35486

Dr. Bernard F. Lyons, Jr.
Director of Training
Knoxville Rape Crisis Center
University of Tennessee
Psychological Clinic
1303 West Cumberland
Knoxville, Tennessee 37916

(They have agreed to serve as a collection and distribution point for reported models on the training of crisis counselors.)

Center for Women Policy Studies
2000 P Street, N.W., Suite 508
Washington, D.C. 20036

Dr. Thomas Lister
Vermillion Hotline
Coyote Student Center
University of South Dakota
Vermillion, South Dakota 57069

Mr. Mark Stephens, Program Director
Coyote Student Center
University of South Dakota
Vermillion, South Dakota 57069

Mr. Clarence M. Kelley, Director
Federal Bureau of Investigation
United States Department of Justice
Washington, D.C. 20535

The Attorney Generals of the 50 United States (for sending their state's laws on rape and rape legislation)

Sen. George McGovern
Senator from South Dakota (for sending federal laws on rape and national rape legislation).

RESULTS OF THE RCC SURVEY

INTRODUCTION

AT the outset of this appendix, the author would caution the reader not to place too much reliability or validity in the data presented herein. This is not because the author misrepresents the results in any way, but, instead, because the results are, at best, sketchy indications of the present state of Rape Crisis Centers across the nation.

The author was plagued by one problem in particular which should cause the reader not to place too much validity in this survey, i.e. of the total of forty-seven questionnaires returned to the author, many were not completed in their entirety; the respondents choose to only answer particular questions as opposed to others. This obviously results in a smaller sample size on which to base any conclusions in regard to specific questions. The author has presented the percentage of the total of forty-seven questionnaires returned on which a particular question was answered.

The results are presented in the order in which they appeared on the RCC Questionnaire itself.

METHODOLOGY

The questionnaire used in this study was an adaptation of a similar questionnaire developed by Dr. Sheila A. Fisher, used in her national survey of suicide prevention and/or crisis services (Fisher, 1972). The questionnaire is contained in the book, *The Voice Of Hope ... To People In Crisis*, 1972 by Sheila A. Fisher, Ph.D., pages 96-101.

The questionnaires were sent to a majority of those addresses appearing on a list of Rape Crisis Centers and women's crisis centers supplied the author by the Center for Women Policy

241

Studies, 2000 P Street, N.W., Suite 508, Washington, D.C. 20036. Only those centers in the United States were included on the mailing list, and then only one questionnaire was sent to one center in a particular city, although there may have been two or more such centers in that city. The author was seeking representation of geographical areas across the nation rather than an exhaustive survey of all rape crisis or women's centers. The final number of centers chosen to receive a RCC Questionnaire was 210.

The questionnaires were mailed in November of 1974. The author continued to receive completed questionnaires until a cut off date of April, 1975.

RESULTS

General Results

Of the 210 questionnaires distributed, only forty-seven were returned in various degrees of completion. This is a return rate of 22.38 percent. Of the forty-seven questionnaires returned to the author, twenty-seven states were represented by one or more questionnaires. Those states from which responses came and the number of responses from each state are shown in Table I.

Table I. Distribution of RCC Questionnaires
Returned According to the State From Which They Came

State	Frequency of Responses
Arizona	1
California	6
Colorado	1
Florida	2
Illinois	2
Iowa	3
Kansas	1
Maryland	1
Massachusetts	2
Michigan	3
Minnesota	1

Missouri	1
Montana	1
New Mexico	1
New York	4
North Carolina	1
Ohio	3
Oklahoma	1
Oregon	1
Pennsylvania	2
Rhode Island	1
South Dakota	1
Tennessee	1
Texas	2
Virginia	1
Washington	1
Wisconsin	2

It can be seen by investigating Table I that, in terms of geographical representation, the Midwest is over represented both in states from which the responses came (8) and in the number of responses (16). The Southwest is under represented both in the number of states from which the responses came (4) and the number of responses (5).

By referring to Table II, it can be seen that cities with a population of 10,001 to 50,000 are over represented in the sample of Rape Crisis Centers.

Table II. Distribution of RCC Questionnaire
Responses According to Population of Cities
From Which The Responses Came

Population of Cities	Frequency of Responses	Percent of Total Responses
10,000 or under	3	6.38
10,001 - 50,000	15	31.91
50,001 - 100,000	3	6.38
100,001 - 500,000	9	19.15
500,001 - 1,000,000	4	8.51
1,000,001 - 5,000,000	10	21.28
5,000,001 and over	3	6.38

Organization

The question asked on the RCC Questionnaire was, "Are you (the RCC) part of a larger organization or service, i.e. a hospital, YWCA, comprehensive women's center, crisis intervention service, etc.?" One-hundred percent of the respondents answered this question. Of this group, 57.45 percent responded "yes" while 42.55 percent said "no." The largest percentage of "yes" responses (51.82%) was included under comprehensive women centers, of which the rape crisis center was a part of their service. Other examples of "yes" responses included YWCAs, hospitals, and crisis intervention services (hotlines, suicide prevention centers, etc.).

The next question asked, "Why did you think it was important to begin a Rape Crisis Center rather than relying on already existing helping services such as mental health centers, social service agencies, YWCAs, etc.?" Again, 100 percent of the respondents answered this question. The major reasons offered as to why these centers began a Rape Crisis Center included: no agency existed which really dealt with the problem of rape or was staffed and trained to handle rape victims (38.30%); existing agencies were not meeting the special needs of rape victims (19.15%); being women and feminist oriented, we can understand and feel compassion for the rape victim more easily (17.02%); and, no one in the community would support or be sensitive to the needs of rape victims immediately (10.64%). Less frequently stated motivations were: our coverage (twenty-four hours/day-seven days/week) was more comprehensive; to provide community education on the subject of sexual assault as well as support the rape victims; we didn't want to compromise our political beliefs; the need was apparent following a NOW Task Force On Rape study; and, the rampant abuses of rape victims by agencies and services organized to assist rape victims caused us to begin our own Rape Crisis Center.

Funding

In regards to funding of Rape Crisis Centers, the respondents were asked to place a check by those funding sources which applied and enter the approximate dollar amount of support coming from this source per year. A total of forty-five, or 95.74 percent, of the total respondents answered this question on the questionnaire.

Those most frequently occurring funding sources from which Rape Crisis Centers obtained operating monies were, in order of frequency: private donations were a source of income for 35.49 percent of the respondents, providing an average of $970.00 per year; university or college funding was a source of income for 11.83 percent, providing an average of $3,160.00 per year; grants from private foundations were a source of income for 9.68 percent, providing an average of $6,225.00 per year to those centers lucky enough to receive one; grants from the federal government provided an average of $7,785.00 per year for 8.60 percent; and, monies from the United Fund/United Appeal were a source of income for 5.38 percent, providing an average of $7,650.00 per year.

Under the category of "other" was included such fund-raising projects as rummage sales, speaking engagement fees, membership dues, sale of literature, awards for community service, recycling campaigns, and conducting workshops on rape. These miscellaneous projects supplied an average income of $2,670.00 per year to 20.43 percent of the Rape Crisis Centers responding to the funding source question.

Very infrequently occurring funding resources included donations from mental health and/or mental retardation associations, state grants, and county and municipal grants coming from revenue sharing monies.

The average operating budget for a Rape Crisis Center was $6,226.00 per year. This average figure excludes a center which had a budget of over $130,000.00. It should be noted however, that almost 44.00 percent of the Rape Crisis Centers responding to the funding question had operating budgets under $2,000.00 per year.

Staffing

Forty-five or 95.74 percent of the respondents answered the

questions relating to the composition of the Rape Crisis Center staffs. The data relating to the questions on staffing is contained in Table III.

Table III. Characteristics of Rape Crisis Center Staffs
According to Average Number and Percentage of Total Staff
Comprising Each Category

Category of Staff	Average Number	Percentage
Paid Staff	4.42	11.03
Professionals	3.29	74.30
Volunteers	1.13	25.63
Unpaid Staff	35.69	88.97
Professionals	3.29	9.22
Volunteers	32.40	90.78
Sexual Assault Victims	6.02	15.84
Nonvictims	32.03	84.16
Females	35.16	91.80
Males	3.14	8.20
Under 18 Years of Age	0.88	2.81
18 - 22 Years of Age	7.65	22.71
23 - 27 Years of Age	12.05	34.83
28 - 32 Years of Age	7.36	21.27
33 - 37 Years of Age	2.89	8.83
38 - 42 Years of Age	1.58	4.82
43 - 50 Years of Age	1.00	3.05
51 - 60 Years of Age	0.44	1.44
61 and Over	0.07	0.24

Length Service Has Been In Operation

One-hundred percent of the respondents answered a question asking how long the Rape Crisis Center has been in existence. This data is presented in Table IV.

Operational Procedures

METHODS BY WHICH CLIENTS CONTACT RAPE CRISIS CENTERS.

Table IV. Time Periods For Which Individual
Rape Crisis Centers Have Been In Operation

Time Period (months)	Frequency of Response	Percentage
less than 12 mos.	21	44.68
12 - 23 mos.	14	29.79
24 - 35 mos.	5	10.64
36 - 47 mos.	4	8.51
48 - 59 mos.	2	4.26
60 - 71 mos.	0	0.00
72 - 83 mos.	0	0.00
84 - 119 mos.	1	2.13
more than 120 mos.	0	0.00

Once again, 100 percent of the respondents answered the question asking how sexual assault victims typically make contact with the Rape Crisis Centers. The respondents were also asked to enter the approximate percentage of contacts made by telephone, through walk-ins, through referrals from other persons or agencies, and other.

The results of the survey indicate that the majority of contacts (80.57%) are made to Rape Crisis Centers via the victim or a friend of the victim calling the Rape Crisis Center. The second most frequent method by which contacts are made with the RCC is through referrals (14.45%) coming from other helping persons or agencies within the community. The least used method by which victims make contact with the RCC is by walking in (4.02%) to the center itself as the initial contact. Under the category of "other" were such things as the center's outreach work or speaking engagements; these accounted for only 0.94 percent of the contacts made to RCCs in these manners.

Days of operation. All of the respondents answered the question asking how many days of the week the RCC operated. By far, the majority or 85.11 percent of the RCCs were open seven days a week, fifty-two weeks a year. Only 14.89 percent of the RCCs operated less than seven days a week. Of those operating less than seven days a week, 71.42 percent operated five days a week, Monday through Friday.

HOURS OF OPERATION PER DAY. Forty-four of the 47 respondents (or 93.62%) answered the question on the questionnaire asking how many hours of each day the RCCs operated.

The majority of the RCCs operated on a twenty-four hour basis (65.96%). Only 12.77 percent of the RCCs operated twelve hours per day and even fewer or 8.51 percent operated less than twelve hours per day. The "other" category included 6.38 percent of the respondents and was comprised of such responses as eighteen, sixteen, and fourteen hours per day.

OUTREACH TEAMS. The question was asked whether the RCCs had an outreach team which would go and meet the sexual assault victim at the scene of the crime and/or be with the victim at the hospital, during the police questionning, preliminary hearing, and trial. Other functions of the outreach team included making presentations to interested groups or conducting workshops on rape prevention and self-defense.

Of the 82.98 percent of RCCs responding to this question, 56.41 percent said "yes" they do have an outreach team, whereas 43.59 percent said "no" they do not have such an outreach team. The author then went on to discover the composition of outreach teams. It was found the teams were composed of 98.19 percent women as opposed to men, and these women comprising the team were 93.37 percent volunteers or paraprofessionals as opposed to being professional personnel.

The author was also interested in whether the outreach team personnel or general staff of those RCCs not having a designated outreach team were allowed to accompany, at the victim's request, the sexual assault victim during the medical exam, police questionning, preliminary hearing, and trial. In regards to the medical examination, 76.60 percent of the respondents said "yes" they were allowed to accompany the victim, with 23.40 percent stating "no." As to the police questionning, 74.47 percent of the RCCs stated "yes" they were allowed to accompany the victim, with only 25.53 percent saying "no." It should be noted at this point that often the person from the RCC was not actually in the same room as the victim during the medical examination or police questionning, but instead was usually right outside the door of the room where such examining or questionning was taking place. This was often done at the request of the RCI so it would be less likely that s/he be subpoenaed as a witness as to what evidence was gathered during these procedures. Finally, in regard to being allowed to accompany the victim during the preliminary hearing and/or trial, 82.98 percent of the respondents said "yes" while only 17.02 percent said "no," they weren't allowed to accompany the victim.

RECORD KEEPING. The author next asked the RCCs to respond to questions regarding their record-keeping policies. Forty-five of the respondents or 95.74 percent answered these questions.

It was found that 95.55 percent of the RCCs keep a record of all calls to their centers, and 66.67 percent of the RCCs also keep case files on all face-to-face contacts with rape victims. It should be noted that none of the RCCs either audio or video record call for face-to-face interviews with sexual assault victims.

Since the majority of the RCCs do keep written records of calls and interviews, the author was further interested in who has access to these files. One-hundred percent of the respondents answered this question relating to access. The responses were as follows: 100 percent of the RCCs gave access to such files to their own staff, 27.66 percent of these same RCCs also allowing access to law enforcement officials. In the case of this 27.66 percent, such access was only allowed with a court order in 38.46 percent of the cases, only with the victim's written permission in 23.08 percent of the cases, and both a court order and the victim's written permission being required by 38.46 percent of the RCCs.

As a result of finding that case files were kept by the majority of the respondents, the author wanted to know how long such files were kept on each case. Thirty-three or 70.21 percent of the respondents answered this question. Files were kept for a period of two or more years by 66.67 percent of the respondents. Files kept for a period of twelve to twenty-three months accounted for 15.65 percent of the respondents, with another 15.65 percent of the RCCs keeping the files only for a period of seven to eleven months. Only 3.03 percent of the RCCs kept their files for a period less than six months.

FOLLOW-UP ON CASES. A question, answered on 85.11 percent of the total questionnaires returned, asked at what intervals of time the RCC staff conducts follow-up interviews on a case reported to them. The most frequently given response (77.50% of the RCCs) was "we follow-up as is necessary following the rape crisis." Seventy-two percent of the RCCs stated they followed-up within twenty-four hours of the crisis. The interval of within forty-eight hours was given by 17.50 percent of the RCCs, with 20.00 percent also following-up within one week of the crisis. Ten percent of the RCCs also follow-up at a period of one month, 5.00 percent follow-up again at six months, and 2.50 percent of the RCCs follow-up on the case one or more years following the crisis.

Of those RCCs conducting follow-up interviews, the average number of such interviews per case was 3.78.

Training For Rape Crisis Interveners

SCREENING. Ninety-five percent (or 45 of the 47 respondents) answered the question asking whether the RCCs screened their personnel prior to acceptance as a staff member. Of those respondents answering this question, 68.89 percent said "yes," with 31.11 percent saying "no." The methods used for screening were as follows: observation during training used by 31.25 percent of the RCCs; as training progresses, volunteers screened themselves out used by 25.00 percent of the RCCs; individual interviews conducted with the volunteers were used by another 25.00 percent of the RCCs; screening by observing volunteers during role-playing exercises was used by 6.25 percent of the RCCs; listening attentively to volunteers during rap sessions and discussions on rape was used by another 6.25 percent of the RCCs; Carkhuff's "Index of Discrimination" (1969) and group interviews were each used by another 3.13 percent of the RCCs.

Those characteristics or traits most frequently sought out in the screening process were: willingness to work, sensitivity to people, concern for women, expertise in counseling/nursing/

caring, knowledge of the subject of rape, motivation, commitment, flexibility, willingness to learn, nonjudgmental attitude, empathy, interpersonal skills, love for women, warmth, stable life situation, desire to work with and for women, common sense, ego strength, responsibility, be a woman, and be a feminist.

SCHEDULING OF TRAINING PROGRAMS. When asked to respond to the question, "When do you conduct your training programs?", 89.36 percent of the questionnaires responded to the question. That data is presented in Table V.

Table V. Periods of Time When Training
Programs Are Conducted by Rape Crisis Centers

Time Period (months)	Frequency of Response	Percentage
once/3 mos.	13	30.96
once/6 mos.	2	4.76
once/12 mos.	0	0.00
whenever a sufficient number of persons have need of training	22	52.38
*other	5	11.90

*Examples of "other" include: every six weeks, each month, as each person applies, every other month.

In a typical training program, there is an average of 13.80 trainees taking part.

LENGTH OF A TYPICAL TRAINING PROGRAM. The respondents were asked to place a check on the blank which is most nearly true of the average time devoted to their RCC's training program. Thirty RCCs or 76.60 percent chose to respond to this question. That data is presented in Table VI.

PERSONNEL INVOLVED IN THE TRAINING PROGRAM. The respondents were asked to note those personnel having input into their training program and the approximate percentage of those personnel contributing toward the total training program. Thirty-nine respondents or 82.98 percent of the total respondents answered this question. The results of this question are given in Table VII.

Table VI. Length of a Typical Rape Crisis
Center Training Program

Length (hours)	Frequency of Response	Percentage
1 - 10 hours	9	25.00
11 - 20 hours	16	44.44
21 - 30 hours	4	11.11
31 - 40 hours	2	5.55
over 40 hours	5	13.89

Table VII. Personnel Providing Input for a
Typical Rape Crisis Center Training Program

Personnel	Percentage of RCCs Using This Source	Average Percentage Of Input Provided By Such Persons
Medical	38.46	13.43
Psychological	53.85	23.70
Attorneys	35.90	7.77
Police	28.21	11.40
Religious	5.13	5.00
Other Professionals	25.64	22.00
Paraprofessionals Not On Your Staff	41.03	21.07
Your Staff	92.31	68.36

In asking the question, "Which of these personnel (in Table VII) do you consider to be most helpful in volunteering time and effort to make your training program a success?", the RCC's own staff was thought to be most helpful.

EVALUATION OF TRAINEES DURING THE TRAINING PROGRAM. The respondents were asked to respond to the question, "What methods do you use to evaluate the progress of trainees during your training program?" Thirty-four or 72.34 percent responded to this question. The data pertaining to this question is presented in Table VIII.

IN-SERVICE TRAINING. In response to a question, answered on 87.23 percent of the questionnaires, asking whether RCCs con-

Table VIII. Methods By Which Trainees' Progress is
Evaluated During Rape Crisis Center Training Programs

Method	Frequency of Responses	Percentage
Observation During Training	9	26.47
Ease With Which Trainees Handle Role-Playing	6	17.65
Use Of Questionnaire	5	14.71
Evaluation Board	3	8.82
Discussion With Coordinator	2	5.88
Self-evaluation	2	5.88
Performance In Communication Games	1	2.94
Intuition	1	2.94
Understanding RCI Role And Center's Policies	1	2.94
Make-up Missed Sessions	1	2.94
No Method Used	3	8.82

ducted in-service training for their staffs, 85.37 percent responded "yes," with 14.63 percent stating "no." The data relating to the scheduling of such in-service training is given in Table IX.

Table IX. Scheduling of In-Service Training
for Rape Crisis Center Staffs

Schedule	Frequency of Responses	Percentage
1 meeting/week	11	31.43
2 meetings/month	5	14.29
1 meeting/month	8	22.86
as needed	9	25.71
other	2	5.71

EVALUATION OF STAFFS. Table X shows the responses to the question asking what methods were used by RCCs to evaluate the effectiveness of their staffs when accepted for duty following training. Thirty-three of the forty-seven total questionnaires or

70.21 percent gave responses to this question.

Table X. Methods Used To Evaluate The
Effectiveness Of Rape Crisis Center Staffs

Method	Frequency of Response	Percentage
Review Of Calls RCIs Have Received And RCI's Casework	8	24.24
Personal Contact With And Feedback From The Coordinator	6	18.18
Self-evaluation	3	9.09
Comments From Rape Victims On RCI's Performance	3	9.09
Observation Of Role-Playing	2	6.06
Group Feedback	2	6.06
Other	5	15.15
No Method Used	4	12.12

Publicity

The RCCs were asked to respond to questions asking what media they used to publicize the existence of their service and to enter the approximate percentage this form of publicity contributed to the entire publicity program of the RCC. Forty-five or 95.74 percent of the questionnaires returned gave a response to these questions. This data is presented in Table XI.

In response to the question asking which of the publicity methods (see Table XI) the RCCs thought to be most effective in making the public aware of their services, lectures and speeches were seen by 29.55 percent of the respondents as most effective, newspapers were thought to be most effective by 22.73 percent of the RCCs, radio was seen as most effective by 18.18 percent, television with 15.91 percent, word of mouth being chosen as most effective by 11.36 percent, and finally, 2.27 percent of the RCCs thought the use of posters and pamphlets was the most effective methods of publicity.

Table XI. Methods Utilized By Rape Crisis Centers
To Publicize The Availability Of Their Service

Method	Percentage Of RCCs Using This Method	Average Percentage Of Method Contributing To Total Publicity Program
Newspapers	91.11	26.55
Straight	100.00	22.32
Underground	31.71	7.19
Gay	12.19	3.50
Radio	88.89	14.06
Television	66.66	8.84
Posters/Pamphlets	82.22	19.45
Lectures/Speeches	82.22	35.74
Word Of Mouth	84.44	17.17
*Other	11.11	10.00

*Examples of "other" include: stickers in women's restrooms, space on advertizing blotters, and newsletters.

Problem Areas

The RCCs were next asked to rank thirteen potential problems experienced by RCCs, with that problem having a rank of one being seen as the most difficult problem area for the RCC and that problem having the rank of 13 being viewed as the least difficult for the RCCs to deal with or overcome. Forty-three or 91.49 percent of the questionnaires ranked the problems.

The results of their rankings were as follows: (1) funding, (2) victim's fear of reporting the assault, (3) volunteer drop-out, (4) liaison with police, (5) handling the reactions of parents, friends, and lovers of the victim to the assault, (6) liaison with hospital personnel, (7) liaison with court representatives, (8) bad publicity about the center, (9) transfer or referral of cases, (10) staff hassels, (11) crank calls, (12) false reports of sexual assaults, (13) obscene calls.

Interagency Relations

Because the work of Rape Crisis Centers necessarily involves the cooperation of the centers with other agencies within the community, the question was asked, "What means do you use to foster better relations with law enforcement, hospital, and medical personnel?" Of the forty-seven total questionnaires returned to the author, 85.11 percent responded to this question.

The most frequently given means and the percentage of the RCCs using this means were as follows: get acquainted with these personnel early and meet with them regularly (47.50%); conduct symposiums, conferences, sensitivity training sessions and invite these personnel to attend (30.00%); work with policewomen (15.00%); make the center's initial approach low key and offer to help these personnel with the problem of handling sexual assaults (12.50%); ask police, hospital, and medical personnel to participate in the RCC training program (7.50%); send letters of commendation to helpful police, hospital, and medical personnel (7.50%); work from the top (hospital administrator, chief of police, nursing director, chief resident) down rather than the bottom (floor nurse, regular police officer, etc.) up (5.00%); and, impliment a program for medical and law enforcement personnel to be presented during their training in medical/nursing school or police academies (5.00%).

Less frequently given methods of fostering better relations were: approach rape crises as the community's problem rather than only a concern of women or only a part of the women's movement; make it well known to those involved that the center's staff trusts them to do their job effectively and sensitively; speak positively about the agencies the RCC has dealt with; work through a recognized social agency, having them act as the center's intermediary; offer immediate feedback to police, hospital, and medical personnel after an interrogation or medical exam; work through the police department's or hospital's public relations department; have a police officer or hospital representative serve on your Board of Directors; have an open-house and invite all interested persons and agencies to attend; and finally, work through the district attorney's office.

Legal Impediments

The final question asked on the RCC Questionnaire was, "What legal restrictions in your state or locale prevent your center or its staff from doing a more effective job in helping sexual assault victims?" Thirty-eight or 80.55 percent of the respondents answered this question.

Those most frequently given responses to this question were: the issue of the victim's past sexual experience being brought out in the trial; RCC personnel are prevented from being in the same room where police are interrogating the victim; RCC personnel can be subpoenaed to appear in court; RCC personnel are unable to obtain the right of privileged communication to protect the victim's statements to the RCI; particular states' antiquated statutes on sexual assault; and, RCC personnel are prevented from being in the medical examination room while the victim is being examined.

Less frequently given responses regarding legal restrictions on the RCCs' functions were: there are no statutes covering males as sexual assault victims; being nonprofit and tax-exempt organizations, the centers have difficulty lobbying for changes in their state's sexual assault statutes; the hospital must always report a suspected case of rape to the police, even if the women don't want to press charges; the district attorney is not required by law to tell the police why a particular case was dropped before a preliminary hearing; there are no "Sexual Offender Treatment Programs" demanded by law; RCC personnel cannot transport legal minors to a hospital or police department without the parent or guardian's permission; lack of legality of "third party" reporting of sexual assaults; questions of legality for a RCI to conduct the questioning of a rape victim while a police officer is present; and, how to best deal with child molestation victims.

SUMMARY

By way of attempting to make the results of the Rape Crisis Center Survey meaningful to the reader, the author will summarize the results by presenting a picture of the typical Rape Crisis Center based on the results contained in this appendix.

The typical Rape Crisis Center is probably located in a city having a population of at least 10,000 people. The center is likely to be a part of a larger organization and began its service because no other agency in the community existed which really dealt with the problem of rape or was staffed and trained to work with rape victims.

The major portion of the funds to operate the center typically come from private donations. The centers have an annual operating budget of approximately $6,226.00.

The staff of the typical Rape Crisis Center is composed of approximately forty persons. Only four of the total staff are paid, whereas the remaining thirty-six persons all volunteer their time and efforts to assist rape victims. The paid staff members are typically professionals while the volunteers are usually paraprofessionals. Of the total staff of a Rape Crisis Center, virtually all of them are women not having experienced a sexual assault themselves and fall between the ages of eighteen to thirty-two years of age.

The typical Rape Crisis Center has been in operation less than two years. The center is open seven days a week, twenty-four hours each day, 365 days a year. Sexual assault victims typically make their first contact with the center via the telephone. With those contacts the center has with rape victims, both in telephone and face-to-face contacts, the center probably keeps written records of such contacts. The center only allows access to such records by the center's own staff. Such records are usually kept for training purposes by the center for a period of two or more years.

The typical Rape Crisis Center also has an outreach team which will meet the victim at the scene of the crime and accompany her to the hospital, and during the police questioning, preliminary hearing and trial. These outreach teams are virtually all composed of paraprofessional women.

A rape victim making contact with a Rape Crisis Center can expect an average of almost four follow-up interviews to be conducted by the center, as the staff of the center and the victim herself feels is necessary.

Those persons wanting to work for the typical Rape Crisis Center will probably undergo some form of informal screening prior to acceptance on the staff. The volunteer can expect to take part in a training program whenever a sufficient number of volunteers also need training and then the training program is likely to be at least twenty hours in length. The training program will typically be conducted by the center's own staff, but input into the training program may come from medical, psychological, and legal or law enforcement personnel. During the training program the volunteer is apt to be evaluated informally by the training staff observing the volunteer's behavior throughout training and in role-playing situations.

Once accepted on the staff of a Rape Crisis Center, the volunteer's training is not over, for s/he is liable to have in-service training at regular meetings each week. While on the staff of the typical Rape Crisis Center, the volunteer will most likely have her/his performance evaluated by having the cases s/he has worked on and calls s/he has received reviewed and receive specific feedback from personal contact with the coordinator/director.

The typical Rape Crisis Center most likely publicizes its services to the public through conventional newspapers, radio, television, poster/pamphlets, by word of mouth, and through lectures/speeches the center conducts. The most effective means of publicizing the center's services is thought to be through lectures and speeches.

Those major problems with which the typical Rape Crisis Center has the most difficulty are finding funding for the center, helping victims overcome the fear of reporting sexual assaults, and dealing with volunteers dropping out of active service at the center.

Those ways in which the typical Rape Crisis Center fosters better relations with medical and law enforcement personnel within the community are to get acquainted with these personnel early and meet with them regularly, as well as conducting symposiums, conferences, and sensitivity training sessions and inviting these personnel to attend.

CONCLUSION

Although the Rape Crisis Center Survey suffered from many methodological problems, it was included in the book. This was done primarily because the author could not find any similar surveys conducted by other researchers. It was also thought that, even taking into account the many deficits in the survey, the survey may begin to shed some light on the phenomenon seen in the growth of so many Rape Crisis Centers across the nation. It may assist those persons thinking about beginning a Rape Crisis Center in their community in taking into account the many considerations necessary to have an effective service for sexual assault victims. Finally, it is hoped that further research, with more stringent and tight controls placed on its design and methodology will result from this admittedly rough beginning.

REVISION OF THE RAPE LAWS

MANY Rape Crisis Centers actively push for changes in their state's present statutes on rape. It is hoped that this material will assist you in deciding what directions to pursue in your efforts to arrive at a more sensible and less degrading set of laws governing the crime of rape.

RESOLUTION NO. 20[1]: SUBMITTED BY THE NATIONAL TASK FORCE ON RAPE

Whereas, rape is an act of subjugation, humiliation and violation of the victim; and

Whereas, rape is now classified as the most rapidly increasing crime of personal violence, yet continues to have the lowest conviction rate of all crimes of violence; and

Whereas, current law enforcement procedures, hospital treatment practices, courtroom procedures, the use of cautionary instructions to juries, and the admissibility of evidence for the purpose of impugning the prosecutrix, often contribute to the victim's humiliation, stress and powerlessness; and

Whereas, the present rape laws, their interpretation and enforcement too often spring from a concern from unwanted pregnancies not induced by a husband, but *should* spring from a concern about any individual's right to personal bodily privacy and safety; and

Whereas, the practice of plea bargaining, whereby a

---

[1]This material was originally contained in *DO-IT-NOW*, Volume 7, Number 10, October, 1974, pps. 10-13 and is reprinted by permission of Ms. Mary Ann Largen, Coordinator-National Rape Task Force of the National Organization For Women.

charge of rape may be dropped or reduced, particularly if it is committed in connection with a felony
such as robbery or kidnapping and the absence of
meaningful rehabilitation contributes to the high
incidence of recidivism among convicted sex offenders; and

Whereas, rape victims and many women's organizations have
advocated a number of reforms to afford victims sufficient protection under the law, as well as recommended changes in the manner in which rape cases
are handled, a general revision of rape laws, including a legal redefinition of rape; and a revision of
courtroom procedures, and

Whereas, many law enforcement officials, civil rights groups,
and members of the legal community agree that rape
laws are in need of revision; and

Whereas, all citizens should be able to live and work in their
communities without fear of violent assault;

Therefore, be it resolved by the National Organization for
Women, as follows:

A. Review of the existing rape laws have found these laws to
deter rather than facilitate convictions of rapists by:

1. Protecting the rights of the accused more than they seek
to protect the physical integrity and freedom of movement of victims themselves.

2. Being overly solicitous of the accused, and overly suspicious of the complainant.

3. Containing overly stringent rules of evidence which impede convictions, by:

a. containing "consent" standards which define rape in
terms of the victim's frame of mind;

b. regarding the nonmarital sexual activity of the accused as being irrelevant, yet allowing the impugning
of the victim's credibility based on such activity.

4. Imposing penalties not in keeping with the particular
acts of the crime, thus deterring judges and juries from
convicting.

5. Placing a web of formal and informal restraints upon

police and prosecutors in pursuing and obtaining the
prosecution and conviction of rapists.

B. Reevaluation and restructuring of rape laws being indis-
putedly necessary, we propose the following model legislative and procedural changes:

Revision of the Rape Laws

Goal

To revise the present laws which overwhelmingly favor the
defendant, impede convictions, allow victims, as witnesses, to
be treated in a manner which is both humiliating and damaging to their emotional health, and which further discourages
victims from reporting the crime to the officials.

1. To revise the present rules of evidence which place the
    victim in the position of being on trial, instead of the ac-
    cused.
2. To eliminate the life imprisonment penalty except in cases
    where the victim met with death, permanent bodily injury,
    permanent mental impairment, and in cases of conviction
    for the third offense, and
    a. To attain a general lowering of penalties, except in gang
        rapes, to fit the severity of the crime, thus making convic-
        tions more possible. Degrees of sexual assault shall be
        defined in relation to the seriousness of a given offense,
        dependent upon the presence or absence of a deadly
        weapon, whether the victim suffers serious injury, and
        whether there is sexual penetration as opposed to sexual
        contact.
    b. To require that parole be granted only after the serving of
        one year for the first offense and five years for the second
        offense, with intensive rehabilitative counseling. In the
        absence of such counseling, a term of not less than four
        years must be served prior to the granting of parole.
3. To redefine "rape" to include oral and anal sodomy and
    penetration by instrument or device, thereby protecting
    women from any form of sexual humiliation and extending

equal protection under the rape laws to men as well as women.

4. To broaden the law to permit the prosecution for rape by a spouse in the case of nonconsent of a spouse to sexual intercourse, when the couple are living separate and apart, and one has filed for a divorce or separate maintenance.

Method

1. Organize a coalition between all NOW chapters and/or rape task forces within a state to strengthen the NOW position and expedite state actions.
2. For a coalition between groups with similar goals and expertise to press for legal revisions.
3. Write letters and visit with state assembly-persons and state senators, stating your feelings and NOW position about the present situation.
4. Gather testimony, both written and verbal, from victims, police, prosecutors, and judges, attesting to the results of the present laws.
5. Press for hearings sponsored by the state legislature to gather evidence of the reality and enormity of the problems.
6. Appoint a special publicity committee to make contacts with local press and broadcast media, with the goal of publicizing the problems and locating more people to testify.
7. Conduct panel discussions and meetings open to the public to discuss the legal problems and advocate action.
8. Speak to community and state groups to educate them to the issues and solicit their support for the desired revisions.
9. The National Rape Task Force, in conjuction with chapter rape task forces, will monitor states for those holding hearings or planning any action on legal reforms.

Rape Defined

Rape is an act of sexual intercourse, however slight, including vaginal penetration, oral sodomy, anal sodomy, and penetration by instrument or device, accomplished by coerced bodily contact between any two persons of either sex.

1. Where the person is compelled to submit or participate by such force that overcomes her or his resistance as might reasonably be expected under the circumstances;
2. Where the person is unconscious or under physical constraints and is therefore physically powerless to resist;
3. Where the person is incapable, through mental defectiveness or other unsoundness of mind, whether temporary or permanent, which renders that person incapable of appraising their conduct or giving legal consent;
4. Where the person is compelled to submit or participates by any threat to themselves or others that would prevent resistance by a person of ordinary resolve; or where the person's power to appraise or control his or her conduct has been impaired by the administering of any substance.

Sexual penetration does not require emission.

Assault with the Intent to Commit Rape

The elements necessary to prove assault with intent to commit rape should consist of:

1. That the defendant made an assault upon the complainant.
2. That this assault was carried out against the will of the complainant.
3. That the defendant intended to have sexual intercourse in some manner with the complainant and that there was a commission of some direct act toward its consummation, falling short of execution of the ultimate intent.

Statutory Rape

Statutory rape shall be defined when the victim is under the age of twelve (12) years.

I. *Pretrial Rights and Privileges of the Victim*

A. A complainant of rape shall have the right to have a

person of their own choosing with them at all stages of police interrogation, medical examination and trial. The victim shall also have the right to exclude from the hospital examining room any person, provided someone is present who is a competent witness and will appear in court.

B. All rape victims shall have the right to receive prompt and free preventive venereal disease treatment and preventive pregnancy treatment and abortion, if desired and if necessary, and must be advised of their rights to these services.

C. Counseling referrals to a local mental health department, or crisis center, shall be an automatic part of treatment, if no counselor is available through the hospital.

D. The cost of the medical examination for purposes of gathering State's evidence shall be borne by the State.

E. Every scientific method currently available shall be utilized by the examining physician to gain evidence from both the victim and the accused.

F. Both adult and juvenile rape victims shall receive medical treatment, upon request, at hospital emergency rooms, without police notification if the victim so desires.

G. Rape victims who are minors shall not be denied medical treatment at hospital emergency rooms due to lack of parental knowledge and consent.

H. If the rape victim is a female, she will be questioned only by a policewoman, if she so desires.

I. Justice for the victim and potential victim shall be recognized as being fully as important as justice for the suspected rapist. Therefore, the complainant shall have the right to be represented in court by counsel of her or his own choosing to fully protect her or his rights in any subsequent civil proceedings which the complainant may choose to instigate.

J. The plaintiff, as well as the defendant, shall have the right to a speedy trial. No continuances, except in the most pressing circumstances, such as severe illness of either victim or defendant, shall be granted in rape cases.

II. Bail

A. There shall be a minimum of $25,000 set, in light of the threat of imminent danger to other potential rape victims.
B. A peace bond shall be levied against the accused if there exists a prior acquaintance between the accused and the complainant.

III. Plea-bargaining

Plea-bargaining, in the form of reducing the charge, or in the form of dismissing some of multiple charges, shall not be permitted in rape cases.

IV. Dismissal of Charges

The charge of rape or attempted rape shall not be dismissed by a state's attorney without the consent of the complainant. If the defendant is not bound over at the preliminary hearing, the victim shall have the right to request the state's attorney to present evidence to the grand jury.

V. Expert Witness

A rape victim may have the physician of their choice testify at the trial concerning interpretation of any medical data.

VI. Jury Selection

The state's attorney shall make efforts to eliminate from juries those jurors who demonstrate prejudice or distrust of rape victims, or special prejudices toward the crime of rape.

VII. Closed Courtroom

The courtroom shall be closed to spectators during the presentation of the victim's testimony, if the victim so desires.

VIII. Evidence

A. CORROBORATION. Special corroboration of the complainant's testimony is not absolutely essential for conviction. The victim's testimony alone should be sufficient to sustain a conviction if it is credible and the guilt of the accused is believed by the jury beyond a reasonable doubt.

B. CONSENT. Previous want of "chastity" of the victim shall be irrelevant in determining consent at the time of the alleged assault. Consent shall be determined solely from the victim's testimony as to her or his conduct at the time of the assault. The victim's past sexual activity with persons other than the accused is irrelevant. The relevance of past sexual conduct with the accused shall be determined in chambers by the judge.

Where a rape complaint is filed, and the complainant has been the victim of another, concurrently committed, crime by the offender, the law shall deem that the victim's consent was absent.

C. CREDIBILITY. Determination of the credibility of the witness shall not be based upon the sexual activity of the witness. Nor shall it be based upon the witness's general reputation as tending to show promiscuity, nonchastity, or sexual mores considered to be adverse to community standards. Such past conduct is irrelevant to show credibility and shall not be admissible in evidence.

D. The accused's history of sex offenses shall be admitted as relevant, as a matter of law, to at least one of the following:
   i. Motive
   ii. Existence of nonconsent
   iii. Characteristic method, plan or scheme in the commission of criminal acts similar to the method, plan or scheme used in commission of the offense in the case at trial.
   iv. To support the credibility of the complaining witness.
E. Testimony of previous victims of the accused, whose cases were not prosecuted to conviction, shall be admissible to support the credibility of the complaining witness.

IX. Instructions to Jury

No instruction shall be given cautioning the jury to view the victim's testimony in any other way than that in which all witnesses' testimony is viewed.

X. Sentencing and Penalties

A. If accused of rape by more than one individual, the defendant shall stand trial on each charge separately, and shall receive a separate sentence for each charge for which convicted.
B. If the defendant is convicted of two or more counts of rape, sentences shall be served consecutively.
C. Maximum penalities shall be reduced to fit the individual acts of the crime, in light of their detrimental effects on jury conviction, except in cases where the assault is committed by more than one offender. The penalty in such cases shall be higher than that for the single offender.
D. Life sentencing should apply to only the most severe assaults which result in death or extreme or perma-

nent bodily injury, or crippling, or permanent mental impairment.

XI. *Rehabilitation and Parole*

A. An intensive study of the convicted rapist shall be made by a psychiatric team of experts within 60 days of conviction. The team shall consist of one-half female experts and shall study the nature of the personality of the rapist and the causes of the offense and possible rehabilitation of the rapist.

B. The convicted rapist shall participate in an individualized rehabilitation program during incarceration and it shall continue as long as he or she is on parole as part of the conditions of being granted parole.

C. Parole shall be granted only upon completion of the minimum sentence or sentences served consecutively, and then only if certain conditions prescribed by law are met, and if the State can guarantee that repetition of the offense would be highly improbable, if not impossible.

* * *

For an example of how some of the propositions made by NOW appear when enacted, the present sexual assault statutes which are in effect in Michigan follow. They are, at this writing, probably the best such laws in the nation. Hopefully other states will follow Michigan's lead.

**STATE OF MICHIGAN
77TH LEGISLATURE
REGULAR SESSION OF 1974**

Introduced by Senators Byker, Faust, Zaagman, Hart, Lodge, Bowman, Toepp, Novak, Pursell, Plawecki, Mack, McCauley, Zollar, O'Brien, Cartwright, Rozycki, Davis, Bouwsma, Brown, DeGrow, Rockwell, Richardson, Ballenger, Faxon, Cooper,

McCollough, DeMaso, Pittenger, Bishop and Fleming

Enrolled Senate Bill No. 1207

AN ACT to amend Act No. 328 of the Public Acts of 1931, entitled "An act to revise, consolidate, codify and add to the statutes relating to crimes; to define crimes and prescribe the penalties therefor; to provide for the competency of evidence at the trial of persons accused of crime; to provide immunity from prosecution for certain witnesses appearing at such trials; and to repeal certain acts and parts of acts inconsistent with or contravening any of the provisions of this act," as amended, being sections 750.1 to 750.568 of the Compiled Laws of 1970, by adding sections 520a, 520b, 520c, 520d, 520e, 520f, 520g, 520h, 520i, 520j, 520k and 520l; and to repeal certain acts and parts of acts.

The People of the State of Michigan enact:

Section 1. Act No. 328 of the Public Acts of 1931, as amended, being sections 750.1 to 750.568 of the Compiled Laws of 1970, is amended by adding sections 520a, 520b, 520c, 520d, 520e, 520f, 520g, 520h, 520i, 520j, 520k and 520l to read as follows:

Sec. 520a. As used in sections 520a to 520l:

(a) "Actor" means a person accused of criminal sexual conduct.

(b) "Intimate parts" includes the primary genital area, groin, inner thigh, buttock, or breast of a human being.

(c) "Mentally defective" means that a person suffers from a mental disease or defect which renders that person temporarily or permanently incapable of appraising the nature of his or her conduct.

(d) "Mentally incapacitated" means that a person is rendered temporarily incapable of appraising or controlling his or her conduct due to the influence of a narcotic, anesthetic, or other substance administered to that person without his or her consent, or due to any other act committed upon that person without his or her consent.

(e) "Physically helpless" means that a person is unconscious, asleep, or for any other reason is physically unable to communicate unwillingness to an act.

(f) "Personal injury" means bodily injury, disfigurement, mental anguish, chronic pain, pregnancy, disease, or loss or impairment of a sexual or reproductive organ.

(g) "Sexual contact" includes the intentional touching of the victim's or actor's intimate parts or the intentional touching of the clothing covering the immediate area of the victim's or actor's intimate parts, if that intentional touching can reasonably be construed as being for the purpose of sexual arousal or gratification.

(h) "Sexual penetration" means sexual intercourse, cunnilingus, fellatio, anal intercourse, or any other intrusion, however slight, of any part of a person's body or of any object into the genital or anal openings of another person's body, but emission of semen is not required.

(i) "Victim" means the person alleging to have been subjected to criminal sexual conduct.

Sec. 520b. (1) A person is guilty of criminal sexual conduct in the first degree if he or she engages in sexual penetration with another person and if any of the following circumstances exists:

(a) That other person is under 13 years of age.

(b) The other person is at least 13 but less than 16 years of age and the actor is a member of the same household as the victim, the actor is related to the victim by blood or affinity to the fourth degree to the victim, or the actor is in a position of authority over the victim and used this authority to coerce the victim to submit.

(c) Sexual penetration occurs under circumstances involving the commission of any other felony.

(d) The actor is aided or abetted by one or more other persons and either of the following circumstances exists:

(i) The actor knows or has reason to know that the victim is mentally defective, mentally incapacitated or physically helpless.

(ii) The actor uses force or coercion to accomplish the sexual penetration. Force or coercion includes but is not limited to any of the circumstances listed in subdivision (f) (i) to (v).

(e) The actor is armed with a weapon or any article used or fashioned in a manner to lead the victim to reasonably believe it to be a weapon.

(f) The actor causes personal injury to the victim and force or coercion is used to accomplish sexual penetration. Force or coercion includes but is not limited to any of the following circumstances:

(i) When the actor overcomes the victim through the actual application of physical force or physical violence.

(ii) When the actor coerces the victim to submit by threatening to use force or violence on the victim, and the victim believes that the actor has the present ability to execute these threats.

(iii) When the actor coerces the victim to submit by threatening to retaliate in the future against the victim, or any other person, and victim believes that the actor has the ability to execute this threat. As used in this subdivision, "to retaliate" includes threats of physical punishment, kidnapping, or extortion.

(iv) When the actor engages in medical treatment or examination of the victim in a manner or for purposes which are medically recognized as unethical or unacceptable.

(v) When the actor, through concealment or by the element of surprise, is able to overcome the victim.

(g) The actor causes personal injury to the victim, and the actor knows or has reason to know that the victim is mentally defective, mentally incapaciated, or physically helpless.

(2) Criminal sexual conduct in the first degree is a felony punishable by imprisonment in the state prison for life or for any term of years.

Sec. 520c. (1) A person is guilty of criminal sexual conduct in the second degree if the person engages in sexual contact with another person and if any of the following circumstances exists:

(a) That other person is under 13 years of age.

(b) That other person is at least 13 but less than 16 years of age and the actor is a member of the same household as the victim, or is related by blood or affinity to the fourth degree to the victim, or is in a position of authority over the victim and the actor used this authority to coerce the victim to submit.

(c) Sexual contact occurs under circumstances involving the commission of any other felony.

(d) The actor is aided or abetted by one or more other persons and either of the following circumstances exists:

(i) The actor knows or has reason to know that the victim 'is mentally defective, mentally incapacitated or physically helpless.

(ii) The actor uses force or coercion to accomplish the sexual contact. Force or coercion includes but is not limited to any of the circumstances listed in sections 520b (1) (f) (i) to (v).

(e) The actor is armed with a weapon, or any article used or fashioned in a manner to lead a person to reasonably believe it to be a weapon.

(f) The actor causes personal injury to the victim and force or coercion is used to accomplish the sexual contact. Force or coercion includes but is not limited to any of the circumstances listed in section 520b (1) (f) (i) to (v).

(g) The actor causes personal injury to the victim and the actor knows or has reason to know that the victim is mentally defective, mentally incapacitated, or physically helpless.

(2) Criminal sexual conduct in the second degree is a felony punishable by imprisonment for not more than 15 years.

Sec. 520d. (1) A person is guilty of criminal sexual conduct in the third degree if the person engages in sexual penetration with another person and if any of the following circumstances exists:

(a) That other person is at least 13 years of age and under 16 years of age.

(b) Force or coercion is used to accomplish the sexual penetration. Force or coercion includes but is not limited to any of the circumstances listed in section 520b (1) (f) (i) to (v).

(c) The actor knows or has reason to know that the victim is mentally defective, mentally incapacitated, or physically helpless.

(2) Criminal sexual conduct in the third degree is a felony

punishable by imprisonment for not more than 15 years.

Sec. 520e. (1) a person is guilty of criminal sexual conduct in the fourth degree if he or she engages in sexual contact with another person and if either of the following circumstances exists:

(a) Force or coercion is used to accomplish the sexual contact. Force or coercion includes but is not limited to any of the circumstances listed in section 520b (1) (f) (i) to (iv).

(b) The actor knows or has reason to know that the victim is mentally defective, mentally incapacitated, or physically helpless.

(2) Criminal sexual conduct in the fourth degree is a misdemeanor punishable by imprisonment for not more than two years, or by a fine of not more than $500.00 or both.

Sec. 520f. (1) If a person is convicted of a second or subsequent offense under section 520b, 520c, or 520d, the sentence imposed under those sections for the second or subsequent offense shall provide for a mandatory minimum sentence of at least 5 years.

(2) For purposes of this section, an offense is considered a second or subsequent offense if, prior to conviction of the second or subsequent offense, the actor has at any time been convicted under section 520b, 520c, or 520d or under any similar statute of the United States or any state for a criminal sexual offense including rape, carnal knowledge, indecent liberties, gross indecency, or an attempt to commit such an offense.

Sec. 520g. (1) Assault with intent to commit criminal sexual conduct involving sexual penetration shall be a felony punishable by imprisonment for not more than 10 years.

(2) Assault with intent to commit criminal sexual conduct in the second degree is a felony punishable by imprisonment for not more than 5 years.

Sec. 520h. The testimony of a victim need not be corroborated in prosecutions under sections 520b to 520g.

Sec. 520i. A victim need not resist the actor in prosecution under sections 520b to 520g.

Sec. 520j. (1) Evidence of specific instances of the victim's sexual conduct, opinion evidence of the victim's sexual conduct, and reputation evidence of the victim's sexual conduct shall not be admitted under sections 520b to 520g unless and only to the extent that the judge finds that the following proposed evidence is material to a fact at issue in the case and that its inflammatory or prejudicial nature does not outweight its probative value:

(a) Evidence of the victim's past sexual conduct with the actor.

(b) Evidence of specific instances of sexual activity showing the source or origin of semen, pregnancy, or disease.

(2) If the defendant proposed to offer evidence described in subsection (1) (a) or (b), the defendant within 10 days after the arraignment on the information shall file a written motion and offer of proof. The court may order an in camera hearing to determine whether the proposed evidence is admissible under subsection (1). If new information is discovered during the course of the trial that may make the evidence described in subsection (1) (a) or (b) admissible, the judge may order an in camera hearing to determine whether the proposed evidence is admissible under subsection (1).

Sec. 520k. Upon the request of the counsel or the victim or actor in a prosecution under sections 520b to 520g the magistrate before whom any person is brought on a charge of having committed an offense under sections 520b to 520g shall order the names of the victim and actor and details of the alleged offense be suppressed until such time as the actor is arraigned on the information, the charge is dismissed, or the case is otherwise concluded, whichever occurs first.

Sec. 520l. A person does not commit sexual assault under this act if the victim is his or her legal spouse, unless the couple are living apart and one of them has filed for separate maintenance or divorce.

Section 2. All proceedings pending and all rights and liabilities existing, acquired, or incurred at the time this amendatory act takes effect are saved and may be consummated according to the law in force when they are commenced. This amendatory act shall not be construed to affect any prosecution pending or begun before the effective date of this amendatory act.

Section 3. Sections 85, 333, 336, 339, 340, 341, 342 and 520 of Act No. 328 of the Public Acts of 1931, being sections 750.85, 750.333, 750.336, 750.339, 750.340, 750.341, 750.342 and 750.520 of the Compiled Laws of 1970, and section 82 of chapter 7 of Act No. 175 of the Public Acts of 1927, being section 767.82 of the Compiled Laws of 1970, are repealed.

Section 4. This amendatory act shall take effect November 1, 1974.

BIBLIOGRAPHY

Books, Handbooks, Manuals:

Alexander, S.: *State-By-State Guide to Women's Legal Rights.* Los Angeles, Wollstonecraft, Inc., 1975.

Amir, M.: *Patterns in Forcible Rape.* Chicago, U of Chicago Pr, 1971.

Bennett, M. E.: *Guidance And Counseling In Groups.* New York, McGraw, 1963.

Birth Control Handbook. Montreal, Montreal Health Press, 1973.

Boston Women's Health Book Collective: *Our Bodies Ourselves.* New York, S & S, 1973.

Brodyaga, Lisa et al.: *Rape And Its Victims: A Report For Citizens, Health Facilities, And Criminal Justice Agencies.* Washington, D.C., Center for Women Policy Studies, National Institute of Law Enforcement and Criminal Justice, 1974.

Brownmiller, Susan: *Against Our Will: Men, Women, And Rape.* New York, S & S, 1975.

Burgess, A. W. and Holmstrom, L. L.: *Rape: Victims of Crisis.* Bowie, Robert J. Brady Company, 1974.

Carkhuff, R. R.: *Helping & Human Relations: A Primer for Lay and Professional Helpers,* (2 vols.). New York, H R & W, 1969.

Connell, N. and Wilson, C. (Eds.): *Rape: The First Sourcebook For Women.* New York, A Plume Book, New American Library, 1974.

Danish, S. J. and Hauer, A. L.: *Helping Skills: A Basic Training Program,* (a leader's manual & a trainee's workbook). New York, Behavioral Publications, 1973.

Delworth, U., Rudow, E. H., and Taub, J.: *Crisis Center/Hotline: A Guidebook to Beginning and Operating.* Springfield, Thomas, 1972.

Fisher, S. A.: *The Voice Of Hope ... To People In Crisis: A National Survey.* Canton, Case Western Reserve University, 1972.

Flakne, G. W.: *Sexual Assualt: A Manual for Law Enforcement, Medical, Social Service, Volunteer and Prosecutorial Personnel and Agencies.* Minneapolis, Sexual Assault Services, Citizens' Protection Division, Office of the County Attorney, 1974.

How To Start A Rape Crisis Center. Washington, D.C., Rape Crisis Center, 1972.

Handbook ... Medical And Legal Aspects Of Rape. Philadelphia, Women Organized Against Rape, 1973.

Ivey, A. E: *Microcounseling: Innovations in Interviewing Training,* Springfield, Thomas, 1971.

Ivey, A. E. and Gluckstern, N. B.: *Basic Attending Skills* (a leader's manual & a participant's manual). Amherst, A. E. Ivey, 1974.

Johnson, D. W.: *Reaching Out: Interpersonal Effectiveness and Self-Actualization.* Englewood Cliffs, P-H, 1972.

Kagan, N.: *Interpersonal Process Recall: A Method of Influencing Human Interaction.* East Lansing, Michigan State University, 1975.

Kelley, C. M.: *Crime In The United States: 1973 Uniform Crime Reports.* Washington, D.C., U.S. Govt. Print. Office, 1974.

Lester, D. and Brockopp, G. W.: *Crisis Intervention and Counseling by Telephone.* Springfield, Thomas, 1973.

Lewis, H. R. and Streitfeld, H. S.: *Growth Games: How to Tune In Yourself, Your Family, Your Friends.* New York, Bantam, 1972.

Lewis, M. O. (Ed.): *The Foundation Directory.* 5th Ed. New York, The Foundation Center, Columbia U Pr, 1975.

McClary, C. et al.: *How To Organize A Women's Crisis-Service Center.* Ann Arbor, Women's Crisis Center, 1974.

Medea, A. and Thompson, K.: *Against Rape.* New York, FS & G, 1974.

Medical Protocol for Emergency Room Treatment of Rape Victims. Berkeley, Bay Area Women Against Rape, 1974.

Mills, P. D.: *Crisis Intervention Resource Manual.* Vermillion, University of South Dakota, 1973.

Pfeiffer, J. W. and Jones, J. E.: *A Handbook of Structured Experiences for Human Relations Training,* (5 vols.). La Jolla, University Associates Publishers, Inc., 1969, 1970, 1971, 1973, 1975.

Planning By Objectives: A Manual For People Working With Student Volunteer Programs. Washington, ACTION: National Student Volunteer Programs.

Rape Task Force Kit. Chicago, National Organization for Women, Inc.

Russell, D. E. H.: *The Politics of Rape.* New York, Stein and Day, 1974.

Specter, G. A. and Claiborn, W. L.: *Crisis Intervention,* (vol. 2). New York, Behavioral Publications, 1973.

Stevens, J. O.: *Awareness: Exploring, Experimenting, Experiencing.* Moab, Real People, 1971.

VD Handbook. Montreal, Montreal Health Press, 1972.

Walker, M. J., (Ed.): *Toward The Prevention Of Rape: A Bibliography,* (Report Number 27). University, Center For Correctional Psychology, U of Ala Pr, 1975.

Periodicals, Pamphlets:

Amir, M.: Forcible rape. *Sexual Behavior, 1*(8):24-36, 1971.

Bohmer, C.: Judicial attitudes toward rape victims. *Judicature*, *57*(7):303-307, 1974.

Brussel, J. A.: Comment by. *Sexual Behavior*, *1*(8):30, 1971.

Burgess, A. W. and Holmstrom, L. L.: *Am J Nurs*, *73*(10):1741-1745, 1973.

Cohen, M. L. et al.: The psychology of rapists. *Seminars In Psychiatry*, *3*(3):307-327, 1971.

Crime Of Rape. *Editorial Research Reports*, *1*(3):43-60, 1972.

Donadio, B. and White, M. A.: Seven who were raped. *Nurs Outlook*, *22*(4):245-247, 1974.

Flynn, L.: Interview: women and rape. *Medical Aspects of Human Sexuality*, *8*(5):183-197, 1974.

Fox, S. S. and Scherl, D. J.: Crisis intervention with victims of rape. *Social Work*, *17*(1):37-42, 1972.

Geis, G.: Group sexual assaults. *Medical Aspects of Human Sexuality*. *5*:100-113, May, 1971.

Goldner, N. S.: Commentary. *Medical Aspects of Human Sexuality*, *8*(2):81 & 88, 1974.

Griffin, S.: "The Politics of Rape," Buffalo, Friends of Malatesta.

Hayman, C. R., (Moderator): Roundtable: rape and its consequences. *Medical Aspects of Human Sexuality*, *6*(2):12, 17, 21, 25-27, 31, 1972.

―――― : What to do for victims of rape. *Resident And Staff Physician*, 29-32, August, 1973.

MacDonald, J. M.: Group rape. *Medical Aspects of Human Sexuality*, *8*(1):58, 65-66, 68, 1974.

MacNamara, D. E. J.: Police and sex: an interview with a criminologist. *Sexual Behavior*, *1*(4):24-31, 1971.

McClary, C. et al.: *Freedom From Rape*. Ann Arbor, Women's Crisis Center, 1974.

McCubbin, J. H. and Scott, D. E.: Brief guide to office counseling: treating the victim of rape. *Medical Aspects of Human Sexuality*, *8*(7):51-52, 1974.

Medical Procedures in cases of suspected rape. *Medical Aspects of Human Sexuality*, *7*(9):65, 68, 70-71, 1973.

Peters, J. J.: Child rape: defusing a psychological time bomb. *Hospital Physician*, 46-49, February, 1973.

Precautions against rape. *Sexual Behavior*, *2*(1):33-37, 1972.

Resolution No. 20 on Rape (suggested changes in rape laws). *Do It NOW*, *7*(10):10-13, 1974.

Roth, E. I.: Emergency treatment of raped children. *Medical Aspects of Human Sexuality*, *6*(8):84-85, 89-91, 1972.

Sadoff, R. L.: Commentary. *Medical Aspects of Human Sexuality*, *8*(2):80-81, 1974.

Schultz, L. G.: The child sex victim: social, psychological, and legal

perspectives. *Child Welfare,* 52(3):147-157, 1973.
Selkin, J.: Rape. *Psychology Today,* 8(8):71-74, 76, 1975.

Newsletters

"Ain't I A Woman"
P.O. Box 1169
Iowa City, IA 52240

"Off Our Backs"
1346 Connecticut Avenue
Washington, DC 20036

"Rape Crisis Center Newsletter"
P.O. Box 21005
Washington, DC 20009

"Rape: Research, Action, Prevention"
Center for Correctional Psychology
Department of Psychology
University of Alabama
P.O. Box 2968
University, AL 35486

"WOAR Newsletter"
Women Organized Against Rape
Trineb Bldg., 420 Service Drive
Philadelphia, PA 19104

AUTHOR INDEX

Alexander, S., 192, 278
Amir, M., 44, 223, 224, 225, 278, 279

Bennett, M. E., 210, 211, 278
Bohmer, C., 280
Brockopp, G., 234, 279
Brodyaga, L., 278
Brownmiller, S., 278
Brussel, J. A., 69, 280
Burgess, A. W., 68, 69, 72, 74, 75, 278, 280

Carkhuff, R., 51, 79, 250, 278
Claiborn, W. I., 279
Cohen, M. E., 280
Connell, N., 278

Danish, S. J., 278
Delworth, U., 51, 212, 229, 278
Donadio, B., 68, 70, 280
Drathwohl, D. R., 79

Fisher, S., 229, 234, 241, 278
Flakne, G. W., 278
Flynn, L., 69, 72, 280
Fox, S. S., 70, 71, 73, 280

Geis, G., 222, 223, 224, 225, 280
Gluckstern, N. B., 279
Goldner, N. S., 225, 280
Griffin, S., 280

Hauer, A. I., 278
Hayman, C. R., 280
Holmstrom, L. L., 68, 69, 72, 74, 75, 278, 280

Ivey, A. E., 279

Johnson, D. W., 213, 279
Jones, J. E., 213, 279

Kagan, N., 79, 87, 88, 279
Kelley, C. M., 7, 279

Largen, M. A., 183
Leitner, L., 51
Lester, D., 234, 279
Lewis, H. R., 213, 279
Lewis, M. O., 228, 279

MacDonald, J. M., 222, 225, 280
MacNamara, D. E. J., 280
McClary, C., 229, 279, 280
McCubbin, J. H., 280
Medea, A., 221, 279
Mills, P. D., 279

Peters, J. J., 74, 75, 280
Pfeiffer, J. W., 213, 279

Rudow, E., 51
Rudow, F. H., 278
Russell, D. E. H., 279

Sadoff, R. I., 223, 280
Scherl, D. J., 70, 71, 73, 280
Schultz, I. G., 75, 280
Scott, D. E., 280
Selkin, J., 281
Specter, G. A., 279
Stevens, J. O., 279
Storaska, F., 222, 279
Streitfeld, H. S., 213, 279

Taub, J., 51, 278
Thompson, K., 221, 279

Walker, M. J., 279
White, M. A., 68, 70, 280
Wilson, C., 278

SUBJECT INDEX

A

Advice giving, 18-19
"Ain't I A Woman", 281

B

Bay Area Women Against Rape (Berkeley, Calif.), 145
Bill of Rights, sexual assault patient's, 153-157

C

Chicago Women Against Rape (Chicago, Ill.), 10, 169, 182
Community Crisis Information Center (Ft. Collins, Colo.), 92
Community education, 5-6
Companion program, 22
Confidentiality, record, 16-18
Counseling, 129-144
 immediate, 22
Court problems, 182
Crisis center (see Rape crisis center)
Crisis Clinic (Bellingham, Wash.), 193

E

Empathy training, 79-95

F

Family reaction, 233
Follow-up care, 21-25

G

Group rape, 222-225

H

Helping skills, 95-112
Hospital assessment, 11
Humanizing procedures, 5

I

Intervener, rape crisis (see Rape crisis intervener)

L

Laws, rape (see Legislation)
Lay advocate, 22 (see also Rape crisis intervener)
Legal procedures, 169-192
Legal terms, 186-192
Legislation
 assessment, 9
 revision, 3-4, 261-277
Listening Post (Salt Lake City, Utah), 193

M

Medical procedures, 145-168
 protocol, standard, 145-147
Mental health centers, community, 7
Miami Dade County Rape Task Force (Coral Gables, Fla.), 147
Minors, 16

N

National Organization for Women (NOW), 10

O

"Off Our Backs", 281

P

Pelvic exam, 159-161
Physical exam, 159
Police
 assessment of, 11
 investigation, 169-179
Pregnancy test, 162
Psychological reaction, 193-195
 adult, 68-73
  acute crisis period, 68-70
  interim period, 71-72
  resolution period, 72-73
 children, 73-79
  long-term, 74-77
  short-term, 73-74

R

Rape Counseling Center (Minneapolis, Minn.), 169
Rape crisis center
 affiliation, 25
 assessing need, 9-13
 cohesiveness, group, 210-213
 establishment, 14-27
  legalities, 14-20
  motivation and philosophy, 20-21
 evaluation material, 198-209
 formation, 3-8
 funding, 226-229, 244-245
 hours of operation, 26-27
 illegal activities, 19
 interagency relations, 256-257
 legal problems, 257
 legal process, function during, 179-180
 list of, 235-240
 nonprofit, tax-exempt status, 15
 omission or inaction, errors of, 19
 operational procedures, 246-250
 phone service, 23
 physical setting, 25-26
 problems, 226-234
  funding, 226-229
  liaison, 231-233
  volunteer drop-out, 230-231
 publicity, 254-255
 referral, 193-197

 services to provide, 21-25
 speaker's bureau, 23-24
 staffing, 245-246
  training (see Training program)
 survey results, 241-260
Rape Crisis Center, The (Washington, D. C.), 14
"Rape Crisis Center Newsletter", 281
Rape crisis intervener
 characteristics, 31-33
 medical information, 157-159
 training, 28-39, 250-254 (see also Training program)
 assistance, outside, 29-31
Rape Crisis Team (Grand Rapids, Mich.), 20
Rape Relief Program (Olympia, Wash.), 180-181
"Rape: Research, Action, Prevention", 281
Rape Task Force Kit (Women Organized Against Rape, Philadelphia, Penna.), 10-12, 279
Rape Treatment and Trauma Center (Miami, Fla.), 147
Rapists
 rehabilitation and therapy, 7

S

San Bernadino Rape Crisis Service (San Bernandino, Calif.), 175
Self-defense programs, 6
Self-protection, 214-221
Statistics, rape, 10

T

Third party reporting, 180-182
Training program, 40-144
 counseling excerpt completion test, 60-68
 empathy, 79-95
 helping process, 77-79, 95-112
 listening skills, 47-51
 means, 41-44
 preliminaries, 28-39
 problem solving, 112-128
 role-playing situations, 42-44

simulated therapy, 52-60
Transportation, 18

V

Venereal disease, 165
Vermillion Hotline (South Dakota), 93
Volunteers
pretesting, 44-47
screening, 31-39
training program, 40-144 (*see also* Training program)

W

Walk-in service, 23
Women Against Rape (Chicago, Ill.), 76
Women's Crisis-Service Center (Ann Arbor, Mich.), 14, 79
Women helping women, 4-5
Women Organized Against Rape (Philadelphia, Penna.), 69, 75, 76, 169, 216
"WOAR Newsletter", 281

Y

Youth centers, 7